Acclaim for
Son-Rise: The Miracle Continues
and the Work of Barry Neil Kaufman

Barry Kaufman's work is inspiring, ground breaking, and visionary. His new book, *Son-Rise: The Miracle Continues,* continues to establish the fact that yesterday's miracles are becoming the science of today. But this new science is not a cold, bleak, objective methodology. Rather it is the science of love, compassion, and insight which will transform the world.
—Deepak Chopra, M.D.
Author, *Quantum Healing* and
Ageless Body, Timeless Mind

Kaufman's work affirms the unlimited potential of the human spirit and offers hope to those who have been challenged by adversity.
—Coretta Scott King
President, The Martin Luther King, Jr.
Center for Nonviolent Social Change

Once in a century a story of such daring and devotion sparks the human spirit. No words could describe my awe while reading *Son-Rise: The Miracle Continues.* The Kaufmans' astounding success in curing their son and helping other families to do the same will inspire us all. If there were a Noble Prize for Love, I'd want the Kaufmans to be the first to receive one.
—Dr. Wayne W. Dyer
Author, *Your Erroneous Zones*

An inspiring book that we all can learn from. It is not only a book for all parents to read, but all of us can use it as guide for dealing with adversity. If you are open to changing attitudes, accepting challenges, and being inspired, read it. P.S. Can you adopt me?
—Bernie Siegel, M.D.
Author, *Love, Medicine, and Miracles*

An inspiring and hopeful book. To see this hopeless youngster gradually respond to the Kaufmans' total investment of themselves is awe-inspiring. The book is beautifully written. I found it so fascinating I devoured it all in one evening. It is quite a contribution.
—Dr. Carl Rogers
Renowned Psychologist

Reading *Son-Rise: The Miracle Continues* has been a profoundly moving experience. It details with clarity the triumph of love over autism in a way that is both convincing and reproducible. As a psychiatrist, I am embarrassed to still hear "experts" in my field describe autism as untreatable and to find that they are unaware of the miracle that the Kaufmans have created. This book is love in action.
> —John S. Weltner, M.D., Child Psychiatrist
> Co-President, Society for Family Therapy and Research

The Option Institute and the Son-Rise Program staff have opened our eyes and our minds just by loving us. They gave us our son! We learned how to join Nicholas in his world. And now he wants to join us in ours. We've never been this happy and at peace.
> —David Valentino, V.P. Sales and Marketing/Father
> Son: Nicholas, Two and a half years old
> Diagnosis: Pervasive Developmental Delay

As a professor in the field of psychology I believe that *Son-Rise: The Miracle Continues* is a mandate for all professionals in helping fields, medical and educational, to change NOW how we help and teach, and to bask in the joy of our own miracles. I look forward to making this book required reading. I cannot imagine a single text that will make such a difference in my students' own learning.
> —Liz Dickinson, Ph.D.
> Professor of Psychology, Michigan State University

Son-Rise moved me enormously. . . . Kaufman's dedication is extraordinary.
> —Joanne Woodward
> Actress, Humanitarian

The Son-Rise Program is the most incredible experience of my life. We came to The Option Institute as a family of unsure, confused people—about ourselves and our son, Gidi—and we leave a strong unit of committed and loving friends. We know Gidi will join us totally—we adore him so—exactly the way he is and chooses to be. Thank you so much—you are the very best—God Bless You!!
> —Toby Greenfeld, Teacher/Mother
> Son: Gideon, Nine years old
> Diagnosis: Autism

An especially important book, not just for parents of autistic children, but for the medical profession, which knows little about the diagnosis and even less about the treatment of autism. To my colleagues in the medical profession: You must read *Son-Rise: The Miracle Continues.* This book will not only make you a better doctor, or a more proficient surgeon, but it will profoundly alter your own personal life and happiness. (Ridiculous? Read it and find out!)
> —Chris Adams, Master of Surgery, Cambridge University
> Senior Consultant in Neurosurgery, Oxford

A kind of love everyone secretly wants but is afraid to ask for.
> —Los Angeles *Times*

How many times will people in my field have to read accounts of the Kaufmans' work before they will tell the truth? *Autism is curable!* Why are we "professionals" so tentative and calculating about admitting the potential healing power of the Kaufmans' love-made-so-practical? After reading this book, I asked myself: Which one of us will ever again suggest that hope is "false"? Read his book and feel the power of yourself unfolding side by side with these special children and their families . . . and the power of being free to believe in the impossible.
> —Elizabeth Shulman, Ph.D.
> Clinical Psychologist

Barry Neil Kaufman champions making the choices to believe in ourselves, to be hopeful, and to seize the power of loving ourselves and others.
> —Lou Holtz
> Head Football Coach, Notre Dame

Son-Rise: The Miracle Continues is must reading for *anyone* in *any* helping profession! Because I have integrated the Kaufmans' work into my own treatment program, my clients consistently achieve lasting changes in speech and their lives that many in my profession have deemed impossible. It has profoundly and positively influenced both my work and my personal life.
> —Catherine S. Otto, M.S., CCC-SLP
> Speech Pathologist/International Stuttering Specialist
> Director, Total Immersion Fluency Training

Son Rise: The Miracle Continues is brilliant, heartfelt, poignant. As a physician working with the developmentally disabled, I urge educators and health-care providers to applaud and incorporate the Kaufmans' methods.
> —Patricia Weber, M.D.
> Fircrest Habilitation Center, Seattle

We are so excited with our Son-Rise Program! One year and five months into the program we found a fantastic thing—a miracle! Our son, Frankie, is now speaking meaningfully in five-word sentences. Last year he couldn't say one word, but by going with him, following him, and inviting him to be with us, he is choosing to talk more and more. We are changing along with Frankie. I never knew what you meant by growing together with your child until now; it is awesome. You guys are very powerful people. Thanks a million for being there for us.

> —Frank Pontillo, Supplier/Father
> Son: Frankie, Six years old
> Diagnosis: Autism

Son-Rise: The Miracle Continues is an uplifting book which recounts the Kaufmans' story and several other families' formidable journeys through pain and anguish to amazing heart-expanding joy with their special children. The powerful impact of acceptance and love and indomitable spirit encourage and inspire all of us to live life more openly, richly, and joyfully.

> —Carolyn Turner Ph.D.
> Clinical and Pediatric Psychologist,
> Graduate Fellow, Harvard Medical School and
> National Center for Clinical Infant Program

A beautiful and healing journey. The Kaufmans' message is one of peace, hope, and possibility. Through their work they demonstrate in very tangible terms the power of love and acceptance.

> —*New Age Magazine*

Heartwarming . . . makes an eloquent statement for human understanding and compassion.

> —*Chicago Sun-Times*

Son-Rise: The Miracle Continues offers concrete, tangible examples of the fruits that can result from a life lived with love, acceptance, and happiness as a priority. As a minister, I often search for "real life" testimony to the fact that miracles occur in our lives every day. This book offers countless such examples and inspired several sermons before I even finished reading it! God's grace abounds in the Kaufmans' work with families and children!! Thank God for the Kaufmans and for the families who were willing to share their stories.

> —The Reverend Elizabeth S. Gombach, M. Div.
> Minister, United Methodist Church

Son-Rise
The Miracle Continues

Other Books
by Barry Neil Kaufman

Son-Rise
To Love Is to Be Happy With
Giant Steps
A Miracle to Believe In
The Book of Wows and Ughs
A Land Beyond Tears
A Sense of Warning
Happiness Is a Choice

Son-Rise
The Miracle Continues

BARRY NEIL KAUFMAN

H J Kramer Inc
Tiburon, California

Published by H J Kramer Inc
P.O. Box 1082
Tiburon, CA 94920

Editor: Nancy Grimley Carleton
Design and Composition: Classic Typography
Cover Design: Jim Marin (Pixel Media)
Book Production: Schuettge & Carleton
Manufactured in the United States of America
10 9 8 7 6 5 4 3

Library of Congress Cataloging-in-Publication Data

Kaufman, Barry Neil.
  Son-rise : the miracle continues / by Barry Neil Kaufman.
    p. cm.
  Includes bibliographical references.
  ISBN 0-915811-61-8 $12 95 (trade)
    1. Autistic children—United States—Biography 2 Kaufman, Raun
Kahlil. 3. Parents of autistic children—United States—Interviews.
4. Option Institute and Fellowship I Title
RJ506 A9K383 1993
818.92'8982'0092—dc20
[B]   93-38530
                                                              CIP

Dedication

To all the special children—
    who too often have been cast aside,
    your lives viewed as tragic events.

To all the special children—
    who gave us opportunities to find
    the most loving and humane parts of ourselves.

To all the special children—
    this book celebrates your wonder,
    your individuality, your magnificence.

To all the special children—
    may God give us all the wisdom
    to see how truly perfect you are.

To Our Readers

*The books we publish
are our contribution to
an emerging world based on
cooperation rather than on competition,
on affirmation of the human spirit rather
than on self-doubt, and on the certainty
that all humanity is connected.
Our goal is to touch as many
lives as possible with a
message of hope for
a better world.*

Hal and Linda Kramer, Publishers

Contents

Foreword
by Raun Kaufman

Do you ever wonder why things turn out the way they do? I do. Every so often, I ask myself why an event in my life occurred, if maybe it had some sort of purpose or reason. I realize that, in the larger scheme of things, I can never really know why events happen or if there is some sort of grand plan for us all. I do believe, though, that each event offers us a brand new chance to change ourselves and our lives, whether the change is slight or sweeping. Even if we can't know whether there is some great cosmic reason for the workings of the world, we can still give events meaning with what we do with them.

When I was diagnosed as autistic (and also severely mentally retarded, with a below-thirty I.Q.), my parents were given ample opportunity to treat the event as a tragedy. The whole world saw autism as hopeless and encouraged my parents to see it that way too. Sometimes it dawns on me how close I came to spending my life encapsulated inside my own head, lacking the tools to interact with the rest of the world. My autism could have been just another event without meaning or explanation.

What turned it around was not a string of events, but rather a wildly different and unheard of perspective: Refusing to accept the age-old view of autism as a terrible catastrophe, my parents came up with the radical idea that my autism was a chance—a great opportunity, in fact—to try to reach a child lost behind a thick, hazy cloud. It was a chance to make greatness out of something commonly viewed as unquestionably sad and tragic. This perspective, combined with a passionate relentlessness on the part of my parents, enabled me to undergo a spectacular metamorphosis and emerge from the shell of my autism without a trace of my former condition.

When I think about what my parents did with my autism, I see what a tremendous role we all play in each event that confronts us. It was not my recovery that made the event of my autism amazing and meaningful (though, needless to say, I'm very happy with the outcome); it was my parents' open-minded attitude in the face of my condition and their desire to find meaning in it regardless of how I turned out in the end. You don't have to "cure" your special child in order for his or her specialness to have meaning and value. The value lies not in "results" but in how you treat your situation and your child.

The question of what is and is not possible has forever been bouncing around in my head. I have definitely had a few times in my life when I chose not to bother attempting to accomplish something because I thought, "That's impossible." At other times, I catch myself thinking this way and realize that it is precisely this type of thinking that could have landed me in an institution for the rest of my life. If there is one thing my life has taught me, it is that anything is possible. I don't mean this idea in the superficial way it is often used. I mean to say that nothing is beyond our reach if we honestly believe that it is within our power to reach it. I've found that I, rather than any external situation, am my own biggest limiter.

One line that parents of special children hear more than anyone else is the "that's impossible" line. The "experts" showered my parents with prognoses like "hopeless," "irreversible," "unreachable," and "incurable." All my parents had to do was believe these "experts" (not a difficult task, since these doctors had plenty of evidence to back their opinions), and my journey would have been over. Instead, my parents defied the professionals, disbelieved their prognoses, and grabbed hold of the belief that they could at least try to do the impossible, reach the unreachable, cure the incurable.

"But your son has a devastating, lifelong condition. He can never come out of it," the doctors scolded.

"So what?" my parents would reply. "We're going to try, anyway, and see what happens."

The word *expert* is the misnomer of the century. The pessimistic outlook that the "experts" show many parents need not be taken seriously. Whatever you've been told about the severity of your child's condition, don't buy it. You and your child can do a whole lot more than any "expert" could possibly know. No matter how much evidence a doctor can show you, it will never be enough to prove that something is impossible. You want to know something?

Evidence is a sham. It can always be defied or demolished. If you really believe in evidence, use it to prove the possible instead of the impossible. (I'm on the debating team at my college, and I've seen how evidence can be used to back up either side of an issue.)

Many, especially the "experts," might claim that I am advocating "false hope." "False hope"? What do they mean by "false hope"? How in the world can anyone put these two words together? When I think about my successful academic career, my fierce tennis matches, my love of Stephen King novels, the fantasy and science fiction short stories I've written, my admittance to the university of my choice, my best friends, my girlfriend, and my complete and ecstatic involvement with life, it occurs to me that each and every one of these is the product of "false hope." Nothing can ever be bad or wrong about hope. Not ever. I advocate giving yourself and those around you as large a dose of it as possible.

So, I bet you're wondering what this product of "false hope" is doing with his life lately. Well, I'm enjoying college (I'm in my sophomore year) more than any other period of my life. I'm having a thoroughly terrifice time choosing my own courses, living away from home, eating school food (yum!). I take courses like philosophy, political science, theater arts, and biology. I took calculus during my freshman year. Definitely not my calling. In addition to enjoying the social and academic scenes at college, I'm also on the debating team, I take ballroom dancing, I'm in a coed fraternity, and I'm in a number of political groups. I recently cast my first presidential vote after working for my candidate's campaign. (I won't say who I voted for, but you can probably guess.)

Here are the answers (and only the answers) to the questions I get asked most often:

- No, I can't stand "Beverly Hills 90210."
- Yeah, I'm an excellent driver.
- Actually, I'm majoring in biomedical ethics. Oh, my career after college? I haven't the foggiest clue.
- No, I only spin plates during really boring physics lectures.
- Sorry, I'm busy this Friday night.

Speaking of questions and answers, I have talked with parents of special children from many different countries and throughout the U.S., and I've had the chance to answer scores of their questions and ask some questions of my own, as well. They all want the best for their child; they all have a strong desire to help their child in any way they can. Many of these families also see their own or their child's situation as horrific. In addition, they want to be "realistic" and not pretend that their child's situation or potential is better than it actually is. It makes perfect sense to me that parents would think this way, but there are other ways of looking at things that might be more productive as well as more fun.

Personally, I see autistic children as possessing a unique talent and ability, not a deficiency. When this talent and ability are embraced instead of viewed with horror, some amazing things can happen. Kids can make leaps people never thought possible.

As for being realistic, it's not all it's cracked up to be. Very often, I wonder how I can be realistic and optimistic at the same time. How can I have boundless hope and aspirations and still keep a down-to-earth perspective on things? Well, many times I can't. Sometimes I choose realism, and when I do, I can always be sure that nothing that happens will exceed my expectations. But when I choose limitless optimism, I don't put any ceilings on my dreams and goals, and, as a result, sometimes I get more and do more than I ever could have accomplished by being realistic. The telephone, the automobile, the polio vaccine—the people who brought these things into being were extremely unrealistic. Realism only preserves the status quo. Nothing was ever accomplished by a realist. Every great discovery and achievement in history is the fault of unrealistic people. My parents' lack of realism is what got me to the place I am now. Consequently, I try never to tell anyone around me to be realistic.

Sometimes, when I think about the continuing savage violence around the world and the pervasive racism in America, I have a hard time being optimistic. Plastered all over my wall in my dorm room are pictures of Bobby Kennedy, my favorite person in history. War and racism were also major concerns for him, but he never let the state of the world bring him down. So when I think of the things I want to be different in the world and I think about being unrealistic and I think about hope, I try to keep a quote of Bobby Kennedy's tucked in the back of my mind: "Some see the world as it is and say, 'Why?' I see the world as it could be and say, 'Why not?'" You can always say, "Why not?" when you're told you can't accomplish something. You can always say, "So what?" when evidence is presented against your dreams. You can always say, "It's possible," when you have a different vision for your child. Your potential is limitless, so don't give up. You have more greatness than you might think.

Letter to Reader

Dear Reader:

Almost twenty years ago, the universe placed in my path a challenge that would irrevocably change my life and the lives of everyone in my family. Our son had been diagnosed as profoundly autistic and functionally retarded. We were offered no hope. In response, my wife and I not only reevaluated the meaning and purpose of our lives but searched ourselves to find the most open-hearted, accepting, and loving place inside. More than anything else, we wanted to help our child. And even when others discouraged such an endeavor as foolhardy and unrealistic, we knew we had to try.

An amazing adventure into the unknown ensued. Instead of trying to discourage what others judged as our son's weird and inappropriate behaviors, we joined him lovingly and respectfully, jumping fully into his bizarre, unpredictable, and fantastic world. Unexpectedly, what began as a journey to find our son became a journey in which we found ourselves.

The publication of the book *Son-Rise*, written eighteen years ago, and the network television movie based on it, brought people to our doorstep from around the world. In response to their pleas for help and assistance, our lives took a dramatic new turn. Soon we were devoting ourselves full-time to sharing what we learned, not only with families with special children, but also with thousands of adults wanting to use the attitude we teach to help themselves find happiness, peace of mind, and inspiration when confronting the challenges in their lives. As I have worked with people at our learning center, The Option Institute and Fellowship, written other books, and traveled extensively presenting talks, seminars, and workshops, I have encountered over and over and over again two pointed questions:

- Question #1: Whatever happened to that little boy who was only four years old when the *Son-Rise* book ended? Did his healing last? Did he continue to develop and thrive?

- Question #2: Was his healing a fluke or were you able to replicate your success with him when you worked with other children?

I wrote this book to answer both of these questions.

Additionally, I substantially rewrote the original *Son-Rise* (which forms the first section of this book), expanding it, deepening it, and adding anecdotes not contained in the original book in order to make the events and what we learned from them more graspable. I feel as if I have matured — grown up — during these intervening years. The people who have come to our learning center have taught me so much about accessing peace of mind and personal power as they faced their challenges and created their solutions. These lessons have enabled me to see more and understand much, much more about our profoundly transforming experience with our own son. I have tried to incorporate those realizations into this book as well.

Reading the following I hope will be as wondrous an adventure for you as living and sharing it has been for my family and all those who have attended our programs throughout the years.

Most sincerely,

Barry ("Bears") Neil Kaufman

c/o The Option Institute and Fellowship
P.O. Box 1180-SR
2080 South Undermountain Road
Sheffield, MA 01257
(413) 229-2100

Acknowledgments

It all began with our son, Raun, whose unique, flamboyant, and Buddha-like presence gave us the possibility of finding so much more to love—in ourselves, in him, and in all those around us. My wife, Samahria, was the heart and soul of our work with our son; she remains a gifted teacher, coach, friend, and cheerleader to families around the world with special children. Our daughters, Bryn and Thea, joined us in our search to help and heal their brother. Their energy and assistance helped make it all possible. Our other children, Sage, Ravi, and Tayo, joined us later in our ever-unfolding journey to find more loving, accepting, and nonjudgmental places inside.

We have held hands with many people who have not only volunteered in our program to help our son, but also assisted us in helping families in towns and cities across the globe. Their love and caring reached out to so many little people. Some of these generous-hearted individuals have joined the Son-Rise Program℠ staff here at The Option Institute and Fellowship, making their commitments more abiding and their contributions more available to others. We salute them and feel a profound gratitude for their giving.

Oh, those courageous families who have come seeking help for their special children—from England and France, from the Netherlands, Germany, and Greece, from Poland and Russia, from Malaysia, Sri Lanka, India, and the Philippines, from Israel, Saudi Arabia, and Syria, from Nigeria and South Africa, from Brazil and Mexico, from Australia and New Zealand, from Canada and from many cities and communities across the United States! We have received so much more than we have given. Those generous families are now the frontier of even greater possibilities; their love and commitment to changing themselves and being passionate teachers of their own special children inspire us endlessly.

ACKNOWLEDGMENTS

And the five awesome, daring, and singular families whose journeys are shared in Part Three of this book! They represent hundreds and hundreds of other families who are using the Son-Rise Program and the attitude of love and acceptance as a basis for helping their children. Carolyn and her daughter Ruthie, Janine and Scott and their son Justin, Jenny and Randy and their son Ryan, John and Laura and their daughter Julie, and Marie and Robert and their son Danny—you take our breath away.

PART ONE
Son-Rise

1

Birth of a Miracle

His little hands hold the plate delicately as his eyes survey its smooth perimeter. His mouth curls in delight. He is setting the stage. This is his moment, as was the last and each before. This is the beginning of his entry into the solitude that has become his world. Slowly, with a masterful hand, he places the edge of the plate on the floor, sets his body in a comfortable and balanced position, and snaps his wrist with great expertise. The plate begins to spin with dazzling perfection. It revolves on itself as if set into motion by some exacting machine. And it was.

This is not an isolated act, not a mere aspect of some childhood fantasy. It is a conscious and delicately skilled activity performed by a very little boy for a very great and expectant audience — himself.

As the plate moves swiftly, spinning hypnotically on its edge, the little boy bends over it and stares squarely into its motion. Homage to himself, to the plate. For a moment, the boy's body betrays a just perceptible motion similar to the plate's. For a moment, the little boy and his spinning creation become one. His eyes sparkle. He swoons in the playland that is himself. Alive. Alive.

Raun Kahlil — a little man occupying the edge of the universe.

Before this time, this very moment, we had always been in awe of Raun, our notably special child. We sometimes referred to him as "brain-blessed." He had always seemed to be riding the high of his own happiness. Highly evolved. Seldom did he cry or utter tones of discomfort. In almost every way, his contentment and solitude seemed to suggest a profound inner peace. He was a seventeen-month-old Buddha contemplating another dimension.

A little boy set adrift on the circulation of his own system. Encapsulated behind an invisible but seemingly impenetrable wall. Soon he would be labeled. A tragedy. Unreachable. Bizarre. Statistically, he would fall into a category reserved for all those we see

3

as hopeless . . . unapproachable . . . irreversible. For us the question: Could we kiss the ground that others had cursed?

*   *   *

The beginning. Only a year and five months ago. It was 5:15 in the afternoon, a time when leaving New York City for home is like trying to pass through mechanized quicksand. Outside, the rush of metal monsters and the scattered hustle of fast-walking, blank-faced people pushed toward their daily release. The rush-hour climax had spilled into the streets, marking the last ejaculation of energy to be spent in the day.

I sat quietly in my office eight floors above Sixth Avenue, exploring ideas and images as I searched for the essential theme of yet another film—now one by Federico Fellini, yesterday one by Ingmar Bergman, last week a Dustin Hoffman film, last month another in the James Bond series. We viewed ourselves as members of a think tank whose mandate was to extract the heart of someone's cinematic statement and design a marketing campaign to reach a targeted audience.

It always began in a darkened theater. Sometimes, at the request of a client, I would sit with four or five members of my staff in the midst of five thousand empty seats at Radio City Music Hall and preview a film in the early morning hours. At other times, we would sit in a private screening room filled with cast members, producers, the director and the writer, as well as executives from the motion picture company involved. I would try to catalog each unfolding scene. I felt like a detective, looking to freeze-frame the heart and soul of a story, hoping a compelling concept or image would emerge, which we would then re-form into concrete marketing tools for that particular movie. I loved the cinema and, oftentimes, felt honored to work on some of the projects we had been assigned.

On this particular afternoon reams of crumpled sketch-pad paper decorated the top of my desk and spilled out of a cavernous wastepaper basket onto the floor. They represented hundreds of rejected ideas that had come to life only fleetingly as a doodle on a white sheet of paper. I kept at it, pushing myself over and over again to search through the nooks and crannies of my mind. For

4

me, the endeavor was at once challenging and totally absorbing. I
felt high on the freedom to originate and create. Turning the words.
Hypothesizing the pictures and graphics. And, then in the end,
mothering their execution in photography, film, sculpture, or illustration. My office had become the birthplace of the favored ideas
that survived as well as the graveyard for all the marketing concepts that fell before the commercial firing squads of my clients
and bled to death on the floors of smoke-filled conference rooms.

As I finished contemplating the solution to yet another project
I prepared myself internally for the evening commute—my dail
hustle through the crowds of humanity that I would encounter
in the street. Wanting to energize myself with a more attractive
scenario, I refocused my attention, now thinking of my wife, Samahria (who in those days was called Suzi), whose warm embrace
would be a welcome and soothing nightcap to my day. I thought
of my daughter Bryn, a seven-year-old young lady who did Chaplinesque routines on the kitchen table at the drop of a hat. I envisioned my daughter Thea, whose dark probing eyes and tiny three-
year-old form embodied the presence of a little mystic. And then,
as always, there would be crazy Sasha and majestic Riquette, two
big, bold, bearlike 130-pound Belgian herding dogs who would
pounce on me as soon as I entered the front door. Friends suggested laughingly that these animals bore an uncanny resemblance
to me.

Suddenly, the piercing ring of the telephone crashed through
my veil of concentration. The buzzer rang—for me.

"Now . . . it just started, and already the contractions are only
four minutes apart. I'll get someone to watch the girls and somebody else to take me to the hospital. Are you okay? Don't get upset. Just take your time. I'll wait for you. Everything will be okay. . . .
The nurses are trained, and they'll help me until you get there."

Samahria seemed so in control. Waves of excitement heaved
through my body. At the same time, I could feel my abdominal
muscles tightening. Not now, Jesus, not now during the rush hour.
As I flew down the stairs, I chuckled at the irony. We had prepared
for this moment with months of practice. Every week, we attended
classes together. Unlike the birth of our other children, this would
be a joint project, a birth for both Samahria and me. We had learned
the Lamaze method. We had become a team, using patterns of

breathing and other support techniques to facilitate a birth mirrored in nature. No drugs. No painkillers. No stainless steel instruments probing and prodding. We were both graduates of an elaborate training program that enabled me to assist and support Samahria from the beginning of labor through the actual delivery. This was the coaching job of my life. I was to be an essential part of this most beautiful process. But first I had to get there . . . to be with her.

The panic set in quickly. I would never make it through the maze of traffic in time. I wanted desperately to support her, to love her, and to consummate this creation as we had planned. The stop-start motion of the car made me feel nauseated. Memories of all our practice sessions and Samahria's excited smiles for the birth we would do together flashed by in a slow-motion montage. Move it! Move it faster! My pulse pounded in my head as if to help the forward motion of my vehicle. Push it! Will it! Wish the traffic away. I talked to God and the universe. Clear the way! Please, clear the way. I imagined Samahria all alone in some cold and drafty tiled room . . . counting and breathing to her own echoes. I knew she would try to hold on and make it through until I arrived. How could all the practice and patience be robbed from us by some arbitrary quirk of circumstances? Impossible! I would not let it be.

The racing of my mind seemed to outpace the speed of the car. For Samahria, this was not just the birth of our third child. It was the culmination of a dream — to share this experience with me and to have me as an integral part of our family's unfolding. Also, this opened the possibility of having a son. She had conspired with her doctor, and both apparently agreed that certain physiological signs indicated this baby would most likely be a boy — our first son. The girls had filled our lives with a new loving and softness. For me, a boy would be an unexpected gift. But for Samahria, the emotional investment was different. She loved the girls with an abiding intensity, but she had always wanted at least one male child. And now she felt sure such specialness was about to enter her life.

My hands began to stick to the steering wheel. One hour had elapsed, snapped from us in what felt like an instant. I turned my car to the right, jumped the curb beside the highway, and catapulted the vehicle onto the grass. Then I pressed down on the accelerator. The car bounced over the curbs by the entrance and exit ramps.

Endless patterns of stilled automobiles whizzed by in my peripheral vision. I felt like a twilight phantom moving through the spaces between molecules, pushing down on the accelerator and then pushing down on it even more.

I had to be there. I knew that I was more than just a significant member of the cast: I was the only one left to her. Samahria's father was consumed by a second marriage, a new family of young children, and a growing business. Four years ago her mother had died at the age of forty-six while developing the fruits of her second marriage. Her sister remained on the other side of a wall. Like Samahria, she, too, had had to endure the lonely years of a childhood immersed in confusion and divorce. The pain of that separation had splashed up against both of them.

But Samahria had also reached for the love and the joy, vowing that she would create a relationship and family far different from the one she had known. However, the disharmony and anger surrounding her left her scared and unsure of herself. At night, alone and lonely in her room, she would talk to God. Her prayers became elaborate conversations with what she described later as a dear and ever-present friend. That relationship enabled her to endure those troubling years. As a teenager, she tried to rebuild her confidence, challenging herself to be more daring and more comfortable. A personal stretch of gigantic proportions occurred when she auditioned and was accepted into the famed High School of Performing Arts in New York City. But even as she traveled alone on the subways for hours to attend classes at this school and was asked to demonstrate her abilities in classrooms and on the stage each day, she could never quite shake the shadow of self-doubt.

Samahria spent years trying to repair what felt like damage within. Her goal had been to reconstruct herself and find new alternatives. But it had been a difficult and inconsistent journey for her in her time as it had been for me in mine. Now most of these events were just memories, clouded in the frosted lens of another era. With each other, we had found new reasons to be.

Finally the wheels of the car slammed over a six-inch cement abutment and landed squarely on the driveway entering the hospital grounds. I stopped haphazardly in the parking lot, getting as close to the entrance of the building as I could, then literally bolted from my vehicle. My legs could not carry me as fast as I wanted to go.

I sprinted up the lawn, jumped up the steps three at a time, and burst through the entranceway, making a mad dash for an opened elevator. Once the doors reopened on the maternity ward, I jumped off at a full run down the hallway. People scattered out of my way, not so much because they sensed my urgency, but for their own survival. This was a tight-quartered version of a football scrimmage. My six-foot-two frame carried its 220 pounds easily as I charged forcefully through the interior of this public building.

The entire experience began to feel like sliding through a time warp. I felt like a metaphysical quarterback reincarnated as a grizzly bear with my thick, wild hair flying behind me as my bearded face bounded up and down to the rhythm of the loping movement. Samahria and my daughters had blessed me with the nickname of The Big Bear, their lyrical and affectionate interpretation of my appearance and size. But eventually this I.D. gave way to the name Bear. Then, deciding the singular was not enough, Samahria started calling me Bears, a name that stuck and became the way family and friends addressed me. So there I was, big, a bit furry, and probably a bit foolish while still on my mad, comic-book surge, dodging doctors, nurses, and visitors as I glided over the polished floor.

Then I heard someone calling my name. The sounds bounced off the floor and walls. In the distance, a nurse frantically waved me on as if she were cheering a long shot in the race at Aqueduct. And for me, it was the last couple of yards, the finish line for the long-distance runner.

No time now. Undress in the hallway. Our child was about to be born. I had just made it.

"Is she okay?"

"She's doing just fine."

Now another nurse was assisting, helping me remove my jacket and slip into the sanitized white garb. The first nurse pulled a face mask out of its plastic wrapping and tied it around my head.

Samahria had in some way decided to wait for me and not to abandon natural childbirth by taking the needle and drifting away. If need be, I knew she would have done it alone. I felt enormously grateful to be there.

There were screams from the other labor rooms I passed — the symphony of emotions seemingly out of control. I walked, almost on tiptoe, into a quiet cubicle, finally arriving at Samahria's side. The nurse put my wife's hand into mine. She was in the midst of a contraction. Her stomach arcned upward into a tall mound while her lips puckered. She rapidly pushed air in and out of her lungs in short, shallow beats. Intense. Quiet. A beautiful pantomime.

At first she didn't look at me, but I knew that she knew I was there. She pressed her hand tightly into mine as I kissed her lightly; then both of us started counting out loud. The corners of her mouth wrinkled in a slight smile.

The doctor came by, measured the dilation of her cervix, and nodded. The time had come to move down the corridor to the delivery room. I kept my focus always on Samahria, counting, pacing, and encouraging her through each contraction—even as they wheeled her through the hallway. We arrived at our final destination quickly. The white tiled walls glistening under the bright lights. A table, filled with surgical instruments, waited nearby, just in case.

Between each contraction, I wiped the sweat from Samahria's face with a damp, cool washcloth. Her smiles came easily now, but she seemed tired.

"You are doing super," I whispered. "And you look enormously attractive in the process."

We both laughed.

"I am so, so glad you're here. I kept holding back. But, Bears, if you didn't make it, I was going to deliver as we planned. No medication. Everything natural for this baby. Really, I had decided." Samahria stopped talking abruptly as the next contraction began. I counted and modeled the appropriate pattern of inhaling and exhaling for her. She winked at me, then pushed her head back and became completely absorbed in the breathing that would help her through the pain. The upward thrust of her abdominal area became more intense than either of us had imagined, but we both stayed with it. Even the doctor seemed to be riding the high of the moment, humming some vaguely familiar romantic Italian tune that he might have heard in his childhood.

We all watched with awe as the top of the baby's head began to appear. It seemed much larger than the opening through which it would exit.

The nurses now moved quickly into different positions. Everyone prepared for the next unfolding event, very contemporary and very theatrical.

Episiotomy. The teacher in the natural childbirth class had never clearly mentioned that—the cutting. As I watched the physician cut the skin with a quick, professional movement and as the blood began to seep out of both sides of the open wound, the room danced before my eyes. Everything around me started to swirl. My focus blurred. The image of myself became fractured and began to crumble. Someone grabbed me as I fell forward and led me from the room. The nurse smiled and told me that "it happens all the time." But it didn't matter. I could not miss it now. I tucked some smelling salts under my face mask and sneaked back in. Everyone smiled, welcoming my return. Samahria seemed so intense, so very much in control. She giggled as I moved to her side and then was quickly lost in the next contraction.

The doctor encouraged her to push now, with everything she had. My insides were pushing with her. She seemed so courageous to me. No cries of pain. No misgivings. She was totally involved. A creator and participant. Suddenly, after a gigantic thrust, a beautiful steel gray child slipped from the womb of her body with the greatest of ease. A boy! He began to breathe and cry at the same time. The doctor put him on Samahria's stomach as he severed the umbilical cord. Unbelievable. He was ours, and we had seen him come into life.

The nurse pronounced him a perfect specimen. We looked at each other in awe. With each second, the color in his face and body changed. As he took in air, the misty gray became pink and his wide-eyed glance beheld the universe. Tears fell from Samahria's eyes. Joyful tears. The culmination. I felt so alive, so connected. We would call him Raun Kahlil.

*   *   *

At home, the first month with Raun was not quite what we had anticipated. He seemed troubled, crying day and night. He was unresponsive to being held or fed, as if preoccupied with some internal turmoil. We shuttled back and forth to the pediatrician, receiving assurances that our baby was perfectly healthy and normal. The Apgar rating was ten at birth, the highest possible score an infant can receive for alertness and reflexes. Yet Samahria still sensed that something was wrong. Her intuitive grasp kept us both alert.

Then, in the fourth week of his life, a severe ear infection suddenly surfaced. Again, we turned to the doctor, who prescribed antibiotics. But the crying continued. And continued. No touch or sound seemed to soothe him. The doctor increased the medication.

The infection began to spread like molten lava, moving through both ears and into his throat. An apparently minor condition of dehydration resulting from the antibiotics escalated quickly into a critical condition. Raun began to lose the spark of life. He held his eyelids at half-mast. His movements became lethargic. Samahria pursued the pediatrician, describing Raun's symptoms and situation in detail. The doctor wanted to wait another day, explaining that our son's current condition could be a normal response to medicine. Yet Samahria wanted Raun checked immediately, and, upon her insistence, the doctor agreed. Since house calls were no longer fashionable, she had to wrap our sick baby in blankets and transport him to the physician's office. She raced through the streets, darting through traffic as she realized that, though Raun breathed normally, his skin had begun to take on a white pallor.

The pediatrician responded with surprise and dismay to our son's appearance. He had not anticipated that the dehydration would progress so rapidly. Raun had slipped now behind closed eyelids; even the doctor could not elicit a movement from him. Preparation was made for immediate emergency hospitalization. Our son was placed in a pediatric intensive-care unit. His name appeared on the critical list. Everything happened so swiftly. We moved with frantic urgency through a blur of uncontrollable events.

Our visits with our son had to be short as dictated by hospital rules. Raun had been locked in a plastic isolette, hidden from us, lost in a mechanized world of tubes and glass. Samahria and I had to dress in white surgical gowns. We bathed our hands and faces in an iodine solution as a sterilizing precaution. Although permitted to enter his glass cubicle, we were not allowed to touch our son. We watched, feeling helpless, as if we had been thrust out of the picture. We knew we could lose him.

All around us little infants were connected to wires and pumps that maintained their tenuous lifelines. In the next booth, a young nurse wearing rubber gloves pushed her hands through the special holes in the side of an isolette. The little girl inside moved restlessly as the young woman worked with great precision and premeditation, adjusting all the valves and devices. Suddenly, the nurse stopped her activity as if awakened from a dream. She looked directly at the baby and smiled at her. Then, placing her face within inches of the plastic container, she began to sing as she softly caressed the infant's belly with her rubberized hands. The little girl's movements became less erratic. Her tiny fingers clutched the nurse's hand. The two of them touched each other in a beautiful vignette of caring—of remembering to care.

This scene lifted our spirits for Raun and all the other children confined to the unit. Each day when we returned, we were given guarded forecasts. Although the ear infection was serious, it was the heavy medication that had created the current crisis. My mind flexed. The same people who had caused the dehydration were now feverishly trying to reverse its effect. How could we know what to do? What judgments could we make? We were lost in a crowd of charts, injections, and unanswered questions.

Several days passed with us all poised at the edge of a cliff. Early morning, Samahria and I sat silently with each other over coffee, consciously avoiding the view of the empty crib. But we were bursting with emotions, and the intensity of those feelings broke the quiet, which always seemed so powerful. We held on to Raun through conversations about him and by sharing our acute sensitivity and love for him.

We spent afternoons and evenings at the hospital. Sometimes we would just sit in the lobby after visiting hours as a way to be close to him. On the fifth day, we heard the first really optimistic forecast. He would get through it. At last, he was holding food and his weight had stabilized. But, unfortunately, the infection had caused damage. Both his eardrums had ruptured from the pressure of the fluids, which could result in a possible loss or impairment of hearing. For us, it would not matter. If Raun was deaf or partially deaf, we would find a way to pump the world's music into his head. All that mattered was that he was alive and thriving again.

Happily, we embarked on our second beginning at home. Raun acted like a different child—exuberant, playful, and free of pain. He smiled all the time. Free from the difficulties that had plagued his first month, his alertness and responsiveness increased profoundly. He ate well and appeared to love the world. We felt alive again, together again. The nightmare had given birth to a new morning.

As we settled in, Samahria and I turned our focus to the girls. We wanted to be sensitive to their wants and needs as well as help them adjust to this new presence in our home. Precocious Bryn, an extrovert, an entertainer, a clown, and sometimes a soothsayer, demonstrated such insight and verbal skills that she often crossed over the line from the profound into the obnoxious. She enjoyed being intense and dramatic. We experienced her more like a friend and companion than a daughter. For her, Raun was not simply her brother; this child became her child as well, to be shared with her mother and father. He would replace the dolls and the afternoon fantasies. She knew he had been rescued from death's door. She really understood and treasured his presence as much as we did.

For Thea, the circumstances appeared very different. Artistic and moody, unpredictable and mysterious, she now had the distinction of becoming the infamous "middle" child. I had held the same onerous position with uneasiness in my family. She could not claim to be the firstborn, thus first to be cuddled and break new ground. Now no longer the youngest child, who usually reaps an abiding harvest of attention as the eternal "baby," Thea had been dethroned. Nevertheless, we did not want her to feel displaced and dislodged. We decided to provide her with extra doses of overt attention and love. We would give her even more now so that she could continue to develop in her very particular and individual style.

The first year of Raun's life whizzed by with incredible speed. He grew more and more beautiful, smiling, laughing, and playing as the girls had. Even his sense of hearing seemed appropriate. He listened to voices and turned his head attentively toward various sounds. Apart from not putting his arms out to be picked up, Raun seemed normal and healthy in every way.

When he was a year old, we began to notice increasing audio insensitivity. He responded less and less to his name and to general sounds. It was as though his hearing began to diminish progressively. Each week, he acted more and more aloof, as if some magical internal voice kept distracting him from being attentive. We had been counseled repetitiously about the possibility that he might exhibit a hearing deficiency eventually. We wanted to intercede, to help him and to help him now. We had his hearing checked. Although it was too early to determine hearing loss accurately, the doctor asserted that despite the possibility of deafness, Raun appeared in "good shape" clinically. He assured us that our son's inconsistent aloofness was of no great concern, insisting that Raun would outgrow any current peculiarities.

Over the next four months, Raun's supposed or possible hearing deficit became compounded by his tendency to stare and to be passive. He seemed to prefer solitary play over interaction with our family. When we picked him up, his arms dangled limply at his sides as if they had been disconnected from his body. Often, he expressed dislike or discomfort with physical contact by pushing our hands away from his body when we tried to embrace or fondle him. He demonstrated a preference for sameness and routine, consistently choosing one or two objects to play with and going to a special area in the house to sit by himself.

And then some obvious inconsistencies appeared in regard to his hearing capability. He would seem not to hear a loud, sharp noise close to him but might be attentive to a soft and distant sound. Then, at other times, a noise that he had not reacted to previously would suddenly attract his attention.

Even the sounds he made and the one or two words that he had mimicked were no longer part of his repertoire. Instead of acquiring language, he had become mute. Even his prelinguistic pointing or gesturing ceased to exist.

We took him back to the hospital. After repeated examinations for audio receptivity, we were informed that Raun could definitely hear but that his seemingly strange, aloof, and obtuse behavior made proper diagnosis difficult. At one point during a test, when the technicians bombarded Raun with a special sequence of tones, he did not react at all. In fact, because there were no evident reflexive responses in his eyes or eyelids, it seemed as if he could be deaf. However, about ten minutes later, while he stared aimlessly at a wall, he began to repeat the notes he had heard before in the exact pitch and sequence in which they had been played—a perfect, though delayed, reaction. To the amazement of everyone present, our son, whose previous lack of reactions mirrored that of a deaf child, could indeed hear.

Was the quality of his hearing intermittent or could he hear but choose to respond inconsistently? Maybe he had difficulty digesting and utilizing what he heard. Even the clinicians shrugged

14

their shoulders in response to our pointed concerns and hypotheses. Ultimately, the tests had raised more serious questions than they had answered.

*   *   *

Sunday afternoons in the park. The glare of the sun bathed the grass and trees with soft yellow hues. A summer breeze brought the foliage alive with movement. Nature danced before my eyes like a twentieth-century Monet canvas in action. Everything around me appeared timeless and perfect. I stopped my racing bike by the swings, extracted Raun from the seat over the rear wheel, and invited him to join me. I did a slow jog into the playground, only to realize that my son did not follow. He stood silently by the curb, eyeing the leaves on a nearby maple tree. I called to him, but he did not respond. Finally, I jogged a full circle, swept him into my arms, and deposited him gently on a swing. Once I pushed the safety bar in place, I gave Raun an easy push. Instead of standing behind him, I remained in front of my son, captivated and confused by his uniqueness. I watched as the swing carried him back and forth. He ignored my smiles, my tickles, even my laughter. He kept flipping his thumb and index finger in front of his eyes. Suddenly, I felt something deep inside shift. It was as if I had always viewed Raun through the eyes of hopefulness and happiness; now I wanted to strip away any romance inside my head and really see him.

With new eyes, I peered at my very special young son, convinced he could hear, perhaps even perfectly. I addressed him, as I often did, as a peer. "Raun, do you know how much Mommy and I love you?" No answer. "Raun, we want to understand. Please, help us." Again, no answer. His little body moved with the swing, but his mind and focus of attention seemed elsewhere. Sometimes, he looked keenly at a point of sunlight reflecting off the seesaw in the distance. At other times, his eyes appeared glazed and fixed, as if he were blind. A strange, almost eerie, humming sound came from his throat.

What was happening to him and to us? "Raun, can you look at me?" He turned his head, not toward me but away from me. Somehow, I knew he could make some sense of my ramblings—

this little big man with profoundly gigantic sensibilities presented himself as a riddle to all who interacted with him. I kept talking. I wanted him to help me know more about his specialness, but my requests fell on deaf ears. Months ago, he had learned a few words, yet even those seemed lost now. Mute. Profoundly inattentive. Was his lack of responsiveness really a sign?

Repositioning myself directly in front of his gaze, I watched him, looking for clues. He kept staring. He seemed to look through me as if I were invisible. His eyes did not appear to absorb my image but merely reflected it back to me. Again I asked him to give me a signal or make a gesture . . . any gesture. My words were carried away by the wind—unanswered.

"I love you, Raun. Please know that I love you." Yet deep inside, even as I spoke, I acknowledged that those expressions probably did not hold any meaning for him. Samahria and I cared for this child so tenderly and yet we had no way to communicate that feeling so that he could digest it and be nurtured by it. Bryn and Thea expressed their love frequently and lavishly. Raun, neither by word nor by action, ever expressed such a sentiment. More than ever, we opened our hearts and minds to this strange child we did not understand.

Moving closer to Raun and peering more intently into his eyes, I found myself actually turning inward and searching myself for answers. Finally my thoughts began to flow. I started to catalog and lay bare all the particulars that were Raun Kahlil.

He could rock back and forth for hours, leveraged on his own eternity. He demonstrated an uncanny ability to spin plates, flapping his hands wildly as they turned in circles. He played hypnotically with inanimate objects while ignoring, even avoiding, people. His self-stimulating smile and the repetitious flipping of his fingers against his lips or in front of his eyes had become ever present. Raun's silent aloneness had a peculiar kind of power, as if he could drop into a deep meditative place from which no one could distract him. He pushed others away, systematically avoiding eye contact. When he did look, he stared and appeared to peer through people rather than at them. And yet, ironically, as he slipped behind what had become an invisible but impenetrable wall, he seemed at peace, fascinated by a world that none of us could grasp.

To expect Raun to have started using language at eighteen

16

months old might have seemed unreasonable except for the fact that he had started using a few words six months earlier and then stopped abruptly. Our concern was not simply that he did not use the spoken word, but that he offered no communication by sound or gesture, no expressed wants, likes, or dislikes. He never pointed toward anything he desired. Raun had become a singular creature afloat in a strange land.

Standing in the playground, I meditated on my thoughts and allowed my focus to dance from idea to idea. I sifted through them as my internal wandering brought me closer to a conclusion. I looked again at Raun; he was so far away. The wooden seat of the swing and its chains had become a substitute for the plate that he would often set into motion by spinning it on the kitchen floor. The swing had become another moving vehicle that facilitated his exquisite ride into a quietly personal and solitary universe.

I called to him and heard the echo in the valley of my thoughts. I laughed and caught the fantasy of an imagined smile. I spoke again. This time, Raun turned his eyes toward me, and for a fleeting and barely perceptible moment we made contact. Then he was gone again. Blond hair in Shirley Temple ringlets framed his face. And, once again, his large brown riveting eyes reflected my image back to me.

A word appeared like a neon sign on the surface of my thoughts. A label that was confusing, frightening, and bizarre. None of the doctors we had seen repetitiously ever mentioned this possibility. I poked at it, focusing my mind's eye on it. Then I drew away and tried to shake it loose. I gazed again at Raun. His softness recharged me. I brought the word into sharper focus. It danced in my head like a vulture inviting me to the last resort. Yet it would only be my last resort and a frightening vision if I chose to see horror, madness, or something even worse. The word became undeniable and I mouthed it into existence.

Autism . . . infantile autism. A subcategory of childhood schizophrenia—the most irreversible category of the profoundly disturbed and psychotic. Could the word destroy the dream, forever limiting the horizons of my son, and damn him to a deviant and sealed corner of our lives?

Just a hypothesis; yet it seemed correct. As I continued to observe my son, my recall sharpened. Suddenly, I could see the words lifting off a page in an abnormal psychology text my professor used in graduate school. I remembered a fellow student giving a short report on autism, saying that all the literature and evidence suggested these children were irretrievable and that most spent their lives locked up in state institutions. The professor chuckled with amusement, calling such children "real crazies." He claimed to have had firsthand experience; so all of us students assumed he knew. But now, I was not considering a statistic in a book or a sarcastic remark about a dysfunctional child. My God, this was my son. A human being.

My mind sped into high gear. Additional scattered pieces of information surfaced. Pieces of a puzzle began to come together. At first I did not want to see what I was seeing. Why hadn't any of the physicians or specialists we had seen suggested such a diagnosis? Had we been wasting time and losing precious moments? I told myself that my memory data could be imperfect and misleading. Nevertheless, I swept Raun off the swing onto the back seat of the bicycle. As I pedaled toward home, I sensed that my supposition was correct. And yet, I wanted to resist.

Like a junkie looking for an angry fix, I searched the cavity of my mind, hoping for a doorway out. There was a difference: The pattern wasn't complete. Raun had always been happy and peaceful, seemingly caught in the mellow hue of a thousand years of contemplation. This serenity placed him outside the classic descriptions of autism, which generally characterized children as unhappy, angry, and even self-destructive.

I submerged myself in this revelation for the remainder of the day, looking through old textbooks and sifting through information I had available. Daylight disappeared and ushered in the last dance of early evening. Samahria sang the final chorus of the day with both Bryn and Thea, saying ten "good nights," negotiating pleas for "five more minutes," and finally wrestling with the girls playfully. I joined in the foray, drinking in all the smiles and pretended sighs. Four hundred kisses were given, each one calculated to buy more time and delay the inevitable "lights out." The girls chattered and meandered while Samahria coaxed and herded them to the stairs as she completed the last chores of the day. I delighted in this sweet ballet, performed each night by my daughters and their loving mom—three women, so energetic and animated. Off to the side, conspicuously disconnected from all the action, Raun rocked in repetitive motions—quiet, peaceful, and very internally absorbed. When Bryn and Thea tried to hug him good night, he pulled away. They smiled at him, loving him anyway.

As I waited for Samahria to finish tucking the children in bed, I rehearsed the word. I said it softly and quietly to myself. I uttered it with authority and conviction. I phrased it as a question. Yes, that would be the way—just a question.

When Samahria returned, she sat opposite me and faced me with a foreboding directness. It was as if she knew that I wanted to talk and that my words would be heavy. The energy flowed from my mouth and rambled over unfamiliar territory. Finally, the word *autism* crept from between my lips. Samahria didn't flinch. She listened carefully to my hypothesis. Her clear blue eyes sparkled with an eagerness to know, to understand, to pin it down so that at least we could move on. Her long blond hair curled softly over her shoulders, while her fingers moved slowly across her bottom lip and her forehead furrowed. The light dipped in and out of the shallow crevices of her face. We looked at each other through the mist in our eyes.

Together there in the living room, we sat silently as the word *autism* settled into the space and spread out around us. It had so much power that I knew Samahria needed a couple of minutes by herself to absorb it. I waited, my eyes traveling from one of the objects decorating the room to another. The woodcut of a four-hundred-year-old man filled the space beside the bookcase. I stared at a piece of sculpture gouged out of onyx. The artist's title, "Anguish," had particular meaning on this night. Our house had always been a collection of ourselves. The toilet bowl I had painted in honor of Samahria's last birthday stood boldly in front of the fireplace. Her charcoal portrait of my face, which she had given to me three years ago from a hospital bed after suffering injuries in a horseback-riding accident, hung just above the couch.

I smiled at the great Murray, which I had created one weekend out of surgical bandage wrapped around an armature—a life-sized, chalk white figure who sat peacefully in a reconditioned antique barber chair near the entrance to the living room. This formidable frozen figure held in his hands an opened copy of Walt Whitman's *Leaves of Grass*. Seven bronze figures, representations of

Yosemite National Park rock formations, sat on a glass table, a gift given to us eight years ago by a California friend who does daily battle there, living his downbeat and painful version of the artistic life. A nine-foot construction I designed and formed out of antique wood type loomed like a gothic pillar beside me. And Samahria's imposing acrylics—dramatic sculptural forms chiseled out of clear Lucite—could be seen throughout the room. They are at once dense and transparent, intense and mystifying. Some of my original photography, rejects from creative endeavors in Manhattan, decorated the walls.

Lifting my feet onto the coffee table, I recalled that even this piece of furniture had a story. It had once been a hatch door on a World War II liberty ship that carried troops across the Atlantic. I felt grateful for the richness of our lives. These objects were wonderful footnotes to our lives, pointing out where we had been, what we had done, and how we had felt. They represented an evolution of eleven years, which at times had been unpredictable and stormy. Those first years were difficult with their up-and-down inconsistencies. But during the last several years, we had come together with more ease and more love. Now, just as life seemed to be almost perfect, we found ourselves contemplating the impossible something that always happens to someone else, never you. We confronted a reality that could last for a lifetime and make a tragedy of all our days.

Samahria's teal blue eyes had been fixed on some indeterminate point in space. Her long, flowing hair framed her radiant face. Old blue jeans, their denim decorated with leather and Indian-print patches, and a long-sleeved polo shirt embroidered with roses and an art deco landscape decorated her trim figure. She was in full bloom, deep and sensuous. Yet the infectious way she would laugh while sitting cross-legged in the middle of the floor or the way she would jump into the air to dance to some outrageous tune on the radio suggested a more adolescent and childlike inclination. The soft pink scent of jasmine filled the room. For me, Samahria meant sunshine and femininity. Even now in this shadow, her exuberance and her love for life danced on the surface. She turned toward me, exhaled a long sigh, and let her head rock up and down as if to say over and over again, "Yes, I know. I know."

Together, we decided to explore and research the subject of

autism. It had always been her belief that Raun could hear and that "something else" was happening with him. We pulled out the old psychology books with their scribbled messages from another era. We took new books from the library. Finally, we had it. Leo Kanner had labeled it first in 1943. Others expanded the initial criteria and recorded a constellation of symptoms. Autism is an illness defined not by origin or cause, but by a collection of associated symptoms or behavior patterns.

The categories: antisocial and aloof patterns of activity; hypnotic preoccupation with spinning, rocking, and other repetitive movements; a lack of verbal communication and sometimes even a lack of prelinguistic gesture language; a tendency to look through people; a fascination with inanimate objects; no anticipatory gestures when being approached or picked up; often seeming deaf, unresponsive, and self-stimulating; desiring sameness; rejection of physical contact. Generally, for no apparent reason, autistic children are often physically attractive children. Thirty years ago, this man had described our infant son who had then not yet been born. Raun fit every category except that he was not self-destructive (he did not bite himself or bang his head).

Samahria and I looked at each other in silence, searching each other's eyes for our reactions. Then we explored our fears, our feeling of despair, and the seeming enormity of our discovery. And finally we decided: We would try to make it all right; we would see it through. If Raun was autistic, we would help him. We would love him. We would, with his sisters, find a way.

The literature argued against our optimistic mood. The literature talked about the noncommunicative child who most often slips behind a veil of his own solitude and becomes unreachable. Bruno Bettelheim, in *The Empty Fortress*, describes autism as trauma and articulates the pessimistic results of his study. The overwhelming percentage of the children he studied had been hospitalized and confined to custodial care for their entire lives. Their personalities disintegrated (or never developed), and the family units they belonged to crumbled. Bettelheim noted the few he had reached but indicated that ultimately all showed severely limited communicative and adaptive abilities. His vision of causality led him to indict the parents of autistic children, for he believed that these children used their abnormal behavior to protest a cold and unresponsive environment. His theoretical suppositions damned the mothers of autistic children; he judged them to have "refrigerator" personalities—all of this without undertaking any substantial investigation or producing meaningful evidence. So much of what he claimed was judgmental and hypothetical. He defined all autistic behaviors as symptoms—statements the child supposedly made to register his rejection of his immediate environment. Clearly, living with and loving Raun yielded distinctly different observations. Our son did not appear to be reacting against or even responding to his surroundings. It was as if Raun had a special calling that originated from deep within.

We noticed all the inconsistencies in the literature and the dismal success rate achieved to date with these autistic children—a success rate measured according to some abstract curve of normalcy. We had to stay open; there was too much to absorb and too much to learn before we drew conclusions. We wanted to stay free of fearing the future so we could understand what was happening to us and our child right now.

Samahria initiated the endless telephone conversations with professionals. Their advice was usually abrupt and contradictory: "He's too young." "We never see them so young." "Go here; go there." "Hopeless." "Great, what we really want is to get them young." "Give him a full psychiatric evaluation." "Face it now: He'll probably have to be institutionalized." "He'll need a neurological workup and an EEG." "He'll probably outgrow it." "It could be a tumor . . . a brain tumor." "We know so little about autism." "There's not much we can do; bring him to us in a year." "Unfortunately, we know very little about these kinds of children."

We had talks with doctors and hospitals in and around New York City. We queried an institute in Philadelphia specializing in brain-damaged and autistic children. There were the specialized environmental schools, one in Brooklyn and one in Nassau County, neither of which would see our child until he was much older, and even then it would be just a "maybe." We contacted a dedicated specialist in behaviorism located at a major California university and funded by a federal grant to study and research autism. We investigated psychopharmacology, psychoanalysis, behaviorism, vitamin therapy, nutritional analysis, the CNS (central nervous system) factor, and the genetic theory. Diverse opinions and non-opinions surfaced, many based on unsubstantiated theories and debatable assumptions.

As Samahria spread her informational grip out over the country, I withdrew into my hermitage of solitude to read everything available on the subject. I examined in depth the writings of Carl Delacato and his concepts of patterning and sensory impairment. He believed that autistic children are not psychotic as Bettelheim described them and defined them instead as brain-damaged with perceptual dysfunctions.

Reading incessantly, I probed the psychoanalytic themes, then explored the work of I. Newton Kugelmass. I delved into the research of Bernard Rimland, stimulated by his concept of impaired cognitive function and the inability of these children to relate new stimuli to old, remembered data. Then I studied Martin Kozloff and his thesis of operant conditioning. I studied behavior modification, whose proponents ignore causality and meaning in favor of restructuring these children's lives by designing a thorough and complex system of rewards and punishments. Was theirs an exercise in robotizing these children?

The research done by Dr. Ivar Lovaas seemed unique and startling. I respected his dedication to designing scientific models, but I had difficulty accepting his methods — especially his early use of electric shock and other abusive techniques to alter a child's behavior. I jumped back into B. F. Skinner and even Freud, rummaging through the basics in the hope of finding a solid footing. The voluminous observations, statistics, theories, and speculation were extensive and contradictory. In antiquity, but certainly not in contemporary literature, Raun would have been considered blessed by a "divine disease" and honored rather than discarded.

We tried to pull everything we learned together, to make sense out of the miasma of volumes, investigations, and lengthy telephone conversations. We tried fervently to synthesize a direction to pursue.

We decided to have an in-depth examination and workup done on Raun. He was almost seventeen months old. We had to plunge in somewhere, but at least now we felt much more knowledgeable. First, we arranged for an interview and a clinical evaluation at a major institution with a highly renowned psychiatric division. They confirmed our son's serious developmental problems and bizarre autistic behavior patterns, but they did not want to label him. They believed that often labels were self-fulfilling prophecies. We were told that if Raun had been officially diagnosed as autistic, his records could result in his being excluded from certain school systems and programs. Additionally, many other professionals often treat such children as hopelessly limited in potential. Come back in a year, they said, and they would have another look at him. We were disappointed, even angry. We wanted help, not an abstract diagnosis.

We scheduled additional examinations. The diagnosis of autism loomed more clearly now. In fact, several physicians and neuropsychologists identified Raun as classically and profoundly autistic as well as functionally retarded in his abilities. One test yielded a below-thirty I.Q. test score. Professionals marveled at our ability to detect the autistic symptoms in a child so young, since usually such signs are not fully recognized before children are two and a half to three years old. And, yet, we found the bizarre and unusual behavior so pronounced that we could see no way not to acknowledge that something had gone terribly wrong.

The professionals appeared solicitous and kind, empathetic and concerned. Like those who first examined him, subsequent doctors told us to return in nine months to a year. Why nine months? Not because Raun couldn't be worked with but because their affiliated facilities did not deal with children so young. A child with these symptoms normally would be three or four years old before being given any professional help. We pushed. Could they make an exception? We wanted help now. Under the pressure of our persistence, one of the doctors suggested we call her facility after the summer but admitted she could not hold out much hope for a child with this condition. Between the lines we detected that a clear message had been given: Why the urgency to intercede when, in fact, whether we began now or later, the eventual result would be the same—a severely dysfunctional human being?

Another clinician shook his head sadly as he viewed Raun spinning happily around and around in dizzying circles. He muttered, "How terrible." I responded by saying that we never wanted to look at our son, or any child for that matter, and think or see "terrible." We were not in a state of denial. Our son looked as if he had just been dropped here from another planet. However, we wanted to see his uniqueness, his singularity, even his wonder—yes, even his wonder. The clinician now looked at us rather sadly and tried to convince us of the unfortunate prognosis for this condition. His associate suggested that we were lucky to have two normal children. In effect, he said, we should focus our attention on them and consider eventual institutionalization for our son. Never, ever, did we want to see our child through their eyes. Samahria and I kept telling each other: "It's just their judgments and their beliefs. No one can foretell the future, not even these specialists."

We decided to be hopeful even if others called such a perspective unrealistic. Without hope, we had no reason to go on.

After the evaluations, we were left with ample diagnoses and test scores—but no help. All our efforts left us with exactly what we already knew. We no longer wanted more confirmations. To suggest that the earlier we help this type of child, the better, and then actually turn the child away because he is too young seemed cruel and self-defeating. Depressing statistics or depressing attitudes? Why should the doctors rush if they believed that autism is irreversible and incurable?

We felt we had to intervene—now. Each day we could see him slipping from us, withdrawing more and more, becoming more insensitive to audio and visual stimuli, becoming more encapsulated. Raun appeared bewildered as well, lost in patterns of self-stimulating behavior that had become increasingly stronger. Medical and institutional help was neither offered nor available for this eighteen-month-old little boy. The endless but futile gesture of finger pointing by the professionals had been incredibly trying and unconstructive. After contacting the National Society for Autistic Children (now called the Autism Society of America) and talking with parents of children similar to ours, we found that most had initiated a search for information and advice and also received little or no help. In most instances, they had learned to accept their predicaments with varying degrees of despair and frustration.

In fact, we attended a local chapter meeting of the National Society for Autistic Children. Other parents and professionals welcomed us graciously. However, once the evening began formally, the mood changed. People shared their difficult and heart-wrenching experiences with their own children. Eyes filled with tears as many gathered around the large conference table nodding their heads knowingly. The atmosphere became gloomy. Some folks warned us that our child not only would become self-destructive but would probably be handicapped further by a seizure disorder likely to surface before his tenth birthday. Then others lobbied for us to understand and acknowledge what had become the party line for this organization: that autism is a lifelong disability. No cure. No complete reversal. They, too, cautioned us to be realistic. We knew they meant well, but we also knew how such beliefs could become self-fulfilling prophecies. How could we reach the stars if we never thought we could get there? We wanted so much more. We never stayed to the end of the meeting. We excused ourselves, wishing our hosts well while simultaneously wanting ourselves and other parents to have a very different vision. The perspectives and fear-of-the-future commentaries expressed about these children had not been challenged, but, in fact, reinforced by professionals present at the meeting. The shared pain had become a black hole, leaving no one left to celebrate these youngsters but only to mourn their existence as they still lived. We knew all the parents in that room loved their children and wanted the best. We also knew we had to travel a very different road.

We believed in Raun; we believed in his peace, in his beauty, in his happiness.

We knew that now it would be up to us and to him. Perhaps it had always been that way. All the diagnoses and analyses might have statistical meaning to a number-hungry society, but they had none to a little boy with staring eyes. If Raun was to get help, if this little autistic boy could be reached and brought into our world, it would have to be done now and by us alone — now, while he was young; now, while we were wanting; now, while he was still happy in his infant playland.

If we waited, the evidence indicated overwhelmingly that he would become just another dismal statistic. We knew that the game would have to be played out while Raun's behavior patterns were still new and unentrenched, while his difficulty in approaching his environment had not as yet created overlays of serious emotional problems, while his peace and his joy were pristine and unspoiled.

We had little to work with but our own deep desire to reach Raun and to help him reach out to us. The professionals offered no real hope or help, but in our love for our son and his beauty we found a determination to persist.

2

The Pilgrimage Begins

Where to begin? We decided to start with ourselves, with the evolution of our own beliefs and feelings.

It was like taking a pilgrimage back in order to come forward—searching and sifting through the memories of my recent past in hopes of recrystallizing essential knowledge that would carry us through. I thought back to the mid-1960s, when I graduated from college with a degree in philosophy. I remembered the months and years of flexing the membranes of my mind, the infinity of questions and the near answers. Then, I pursued graduate work in psychology. I lost my way in a world that became increasingly confusing, never believing that I could fully trust myself and move from my own awareness.

I built barricades around my feelings as I helped nurse my dying mother in her last years, taking long rides to Manhattan to be with her during the endless series of cobalt radiation treatments and then stopping beside the highway to allow her to puke her guts out, overcome by the intense nausea they caused. I watched in agony as her world crumbled. I did not know then to talk with her about her suffering, to tell her that I loved her, that I knew her life was coming to an end, and that her pain felt like a knife turning mercilessly inside me. We cluttered our lives with bedside smiles, chatter of trivia, and fabricated busyness. I never told her how much I cared. Our family created a conspiracy of silence, a gesture we had thoughtlessly envisioned as distinctly humane. But, in our kindness, perhaps we left her alone with her thoughts and fears. When the end came, my system erupted in an upheaval and a protest against the universe for taking her into its womb, where my imagination could not penetrate. I screamed at myself through my sorrow for not having been with her openly and loving her as the odor of death enveloped her.

Twenty-one years old, and the walls had come tumbling down.

My eyes clouded over with a melancholy vision of existence. Although I supported myself by working in the film industry and eventually created a think tank design and marketing organization to serve motion picture and related companies, I saw it as less important than my continuing education, which held center stage for my personal growth and salvation. I loved ideas, the mind, and the unseen potential that surrounds us. Most important, I wanted to make sense out of my existence and all human existence. What was our purpose in life? Why did we live and why did we die? As I attended graduate school and participated in workshops in human dynamics, I also trudged to a secluded Park Avenue office to choke out slightly abortive sessions with a Freudian psychoanalyst. Ostensibly, I initiated the contact for educational purposes, unwilling to admit that deep down I felt a gnawing desperation. Though I demonstrated strength and success in both academic and business pursuits, the death of my mother and years of anguish and confusion that followed had taken their toll. I searched for old bones beneath the pillows of my unconscious, free-associating, then pushing myself to synthesize new alternatives and understanding.

The weight on my shoulders lifted somewhat as I developed increased clarity and comfort. However, despite my insights and the fragile truce I made with the enigmas of life and death, even after years of exploration, I still felt vulnerable, as if I dangled precariously from the end of a rope. Whatever I held as true appeared limited and tentative.

Eventually, I terminated this analytical version of therapy with its half-measure vision of life. I can still remember the words a well-meaning psychiatrist told me as I left his office for the last time: "You will always have times when you are anxious and fearful, but you are now better equipped to handle it and to cope." Disillusionment. This sounded like an intellectual and emotional compromise. To leave this soul-searching while still seeing pain and discomfort as inevitable felt untenable. I knew there had to be more if I could only find it.

My earliest dream had been to be a writer. I had formulated that idea at the age of fourteen. I wanted to go beyond the walls of my own skin and improve the quality of life for perhaps just one other person. To make that mark had been an adolescent fantasy. The second dream had been different. It had come to life with my pursuits in the area of psychotherapy and education. I had considered a career in psychiatry once, but as I took a closer look, the medical model seemed limited and antiquated. Graduate schools were cluttered with brittle books and strange approximations of reality. The whisper within encouraged me to search for my own path.

In some of these diverse explorations, which occurred during the first years of our marriage, Samahria would come, too. We created a joint venture into what seemed to be an endless abyss, experimenting first with hypnosis and trying to realize that second dream. Then we explored autohypnosis. I developed this tool so exquisitely that I could put myself "under" by merely touching my eyebrow with the tip of my index finger. What a beautiful and useful skill, but incomplete—certainly not a panacea, though definitely a soothing internal massage.

The questioning that fueled our diverse and varied explorations occurred prior to Raun's birth and subsequent diagnosis. It was as if something, back then, beckoned from the future, driving us to prepare and transform ourselves for our son's auspicious entrance into our lives. I read ferociously, consuming countless books, and experimented with new theories in practicums and seminars. Freud. Jung. Adler. Then on to Sullivan and Horney, a left turn to Perls and the dramatic confrontations of Gestalt. I had a fleeting love affair with the work of Sartre and Kierkegaard, then dove deep into the loving simplicity of Carl Rogers. After flirting with Eric Berne's trinity of parent/child/adult, I found myself beguiled by the fascinating and theatrical screams of Janov. I charged through courses in group dynamics and workshops in interpersonal communications, then fell in and out of Skinner rather quickly but lingered with Maslow. Finally, bathing in the quiet wisdom first of Zen and then of yoga, I walked an ancient path, trying to forge a new grip on an old reality.

Taoism. How I delighted in the beautifully perceptive teaching, "Life is not going anywhere because it is already here." Soon I moved on to meditation and solitude, then dabbled with the insights of Confucius—"To know what you know and what you don't know is a characteristic of one who knows"—slid through the philosophical basis of acupuncture, then moved back to study the collective unconsciousness of humankind and its genetic implications.

All these, whether philosophy, psychology, religion, or mysticism, were moving and arresting attempts to make sense out of the human condition. Though I found them helpful and even momentarily enlightening, I knew to go on, believing that I would someday discover something that would penetrate the core of me and unravel many more of life's perplexities for me. Although I had gained much, I chose to push on with this purely personal pilgrimage.

My cynicism had abated somewhat, but I remained a fool-hardy skeptic reaching for the ring of gold. Then one day I sat in the classroom of a school that has since disappeared and heard a man talking about the impact of beliefs and attitude on all that we call the human condition.

As I listened and became a student of this new awareness, I felt a surging from within, as if a seed had sprouted or a knowledge I had always possessed suddenly came into sharp focus. This knowledge crystallized rapidly for me. I began to recognize and acknowledge that my feelings and behaviors did, in fact, come from my beliefs and that those beliefs could be investigated and changed. Samahria and I internalized and used what had been presented to us as an expansive process. Later, we would apply, adapt, and then modify what we had learned to many diverse endeavors. Our new vision and way of thinking, called The Option Process®, flowed out of the attitude "To love is to be happy with." More than a philosophy, it presented a vision that drew us toward a new way of life and it served as a foundation for our efforts to help Raun. Ultimately, our developing awareness would enable us to see our son and ourselves with heightened clarity and comfort.

Each of us has the power to choose our perspectives and, thereby, create the resulting emotional experiences (the resulting life experiences) that flow from them. This simple empowering insight opens the doorway to a completely different way of embracing life. Happiness is a choice. We no longer have to wait on the sidelines for the experiences we want to happen to us. We are in charge of creating our state of mind; we have only to make new choices. For me, this was the ultimate romance! For the first time in my life, I saw old beliefs, such as "I do not choose my feelings; they just come upon me," "I am a victim of what happened to me in my past," and "I can't help it, that's just the way I am," as open to question and began to challenge them.

A person's personality could be viewed as a constellation of beliefs. Between any event (whether real or imaginary, perceived or performed) and the reaction to it (whether fight or flight, fear or joy or a neutral calm), there is a belief. That belief fuels our feelings, our wants, and our behaviors. Change the belief and we change the feelings as well as the behavior.

As Samahria and I began sharing and then teaching others, our own grasp of the power of the sweeping personal changes we were making deepened significantly. Had our son Raun entered our lives before we had challenged and changed ourselves in this way, I have no doubt we would have been emotionally paralyzed, devastated, and overwhelmed by the apparent enormity of our child's difficulties. Instead, changing our own beliefs and judgments first prepared us to try to help him change and provided the necessary energy and insights.

The beauty of the process began with the extraordinary wonder of exploring in a manner that encouraged letting go of judgments — not assigning a good or bad label to people or events, just being open and accepting.

No diagnosis. No pushing people according to a predetermined agenda. The backbone of this process was nondirective and Socratic in nature. Questions became simple, respectful, transformative gifts. Each question flowed naturally from a student's or client's previous statement or answer. The banter back and forth would become a dialogue; its intent was to help ourselves and others to see through unhappiness to the underlying beliefs and judgments that fuel it. We could learn to go beyond just coping and adapting to feelings we did not want, such as anxiety, fear, anger, frustration, jealousy, and the like. We could reeducate ourselves to dispense with them cleanly and completely.

No vision or process can necessarily be trumpeted as the ultimate panacea. I still stumble and fall, certainly not the perfect incarnation of what I know to be possible. However, most teaching approaches I had explored previously encouraged pain and suffering as a transformative tool. No pain, no gain. Suffering will get us to heaven. Well, suffering never got me to heaven; it just bathed me in more grief and distress. I felt truly excited — no, more than that — truly blessed to have found this gentle, quick, and easy way to change without pain. And I felt awed to realize that the attitude of love and acceptance made this process work.

This probe or style of inquiry into human dynamics revealed one profound commonality in many of us: We believe that we have to be unhappy sometimes and that it is even good or productive to be unhappy. Our culture supports it. Unhappiness is the mark of sensitivity, the tattoo of a thinking person—considered by some to be the only "reasonable" and "human" response to a difficult and problematic world.

We can see this type of mechanism operating all the time: being unhappy and then using our discomfort as a way to deal with ourselves, other people, and circumstances that greet us. We fear dying so that we can motivate ourselves to stop smoking. We dread rejection in order to encourage ourselves to stop eating and not become fatter. We become anxious as a way of pushing ourselves to work harder and achieve more. We get headaches in order to have a reason to avoid something we don't want to do. We feel guilty to punish ourselves in order to prevent ourselves from doing the same thing in the future. We get unhappy when someone we love is unhappy in order to show how much we care. We get angry at our coworkers to make them move faster. We scream at our children, even hit them, so that they learn to do the "right" thing.

We punish in order to prevent. We hate war in order to stay in touch with our desire for peace. We fear death in order to live.

These are just some of the pressures we might put on ourselves in order to stay in touch with what we want or to motivate ourselves to go for more—all of this so that eventually we can be happy or fulfilled. Ultimately these dynamics of distress and discomfort become a familiar part of the sophisticated internal system by which we function.

I remember a fascinating incident with Thea when she was about three years old. She came to us quietly one afternoon and asked for candy. Since we did not keep candy in the house and we didn't want to go to a store when we were busy, we denied her request. Perhaps, we suggested, we could buy her the candy another time. However, this determined and resourceful young lady found our response unsatisfactory. Consistent with the fiber of her personality, she persisted. Her initial gentle request turned into a series of pleas, accompanied by whining and grimaces. Her posture stiffened, and her body movements became frenetic. Thea might have been preparing for some great challenge or battle.

Still intent on achieving her goal, Thea escalated her efforts by demanding the candy. She substantiated her demands with a complex succession of arguments. Again we explained our situation. Samahria stroked Thea's hair and told the little dynamo how much we loved her. For just a moment, Thea relaxed and seemed satisfied. But then she decided to pay the highest tribute possible to her wanting and started to cry. It astounded us to watch the progression of her efforts. She worked very hard to achieve her goal.

I did not want her to be unhappy, so I sat beside her, letting my fingers dance all over her belly and tickling her under her arms. As she began to smile and allow herself to giggle, she pushed my hands away. Then, as I continued, she moved to the other side of the room in protest. For two frozen seconds, she looked at me through her tears, and then another smile broke through the clouds of her "unhappiness." Her eyes carefully avoided mine as she began to cry again. It was as if she were saying, "Don't spoil it for me; I am trying to get candy by making believe I am unhappy."

She turned her tears on and off like a water faucet. She could laugh as easily as she cried. She used the game of unhappiness as a tool. Later that day, Thea, Samahria, and I discussed the episode. How ironic and amazing that Thea really had been aware of exactly what she had been doing. She casually informed us, "You know before, when I was crying and everything—well, I was really just making believe so you would buy me candy."

In addition to using unhappiness as a tool (as Thea had), many of us also tend to use unhappiness as a gauge to measure the degree of our desires or even of our loving. The more miserable we feel when we do not get what we want or when we lose something we love, the more we believe we cared. Conversely, if we don't feel unhappy about not getting something or about losing it, then we believe maybe we did not want it enough. Even more fearful might be the belief that if we allowed ourselves to be happy under most or all circumstances, we might, thereafter, not want anything or care about anyone. If we were perfectly satisfied with our situation, we might not move toward new opportunities. Additionally, we might judge ourselves as cold, insensitive, and unfeeling if we weren't unhappy in circumstances most might consider difficult, stressful, or tragic.

I think that my biggest fear was that if I did become perfectly happy, I might stop moving. But as I accepted and trusted myself more, I found the opposite to be true. I became more energetic and passionate in expressing and trying to achieve what I wanted. My feelings were no longer at stake. Whether I got what I wanted or not, I could still be comfortable. And, yet, in permitting myself to freely want more as I became happier, I noticed myself getting more of what I wanted.

*   *   *

The key to what we could and might choose to do with Raun would be grounded in our beliefs. Understanding the power of those beliefs and digesting the beauty of that awareness would facilitate our comfort and willingness to view our son clearly, to trust our decisions, and to pursue our wants.

Each belief lies atop a mountain of beliefs. And unhappiness, which is the experience of certain kinds of beliefs, is based on a logical system of reasoning. Those reasons or beliefs are therefore available for investigation. Once we unveil the system of beliefs that we have been taught, the path to discarding the short circuit of unhappiness becomes apparent. Pull the plug on those self-defeating judgments and concepts, and the "attitude" will evolve. Buddha once said, "Remove the suffering, and you get happiness." It is what remains when we have worked through the misery, the discomforts, and the fears. It is what we find beneath the debris of bad feelings and unsettling visions.

An opened doorway loomed before me, beckoning with its intrigue. I had found more than just a tool or technique to help me solve problems. This approach—philosophical, but not just a philosophy; therapeutic, but not just a therapy; educational, but not just an education—allowed me to let go of judgments in order to see and freed me to want in order to get.

We can recreate ourselves again if we want to. We are fully equipped to do what many philosophers, teachers, and therapists represent as impossible.

What a different and original perspective, not only a dynamic, beautiful, and free-flowing investigation into self-defeating attitudes and crippling beliefs, but a new beginning. I no longer had to accept half measures. I knew that I could choose to believe or not to believe anything that I wanted to—that I was the designer and the ultimate interpreter.

Unlike other disciplines (Freudianism, Gestalt therapy, behaviorism, primal therapy, and the like), The Option Process® was not a painful pursuit with only the therapist or teacher knowing the right answer for sure. Not a treatment or a miracle, this process maintained an infinite respect for the student or client. We no longer had to wait in a classroom or in an office for someone else to give us the message—to tell us about ourselves and make judgments. I knew it to be a joyful adventure into myself to uncover, discover, and recreate. In this enterprise, we became the experts on our own dynamics.

We saw we could rechoose old beliefs or create new ones. What an emancipation! The interior landscape within became accessible and user friendly. I had found new ways to be with myself.

During this time of great personal change, a close friend informed me that his cousin had just died. I asked him immediately how close he felt to the deceased, since it was not obvious. It was as if I wanted to know how bad I should feel. If my friend had told me that the relationship was close and important, I might have cried with him as a way to share his grief. If he had described his relationship as distant and unpleasant, then I would know to treat it casually. I realized that I used cues from others to dictate my responses. I would choose my degree of unhappiness or happiness or neutrality based on what I believed to be appropriate to the situation. With that type of growing awareness, I could now challenge the beliefs and reasons underlying my discomforts in all situations and decide whether or not to modify them or discard them as the basis of my feelings and my behavior.

For example, I realized that going to work and making a living was not a "must" or a "should" anymore but something I really wanted to do and chose to do. I began to look beneath my stress about work and understood that in believing that work was a "have to," I had never allowed myself the freedom to enjoy my choice to be gainfully employed. Additionally, I dissected and discarded my beliefs that anxiety and tension fueled creativity and industriousness, resulting in success. In fact, my discomforts often distracted and even blinded me. When I relaxed, dropped my worry about the future, and taught myself to stay present with each unfolding moment, new ideas and insights bubbled easily to the surface. Then I worked through all the "good" reasons I believed I had for feeling economically deprived, rejecting many self-defeating concepts I had adopted previously about needing things and about making myself unhappy if I didn't get them. I immersed myself in this very considered and studied liberation.

Had I grown wings? Everything in my head felt different, changed for the better, lighter and freer. I opened doors that I never knew existed. Samahria and I evolved rapidly, creating a new way of being and interacting, discarding much of our old unhappiness by continually investigating our beliefs and making new choices. We spent almost three years redesigning our lives and deepened our growing awareness by teaching and counseling others. In addition to working with people individually and in groups, we supervised some students who wanted to use this process to redesign themselves as dramatically as we had. Years later we would establish a learning center, The Option Institute and Fellowship, in Sheffield, Massachusetts, in response to the requests of others seeking input and help. However, during this time, we focused on teaching ourselves to come from a more loving place inside and were excited by the limitless opportunities we had to plant the seeds of such possibilities in others as well.

We allowed ourselves to enjoy more and to want more. Samahria and I rebuilt our relationship and our marriage on a new basis. We no longer exchanged comments like "If you loved me, you would do this or that." Both of us grew more comfortable with ourselves and with each other. We took our togetherness and stripped it of all the elaborate expectations and conditions. We thereby eradicated many disapppointments and conflicts and were more nonjudgmental with each other, more accepting. And the benefits of our growth flowed over to our parenting of Bryn and Thea. More highly sensitized to the beliefs that we "sold" them each and every day, we became more tolerant and more appreciative of their individuality. These very attitudes constituted a firm foundation for ourselves and formed the springboard for the entire approach we developed with Raun.

*   *   *

All of the decisions we made, all of our comforts and discomforts, all of our concerns and confusions, the exploration of ourselves and our family, and the pursuit of Raun began here—with our beliefs.

Perhaps the following example can illustrate in a grossly simplified way how diverse our beliefs can be about the very same occurrence and how those beliefs determine our feelings and responses. A girl stands on the steps of a train about to leave for college for the first time. Her family gathers on the station platform nearby. Her father is very proud and feeling good that his daughter has grown into such an independent young woman. Yet, at the same time, he feels bad, believing he will miss her and be lonely. Her mother sobs, quite overwhelmed with her sense of loss and the passage of time. In contrast, the girl's little sister displays absolute joy, aware that she will inherit her sister's room and become a more significant member of her family simply by default. Just at that moment, a stranger walks past, observing the entire event. He has no feeling whatsoever about the matter. Though involved in the same experience, all of these people react according to their beliefs. The father believes the situation to be both good and bad, the mother judges it to be bad, and the sister judges it to be good for her. The stranger makes no judgment. He is not involved and therefore does not activate a belief about the situation; thus, he develops no feelings about the event.

What we feel and how we act are dependent on our beliefs, which we freely choose. We continually adopt beliefs from parents, peers, teachers, magazines, television, governments, religious organizations, and our culture. We form our own conclusions and make up our own beliefs as well. Then we amplify the belief-making process by using labels as a sort of conceptual shorthand, putting people and events into simplified categories such as good and bad. However, no act, event or person is intrinsically good or bad—we call it what we will; we define it, love it, hate it, embrace it, reject it, and become unhappy or happy about it in accordance with what we believe. I used to see the "goodness" or "badness" of things as located outside myself and constituting, somehow, an integral part of people and events. But my son's presence in our lives taught me something very special. Though Samahria and I would listen to physicians, family, and friends use words like "terrible" and "tragic" when talking about him, we saw someone very different from the child they seemed to see. To us, Raun was a wonder, an opportunity, and an extraordinary creature for us to love. Truly, this child was neither terrible nor wonderful. What we could observe was people making up different beliefs about him. And, wow, I liked our vision much better than theirs. Ours led to exuberance and even optimism, while theirs led to disappointment and distress.

If my beliefs are ones that I can choose, if I can be the expert in understanding my own dynamics, then I can uncover, discover, and recreate my beliefs and personality dynamics if I want to. I can choose old beliefs of my own, choose the beliefs of others, or create absolutely new ones.

If we were unhappy about Raun, it would be because we believed or judged Raun's condition as bad—for us, for himself, and for others. Our unhappiness about him or any other child who did not meet our standards of behavior or acceptability could result in disapproving and punitive actions on our part. In the extreme, people's adverse treatment of an autistic child often produces adverse ramifications. Because the child does not behave "normally," he is oftentimes discarded, put behind the walls of cold and faceless institutions. His existence is considered a burden. Frequently, these children are seen as the cause of unhappiness in others. Many families and parents, drawing these conclusions, crumble under the pressure of their despair. They hadn't discovered, as we had, that no one outside of ourselves causes our unhappiness or happiness. Only we have the power to do that for ourselves. And that's not bad news; it's good news—because if we are the architects and designers of our feelings and responses and we have lived with much distress and discomfort, we can reeducate ourselves and choose a different vision or perspective from which to see ourselves and the challenges in our lives. We can teach ourselves to see the gifts and experience the joy and hope that come from holding such a perspective.

What was the main question for us? Was there ever any other than our wanting to be happy? Yes, we had called it by other names—comfort, peace of mind, fulfillment, excitement, communion with God, and so on. Yes, we made it only a shadow priority at best, believing that our intense hustle to be successful, popular, respected, loved, and financially solid would get us that desirable feeling. But, ultimately, no external event determines our internal state of mind. And sustained happiness, comfort, and ease do not have to depend on the outcome of events or the charity of others. Such a perspective leaves us vulnerable and easily victimized. We don't have to be emotional victims anymore.

The Freudian might have called for adaptation and adjustment. The Gestaltist for awareness and being in touch. The humanist for self-actualization. But why? What is it that we chase with such haste and fascination? Isn't it just our wanting to be happy—to feel good with ourselves and those around us? And if that is where we want to go, why wait? Can't we have it now? For us, for Raun, could we be happy now, while we still continued to pursue our wants and clarify our directions? Indeed, wouldn't our coming from happiness instead of disappointment or guilt or fear or anxiety probably increase our effectiveness with our son and with what we might be wanting for him? If we were not confused or diverted by fears about Raun, wouldn't we be able to see him more clearly? Better for him and more useful for us.

I have heard it said that there are no stupid people on the face of the earth, just unhappy ones. Fearing to see too much or too little. Afraid to allow themselves the freedom to want and not to get. Concerned with the judgments of others or their own recriminations. All these considerations before taking their first step. Happy people, unencumbered by anxiety or fear, can allow themselves to absorb everything, so that when they decide to act, they do so with the maximum information available. They understand that the more they know, the better equipped they are. They can allow themselves the freedom not to worry about their future, the freedom to be okay with themselves whether they win or lose. The freedom to succeed. The freedom not to succeed and yet be content.

Does it sound too easy, like some groundless daydream or the pop fantasy of a contemporary Wizard of Oz? The question to ask is, "Do we freely choose our beliefs, or are they cast into the cement of our genetic structure?" Are they understandable and knowable or mysterious and lost in some inexplicable subconscious? Is our son confined by some irreversible malady, or could he be a fountain of new inspirations? What determines what we feel about him—whether we feel good or bad, whether we are happy or unhappy with him? What is the genesis of our feelings? Is our particular vision of our son going to be the direct result of a medical-psychiatric vision of mental health or the result of our own self-generated beliefs and attitudes? Do we learn to be unhappy, fearful, anxious, angry, and so forth, or is there an "unhappiness virus"? Could we choose to be perfectly happy about Raun as he is—and still try passionately for more?

One Friday afternoon, Bryn came home after spending the day at a friend's house. She wanted to talk. She had overheard a conversation between her friend's mother and another woman. My daughter was visibly distressed and confused.

"Daddy, what did Dana's mother mean when she called Raun a 'tragedy'?" She looked up at me with unusual softness and concentration. Though it was apparent that she knew what the word meant, she did not fully understand all its subtle and far-reaching ramifications. She had, in fact, intuitively grasped the tone and attitude that had probably been implicit in the conversation.

"Bryn, when someone believes that what happens or the way something is, is bad or terrible, they call it a tragedy. It's their way of describing something they would feel miserable and sad about if it ever happened to them. I guess because Raun is different and behaves differently from other children, they thought that was bad. Do you think that it's bad or sad that your brother is different?"

"Oh no, I love Raun. I would like to be able to play with him the way my friends can play with their little brothers and sisters. But that's okay; he's so cute and funny."

The beliefs and fears of others had created a tide of commentary about this delicate little boy that had filtered through to our children. Whispers and innuendoes. And what about their vision of tragedy? Was it just a word to label the feelings they had after judging the situation as bad? Perhaps. But, perhaps such a perspective, with its many ramifications, could be devastating. Unfortunately, many of us are never fully aware that many beliefs embody judgments so potent that they become self-fulfilling prophecies. If we believe a child's disability is tragic, hopeless, and irreversible, we act accordingly. We don't try to help someone we believe can't

40

be helped. We don't try to fix what we believe can't be fixed. We are dead in the water before we even start to swim.

Couldn't we be happy about Raun right now without having any answers, without solving the problems of his behavior and our relationship to him? Why should we need Raun to act or perform in certain ways before we would allow ourselves to feel good about him and ourselves? Why did we have to believe something must change in a favorable direction in order for us to be joyful about our son? Why do we so often make happiness a reward, the bonus we allow ourselves to feel after we accomplish or get what we want?

I am not suggesting that unhappiness is bad, nor am I implying that anyone should or must be happy or that everyone even cares to be happy. However, for those of us who want to feel good, there are new choices to be made. Change our perspective or point of view and we change our lives.

One last aspect of unhappiness that most of us fail to recognize: Unhappiness is lethal. Sure, discomforts and distress are acceptable, if not applauded, reactions to many situations judged to be bad for an individual or the fabric of our communities. We often use unhappiness as a device to motivate ourselves and others and to measure our concerns and commitments. However, those same discomforts in the form of anger, anxiety, hate, prejudice, and jealousy have awesomely destructive power. Rape, child abuse, drug addiction, and drive-by shootings are just some of the faces of unhappiness expressed outwardly. When embraced internally, the pain and suffering become high blood pressure, bleeding ulcers, chronic colitis, migraine headaches, and the like.

Living the attitude of love and acceptance, even as imperfectly as we do, became our antidote to all the teachings which had supported and encouraged misery. What began as a pilgrimage into our hearts and minds became an integral and liberating part of our life-style.

Although we were still in the initial stages of reckoning with our dilemma and dealing with Raun, a decision to intervene ourselves developed. We wanted to find a way to make contact with our son, and we wanted to make that contact significant. Could we pierce through a seemingly invisible, impenetrable wall and touch him so meaningfully so that he could get to know us and the world around him? We wanted to let him know how much we loved him.

41

Samahria and I spent endless hours exploring our fears and anxieties with each other. We omitted no thoughts or speculations, no matter how hard to face. If we felt like crying, we cried. If we felt like cheering, we cheered. We belched up the bile of guilt. Had we done something wrong? Nothing surfaced. We continued. Had we missed opportunities to stop his fall? Could we have done anything differently? We looked beneath every stone we could find. We knew the more we understood, the more we could help. We had to clear our vision.

Questions. Probing. Our after-dinner conversations spilled over into the bedroom. We would lie awake together until three or four in the morning, talking and talking and talking. From time to time, we would pause, stare out the sliding glass door beside our bed, and catch a glimpse of the night sky. Moonlight infiltrated our room and lit the walls and ceiling. And just above us, on that ceiling, we could see highlights of a Daliesque landscape that one friend designed and another painted on the Sheetrock. A huge, three-dimensional spoon, part of an abstract creation of geometric forms, dangled just above our heads. We laughed at the silliness of it all, then returned our attention to our explorations. What about institutionalization? What about responsibility? What about the future?

Evenings passed into the early morning hours as our eyelids drooped over half-covered pupils. We drifted off to sleep only to reawaken in the morning and continue to talk as if there had been no interruption, no sleep.

Psychoanalytical theory suggested that autism resulted from a cold and hostile environment. Reviewing all the particulars of that first year with Raun, we knew we had been with him warmly and lovingly. Saying it aloud to each other helped—hearing it and knowing that it was true. We had welcomed him, played with him, and cuddled him as we had the girls. Our first reactions to his withdrawal had been gentle and tender. We never moved away from him. Initially, we viewed him as independent and self-reliant. We were proud of his fortitude and excited about his strength. Who knew then it was just the beginning, like sand drifting through our fingers. Throughout his mysterious slide over a period of four months, we pursued him but never with a heavy hand. Perhaps that had been a mistake? Possibly, but it did not seem to be so.

And what about the pediatricians and hearing specialists who said he would outgrow his detachment and his unusual behavior? At the time we had felt skittish about those assessments, yet we bought them anyway. Time! We listened, stood by, and waited. Could we have acted even sooner? We let it go. We're here now· that was yesterday.

Samahria sat on the grass. Another evening of soul-searching in the warm, still summer air. Tears splashed from her eyes and cascaded over her cheeks. Yesterday, she realized something she had not remembered about her nightly conversations with God.

"Bears, when I was pregnant with the girls, I just asked God that they be healthy. That's all. This time I asked for something else. Please, please make it a boy!" She started to sob. I held her until the heaving of her chest subsided.

"Honey, why are you crying?" I asked.

"Well, I don't think I asked that the baby be healthy. I can't believe it. I was so set on having a boy."

"Samahria, do you believe that God in all his infinite wisdom didn't know you also wanted a healthy baby?"

She nodded. Of course. And yet it irked her, haunted her. Did her omission cause the flaw? But then, was it a flaw? We battled the issues back and forth, whipping them over some invisible net until each of us could field the other's serve. We could feel the evening dew settle on our skin as the night air cooled.

I thought of Raun, his little face looking out through the bars of the crib. What about my interactions with him? My participation? I had given each child similar amounts of time and involvement when they were infants. Maybe I could have given more? Maybe I could have made the difference? And yet, after investigating the beliefs that underlay my fear, I found that my anxiety had stemmed from the following thought: Time involvement might be more important than quality involvement. Since I knew that this was not so, I discarded it and moved on.

Did the doctor overdose Raun with antibiotics during his bout with the ear infection? Did that cause brain damage? Could this be the result of severe dehydration during infancy? Had we been lax in choosing a physician and foolish in allowing him to prescribe medication without interfering? Had we embraced the theory of a hearing deficiency to keep the truth at a safe distance? We worked and sweated through each idea, finally exhausted.

We baited each other, pushing ourselves to dig into the deepest recesses of our minds, saying whatever we could think of that was negative or bad. Throw it all on the table. If it would be a house cleaning of our feelings, we would go all the way. We even tried to fertilize any lingering unhappiness. Get it out! Deal with it so we could be free! We played devil's advocate for each other, confronting the phantoms of fear. In the end, though drained and tired, we felt free and alive with desire. This was our family, our life, and we could make it an adventure.

Summer had just begun. The warm air was moist and heavy. The taste of newborn green scented a fertile earth. We grabbed the girls for a weekend on Shelter Island, leaving behind all the projects Samahria and I had worked on together in preparation for classes we taught. Raun stayed with Nancy, a seventeen-year-old girl who, over the past five years, had become so close to all of us that we considered her part of our family.

We wanted to share our feelings and reflections about our family and Raun with Bryn and Thea. We were about to open a new chapter in our lives and make radical changes in an effort to help our special son. Additionally, we wanted to give them our full and focused attention.

Bryn had tried continuously to make contact with her brother. Often, she accepted his lack of interest, but, more and more, she became frustrated and melancholy over his rejections. Just before this weekend, she became extremely upset after yet another refusal to interact with her.

Roundtable discussions. Even Thea, now just five years of age, was a concerned participant and peer in our little group.

"Daddy," said Bryn, "maybe Raun really doesn't like me; maybe there is something wrong with me and he doesn't want to be with me."

"Okay," I answered, "could you imagine Raun sometimes not answering you because he didn't hear you? Suppose he was deaf; would you be angry if he didn't look at you when you called?"

"Of course not, Daddy."

"Good," I replied. "We don't know why your brother is the way he is. Many doctors who have seen him call what he does autistic behavior, which simply means there is a name for how Raun behaves. Maybe Raun can't help himself right now. For some rea-

son, it's hard for him to look at us or play with us. He is really doing the best he can. So when you call him and he doesn't answer,
it just means that he can't respond or doesn't know how to respond.
It has nothing to do with you or with his loving and caring about
you." Tears began to stream down Bryn's cheeks. There was no anger
or frustration in her expression, just the dawning of a new realization. Samahria held her close while I stroked her hair. I held Thea's
hand tightly as her eyes glazed over.

The next morning the hot sun baked our bodies on the sand.
The sunlight danced on the surface of the water. We shared tuna
sandwiches and warm soda and enjoyed each other. Bryn and Thea
dared the soft turf with their toes, laughing and giggling. Sometimes they found time or interest to gesture or wave in our direction. Thea had not really discussed her feelings. Her relationship
with Raun was less problematic. Thea was the family Gauguin and
a worshiper of privacy. She had little trouble with Raun's apparent desire to be alone. If he did not heed her beckoning, she would
play and make her little drawings as she sat beside him in the same
room, willing to be near him, not needing him to participate.

Yet Samahria continued to probe Thea gently. After two
hundred staccato introductions, she made her first statement of
genuine concern. Thea noted Raun was getting more and more
of our attention. The weights on the scale seemed to have changed.
Notes of jealousy. We explained to her how Raun's special condition required special responses, all of which would never diminish
our caring and our love for her. She smiled sheepishly with visible
relief. She had tested the waters and, apparently, felt comfortable
with our response.

On our last evening, we borrowed a motorcycle and cruised
the perimeter of this small and quaint island. Images of other times
whizzed through my mind. During the first years of our marriage
we had ridden another motorized two-wheeler over the mountains
of Vermont and across the landscape of Canada. We ate our dinners at roadside stands. The curbs became our seats, the streets
our table. We saved up pennies each week to buy cigarettes as I
played out the contemporary drama of a struggling young writer
while Samahria supported both of us. Throughout college and in
the immediate years that followed, I worked feverishly on a single
saga that I tried to bring to life in the form of a novel and play

simultaneously, only to discover that Hermann Hesse had written a story of similar structure—and had done it much better.

The wind against our faces caressed and massaged our skin. Samahria locked her hands around my waist. I leaned the machine into a sharp turn and banked with the curve of the road. I could feel her begin to cry. We stopped and walked along the water. She was letting the rest of it go. Diamondlike lights from the sky shone across the water and danced on the tears gliding down Samahria's face.

Sunday night we arrived back at home, settling into the changing style of our lives and putting our hands firmly to the wheel.

We picked apart all the notations and diagnostic concepts, then reviewed all the articulated theories and procedures. We had heard all the professionals give their talks about hopelessness and limited futures. Even our family doctor looked listlessly at the floor and shook his head from side to side upon learning about the diagnosis. We met with other parents of similar children. We heard their outcries and accusations, their anguish, their guilt, and their confusion. They, too, had not received any substantial help or meaningful advice, nothing but the traditional negative beliefs. Some gave up. Others stumbled through halfhearted starts. In the end, for most of them, came the inevitable and tragic institutionalization.

We queried the man who had taught us about the power of beliefs, and even he suggested that we leave Raun alone. He thought that if our son could or wanted to come to us, he would. We disagreed. We did not believe that Raun had the receptive apparatus or conceptual capacity to decide whether he wanted to join our world or not. We knew there was more that we could do, more that we wanted to do. Why couldn't we take the principles of acceptance, love, and letting go of judgments that we had been teaching adults and use them as a basis for designing a program to reach and educate children like Raun? For us, acceptance never meant passivity or inaction. Adopting such an attitude helped us open our arms and our hearts to people and circumstances we might once have judged and avoided.

All alone. Samahria and I. Holding it together. What did we know about our son? Definitely distant and encapsulated, but gentle, soft, and beautiful. He appeared happy with himself and the fantasies of his solitary universe—a peaceful journeyman with an incredible talent for concentrating on a single object for hours. Raun was a flower, not a weed; an adventure, not a burden. What others portrayed as an affliction, we began to hold as a gift. We never felt obsessed, just dedicated and committed. Samahria and I held hands together late one night as we watched Raun sleep in his crib. We glanced at each other. We knew. We had decided. We would intervene and try to reach for our son, no matter what it took!

We realized that we could have special and different wants for Raun but that our relationship with him would not be conditional upon his fulfilling them. To be happy and not judgmental—this would be the place to begin with Raun. Although this had been our attitude all along, our reaffirming and verbalizing it helped us to be more aware of the fundamental perspective that would characterize our way of dealing with our "special" son.

We would kiss the earth that the literature had cursed. We would embrace all the wonder and individuality of our son. Raun would open us to a beautiful and enriching journey into our own humanity. We would walk together.

3

Embracing an Alien Universe

No conditions. No expectations. No judgments. This attitude would guide all our actions and interactions with Raun. We would continually dedicate ourselves to this vision of acceptance and approval. We decided that his "isms" (his ritualistic behavior of rocking, spinning, finger flapping, and so on) were perfectly okay with us. In fact, as a result of our initial observations, we sensed that he could be using his "isms" to help himself make sense out of a conglomeration of perceptions that he found complex, bizarre, and confusing. Perhaps they represented a healthy way of coping with his world and he never meant them to serve as a commentary on us or his environment. Even his excessive mouthing and drooling, the hours he spent examining his fingers, his compulsive desire for sameness—perhaps they were all just adaptive processes his dysfunctioning system developed in its attempt to meet and digest an unpredictable world.

First we must know him completely. We decided on marathon observation sessions. Samahria and I spent endless hours sitting with Raun and observing him, writing elaborate notes, which we reviewed at the end of the day. In the mornings, we watched him closely as he sat on the kitchen table with the light dancing through the picture window and bouncing off his rocking form. We walked around him, catching his silhouette against the wall-mounted stained-glass window, whose New England ecclesiastical imagery served as a muted backdrop for his bizarre ritual. Afternoons were spent outside with Raun sitting between us in the woods behind our house. Under one-hundred-year-old oak trees, which created a huge umbrella shielding us from the summer sun, our son fluttered his fingers hypnotically close to the outside corner of his eyes.

He appeared captivated by the flickering motion he saw peripherally but remained oblivious to the scenery directly in front of his eyes.

We watched him as he rocked his body passionately in a repetitive motion and tried to spin every round object he could find. We started to imitate him — for him, but also for us, hoping in this way to find some relevant insight or understanding. We also believed that imitating him was one of the few channels open to us through which we could let him know that we were with him. We wanted to pick up on his cues in order to communicate with him. If he couldn't follow us, we wanted to follow him.

Evenings in the den, Raun sat in the middle of a multicolored Navajo rug, fine-tuned the position of the plate he held expertly in his fingers, and then sent it spinning across the intricate, geometric patterns of tightly woven fibers. He never once looked up to see us or the paintings hanging on the walls created by his mother. He never glanced out the windows to catch the fleeting image of the sky or the trees set in motion by the wind. He never departed from his circle of activity. When the plate slowed and wobbled, finally falling flat on the surface of the rug, Raun retrieved it quickly and set it back in motion. He repeated the process hundreds of times over a period of several hours. Try as we might, we could not distract him from his solitary play.

We initiated a very elaborate imitation format that extended beyond our periods of observation. When Raun spun plates for hours at a time in a room, Samahria and I and whoever else was in the house gathered up plates and pans and spun beside him. Sometimes as many as seven of us spun with him, turning his "isms" into an acceptable, joyful, and communal event. It was our way of being with him, of somehow demonstrating to him that he was okay, that we loved him, that we cared, and that we accepted him wherever he was.

What we did contrasted dramatically with a technique developed for dealing with autistic children that had recently come into vogue and still remains popular, a psychological and educational discipline called behavior modification. Thus far, it had had only limited success in controlling what was labeled aberrant or inappropriate behavior. Nevertheless, more and more professionals used it exclusively in approaching autistic and developmentally impaired children. Although we believed that it could at times be a useful educational tool, its essential premise and philosophy made its use as the sole basis of a program very questionable. Behaviorists at the outset make many judgments about an autistic or deviant child and his or her behavior, categorizing and labeling some activities as "bad" or undesirable while deeming others good. They do not consider the underlying reasons for the behavior to be applicable in planning treatment but deal only with what is concretely observable. So, if they find "isms" undesirable, they extinguish them through an elaborate system of rewards and punishments.

Oftentimes aversion conditioning techniques utilized in behavior modification programs include yelling, pinching, and slapping, squirting children in the face with a water gun, locking them into a "time-out" closet, or prodding them with electric shocks. One behaviorist I observed dismissed our sensitivity to the child's inner world and called me a foolish romantic. However, though he identified himself as a scientist, not a bleeding-heart humanitarian, he wished me well. His programs were experimental models funded lavishly by government grants.

What this man and others like him did not consider was the dignity of the child — the right of the child to be who and how he or she is. What he did not consider was the message of the child and the tone of his own statement. If just part of a program starts with disapproval, even if only implicit — if it is based on the idea that these little people are bad and their behavior is somehow wrong — what then can possibly be the result? When you push people, they tend almost automatically to push back.

Behavioral programs send the child a strong message that the little person "must" conform to the directives of the therapist or teacher or suffer the consequences. The child's wants are ignored or dismissed. The so-called maladaptive behaviors of the special child, which the youngster might have instituted as a way to soothe or center him or herself, are rudely and sometimes violently restricted. Why would any little person, especially one who demonstrates difficulties in digesting and relating to the world, want to communicate with and embrace someone who disapproves and threatens him or her? How could any developmentally impaired little girl or little boy want to learn from someone who does not allow that youngster basic human rights in the process? Why ignore the child's interests and wants? What I have seen done to special-needs children in the name of therapy or education would be viewed as child abuse in any home or school environment.

How could I, or anyone else for that matter, sit in judgment of my eighteen-month-old son, label his behaviors inappropriate or bad, and then proceed to hold him, bind him, or hit him in order to get him to change? If Raun could look directly at me, I knew he would. If he could talk, I knew he would use language as other children do. He spun and rocked and flicked his fingers as his way of taking care of himself. Why, I reasoned, would I ever want to attack what I don't understand? Why make an enemy of his illness? Why not be open, learn about it, and make it our friend?

We reasoned that so many professionals working with special children never ask themselves simple, basic questions. They mean well but trip over fundamental human considerations they never even entertained. They might win a momentary battle by making war against aberrant behaviors, but in the end they lose the person they had hoped to rescue. We approached Raun very differently. We respected him and honored him, although he was just a toddler. We believed that demonstrating to Raun in every way possible that we accepted and loved him was the first and most important step in our journey to reach him. If he couldn't come to our world, then we would gladly go to his.

The fruits of our labor would be slight if we pushed or pulled him. If we intervened in his world, it would have to be with him, with his allowing. We wanted our action to harmonize with his wanting. Like all of us, Raun did the best he could. If we wanted him to do more, we would first have to facilitate his wanting more. Help him. Show him. Love him.

More days of observing. Samahria and I sat on one side of the den floor with Raun on the other side. First he rocked, then he spun himself in circles. His movements were well defined; nothing seemed arbitrary. We felt like frontierspeople exploring the dynamics of an entirely new universe. A little boy lost in the complexity of his self-stimulating activities. We noted his mood. Really happy. Although the literature at the time—at least an overwhelming percentage of it—defined autism as an emotional and psychotic condition, Raun did not fit the mold. Autistic, yes. Psychotic, no.

What I had read seemed contradictory. Some authorities

defined the autistic child's "isms" as symptoms—items not to be dealt with but merely discarded as the arbitrary topping of underlying feelings. Others saw them as definite statements being made by the child as a disapproving protest against his world. I wondered if anyone sitting with a child like ours with no preconceived notions or judgments could ever come up with such hypotheses. What Raun did he did all the time whether in our presence or alone. His movements were exacting; they seemed to comfort and console him. Only in isolated and fleeting moments did he venture outside himself and dare to make contact with others. Each time he did, he seemed to do it with great difficulty. Our growing awareness of the usefulness to him of his behavior patterns excited us and helped us penetrate his universe.

Traditionally, the autistic child is not clearly identified and diagnosed until the age of three or four years. Some parents do not become motivated to seek formal testing until their child's behavior becomes more obviously deviant. Others resist recognizing their child's problem because of their own fears and anxieties. Still others seek early consultation, only to be confronted by the wait-and-see attitude that many pediatricians and professionals adopt.

The child does not know how to deal successfully with his surroundings, and well-intended family members and friends do not know how to cope with this little person's bizarre and enigmatic behaviors. Therefore, after a few years of being functionally autistic, the child intermixes a good deal of frustration, anger, and pain with his fantastic array of special behavior patterns in response to the anxious and even disapproving people around him. The child's display of discomfort, once interpreted as a causal factor of autism, represents the possible explosive and painful results of two worlds colliding.

Even the more recent and enlightened perspective of autism as a neurological and/or genetic malfunction does not soothe the aching heart of an overwhelmed parent or liberate a child from isolation and self-encapsulation.

If these children who cannot put the world together in a functional or meaningful way are forced to participate in an environment where "putting the world together" is expected and stressed, then their deficiencies, conjoined with this pressure, may easily create anxieties and fears. Unrelieved and uninterrupted, their emotional problems can escalate until their unhappiness grows so acute and pervasive that their behavior and attitudes reflect it, becoming so strange and unacceptable that professionals then additionally label them schizophrenic.

None of these developments, however, characterized Raun, who at seventeen months appeared tranquil and comfortable. We did not pressure him or judge him. We did not disapprove of his unique repetitive behavior. Although we wanted to make eye contact with him, we did not force him to perform. He had slid into his alien world over an eight- to ten-month period. The rampant autistic behavior patterns were still relatively new. Our worlds had not collided. Samahria and I had reevaluated the basic premises of our lives and adjusted our life-style to meet the challenge of our son's dilemma. We learned to see with new eyes. Raun never displayed anger or anxiety. Playfully, we referred to him as our little Buddha from another planet. He appeared delightfully happy and meditative when he rocked on the kitchen floor or continuously sang a two-note serenade. We had no reason to assume his functional deviance had been born out of emotional trauma and stress—no reason to define his malady as a response to inner turmoil.

Most professionals are not present at the birth of autism, during the early months in which the child begins to detach him or herself from human contact. Most professionals do not witness the child transforming simple, normal, everyday behaviors into compelling theatrical events. They see a child, usually, who has exhibited these behaviors for many months and many years. By that time, the traditional social fabric of the family has been understandably traumatized. Those stresses impact on that little person's world, leaving the child enveloped in many emotional overlays that can no longer be easily distinguished or separated from the underlying autistic syndrome. With Raun, we felt we had a child as yet untouched by a judging or disapproving world. We could meet him openly, lovingly, and without fear.

Every morning, as he stood in his crib, Raun stared into the looking glass of himself, eyes sparkling in their porcelainlike setting. The breeze moved gently through his curly hair and bathed his face in its coolness. He seemed otherworldly, a visitor from another galaxy or another time. When Samahria changed his diapers and washed his face, he accepted the distraction passively, looking fleetingly at her and then returning to his private universe. Brain-damaged or brain-blessed? Now was the time to begin working with him if we wanted to reach him, love him, and touch him in a meaningful and lasting manner.

On the tops of tables, sitting on the tile floor, rocking on the rug, spinning outside on the cement walk, we were with him, participating and observing. From early morning to early evening, we stayed with him continually until he went to sleep. We skipped meals or had them on the floor next to him. We made every second count, taking notes and writing down questions for our nightly discussions. The hours became days. The days became weeks. We tried to know him as if we were inside him. We found our love increased with each passing week as we grew infinitely more respectful of his dignity and specialness.

It happened during the second week of our marathon observation period. He had spent hours spinning every round object he could find on the kitchen floor. Dishes. Bottle tops and plates. Pans and balls. But this one time he came upon a rectangular shoe box. He picked it off the floor and held it in his hands for almost twenty-five minutes. He did not move, except to occasionally stroke the cardboard with his fingers while moving his gaze back and forth along the edges of the box. Then, quite suddenly, he put the tip of one of the corners of the box on the floor, balanced it firmly with his left hand and set it expertly into motion with his right. No trial and error. No practice run. He had actually used his mind analytically and with great sophistication in order to create the movement he had wanted. Before he moved or made a single test, he had analyzed the potential of the box as a spinning object and then synthesized a method to achieve his goal. Still only seventeen months old. Incredible. Amazing and slick. This significant piece of behavior just hinted at the vast field of intelligence that we sensed existed beneath the surface of his bizarre patterns.

As we continued to observe Raun on the floor, we found ourselves asking many questions about the fundamental symptom most characteristic of autistic children: their simultaneous fascination with inanimate objects and tendency to ignore the world of people and social interaction. When he was not engaged in self-stimulating antics, he might stop and stare for ten or twenty minutes at a time. One time he focused on a blank portion of the wall.

Samahria sat beside him to see what had so riveted his attention. She saw nothing apparent. No mark. No crack in the plaster. I actually brushed my hand along the surface of the wall, trying to feel what might not be visible to us. The texture felt perfectly smooth. Raun maintained his intent gaze. We wondered whether he could look into a sleeve of reality hidden from our eyes. What was it about him that so dazzled us? Raun appeared like a majestic human sphinx poised in a timeless posture as he surveyed invisible pyramids more fantastic than any tangible, three-dimensional monument.

Now Raun fixed his gaze on the base of the dining room table, which was richly ornamented with antique scrollwork. His eyes became glued to it, though this object of interest did not move or emit sounds. The base would move only if someone moved it—a highly unlikely possibility. Therefore, in its inertia, this inanimate metal pillar was highly predictable and secure. He could deal with stationary objects, or, as with the plates he spun, he would interact with a limited selection of items as long as he could control them and use them for his very own special purposes.

In contrast, when people entered the room, they were usually moving. Erratic. Noisy. Unpredictable and clearly uncontrollable. If one of Raun's organic deficits was a thinking deficiency or problem—a confusion of memory and recall—an inability to hold life experiences together in time and space—then surely objects would be easier to deal with than people. If each person entering the room became a new and unrelated experience to Raun, then each one of us might be a hundred different people to him. What a confusing and perplexing bombardment of data we must create, a diverse spectrum of sporadic images! Although we loved Raun and spent long hours with him, he did not appear to recognize us or prefer us to anyone else who might fleetingly enter and then exit his world, whether that be the plumber or the postman. Even Bryn and Thea, who poured their little hearts out to him each time they encouraged him to play, did not gain any detectable favor in his eyes. Mostly, he ignored us or looked through us. On many occasions, he clearly avoided looking at us.

To complicate things even more, each time we moved, we did so at a different speed, turned in different directions, and made different sounds. If Raun could not make sense out of us, if he found us a perplexing jumble of perceptions, then why should he not shut us out? Why shouldn't he prefer the infinitely more peaceful and predictable world of inanimate objects?

As he poured his energy into manipulating objects, he remained aloof and separate from people. He did not observe them. And, unlike other children, he did not imitate them. Therefore, we saw his learning would be severely curtailed and, in many instances, simply not occur at all. Language acquisition, which also depends upon listening and imitating, would be profoundly affected. In the end, manipulating and communicating with others in the environment would hold no meaning for Raun in his peopleless world.

Observing Raun, we agreed with the assumption that children like him do not relate to people because they choose not to, but we developed one major and essential qualification: they hesitate doing those things that they find extremely difficult and problematic to do. Unfortunately, this often includes most normal behavior patterns and simple tasks. We compared Raun to a person who has an inner-ear balance dysfunction and gives up tightrope walking after trying numerous times and finding the task extremely difficult, if not impossible. Raun, too, would choose what he could work with. Ultimately, he would need incredible desire and drive to leave the graspable universe he had created for one that might be unintelligible.

We finally hypothesized three areas of apparent dysfunction. First, his ability to perceive and digest data from people and events appeared severely inhibited. Second, he did not seem capable of using whatever information he could absorb in a manner meaningful to others. And third, he had designed compelling internal systems to stimulate himself, creating an avalanche of alpha waves and endorphins, enough to satisfy any earthly creature—all of which drew him further inside.

Often, Raun would sit in his crib after awakening and fix his eyes on his hand. He usually concentrated on only one hand— moving it close to his eyes and alternately moving his fingers up and down. He did this throughout the day. At times, the flexing had a rhythm to it. Each time his hand came into his visual field, he stopped and visually investigated it. The surveying could take hours. If he had been four to eight months old, we might have considered this behavior normal and appropriate—a child discovering his limbs. But what did it mean if at seventeen months old this little boy still seemed to be discovering those same limbs? Every time he saw his hands, it was as if he saw them for the first time. If that was so, then of course they would be a source of endless contemplation. Each time his hand appeared, it became a new and disconnected experience, unrelated to his past, to his memory, or to any other piece of meaningful data.

Could this sweet and solitary child be cemented to each experience as an isolated event with no capacity to draw upon a previous situation or understanding? If he couldn't put it together, of course he might spend hours or days or even years going over the same experience. And then, obviously, he would have no time to learn new things. He would live in the present without any resource from the past or possibilities beckoning from the future to assist him. Something about that hypothesis was attractive. Most of us have difficulty staying present, being in the moment, focusing on unfolding events. Oftentimes, we are "in our heads," reviewing the past or anticipating the future. In our self-explorations, Samahria and I came to see that all our unhappiness was either a regret about the past or a worry about the future. Happiness exists in the present, we concluded. Certainly, Raun could stay very, very present. Perhaps that accounted for his easy attentiveness and delight in all that he did. At the same time, he had lost access to a significant reservoir of information and understanding.

One clinician, whose test scores put Raun's I.Q. at under thirty, shook his head compassionately and informed us that, in addition to being autistic and developmentally impaired, our son was severely retarded. Of course! We could see. And yet, so what? We had long decided to believe that anything was possible and that any effort we made to help our son, whether successful or unsuccessful, would never diminish us or our family or the special little boy who had become such a mystery.

We continually tried an experiment with Raun: We would establish good eye contact with him by getting him to focus on a cookie; we would bring it in front of his eyes, let him fixate on it, and then move it slowly so that he could track it. Samahria would then hold up a piece of paper, and I would hide the cookie behind it. Raun would follow until he lost visual contact with the cookie. Then his eyes would remain fixed on the last place he had seen it. He would stare confused into empty space, lingering for a period of time, and then turn away. Once the paper blocked his vision, he would lose contact and become disoriented, even after we showed him carefully that the cookie had been put behind it.

According to Piaget, the average eight-month-old child has developed an intellectual maturity and skill that enables him or her to sustain images in his or her mind even if objects envisioned are out of view. In most cases, an eight-month-old will pursue a hidden object. Raun, at seventeen months, could not retain an object in his mind without seeing it, and he never pursued what he could not see. When an object disappeared from his vision, it disappeared from his mind and from the face of the earth.

A variation on the same theme: Raun's most consistent interest, besides his "isms," was certain foods. Yet he never asked for or cried for food; in fact, he never expressed any wants. If he was not fed, he made no protest or plea. But, when we placed food before him, he did know he could eat and he would eat if hungry. Perhaps Raun did not call for food because he did not know how. When soft baby food (the only kind of food he could eat without choking) was introduced to him, he would always eat with some apparent interest. Still, when he finished, no matter how much or how little he had eaten, he never called for more.

Each time, eating appeared to be just another new and disconnected experience. So, although his internal system registered hunger, his mind could not connect it with a remembered remedy. It would be as if he forgot each time that food had satisfied his hunger. He would not do anything to get food because, for him, there would be nothing he knew to do. The environment provided no meaningful cues for him in most instances.

And what of his spinning and the rocking? Possibly those repetitive behaviors soothed him as he faced an unending bombardment of sensory experience. As Raun leaned over the objects he set into motion, he would rock as if one with them. His hands and fingers created erratic and jerky patterns as they moved. Could Raun be living in a world that always turned? Could his early ear infection have disrupted the proper development and the stabilizing function of his inner ear? Was he always in a state of dizziness? Although he had learned to walk at the age of a year and moved with apparent balance, often he walked on his toes. Was this his way of trying to establish better equilibrium? Perhaps he spun to make the world catch up to his way of perceiving it. If so, in effect, he would be making the world stand still.

These self-stimulating activities, which he controlled, also had their own built-in sensory feedback. In many ways, they parallel the comfort or delight most of us might feel when humming to ourselves or rocking in a rocking chair or snapping our fingers continuously to music. These, too, are self-stimulating behaviors, though widely viewed as socially acceptable, and most people do not engage in such activities in "apparent" excess. The questions! The unanswerable questions!

What meaning could we find in our son's audio insensitivity and staring? This sweet little boy could see but appeared blind; he could hear but appeared deaf. Samahria would call to him, and he would not respond. Once, I slammed a book on a table no more than a foot from his head. He did not seem to hear it; he did not blink or move. Yet, at times, low music coming from another room could grab his attention. The inconsistencies abounded. The same enigmas held true for his vision. He stared—even appeared blind to some objects, yet was visually alert and attentive to others. One morning I moved my open hand quickly in front of his eyes; he did not even blink. All his sensory intake systems appeared intact, yet he could turn off his sight or hearing at will. He demonstrated extraordinary capabilities. He could cut off perceptions and successfully, as well as selectively, nullify his sensory apparatus. What amazing self-mastery! And yet, the reasons for his internal switches being thrown "on" or "off" at any given moment remained a mystery.

Although no simple answers surfaced, we saw we could form a tentative hypothesis as a result of our observations. Perhaps Raun was overbombarded with stimuli or oversensitive to his perceptions. If so, perhaps he stopped reception to protect himself by actually cutting off signals to his brain. But then again, perhaps the opposite could be true: He could have a low-volume intake system, and, if so, perhaps he cut one sense off temporarily in order to heighten or concentrate on another. While he looked at something, perhaps he cut off his hearing so as not to be distracted. Sometimes, while he listened, his eyes appeared vacant. Did he have a regulatory problem that led him to simplify input for easier digestion? Sometimes we speculated about a third possibility: that the replay system in his mind of memories and past sensations was so vibrant and active that he stopped perceiving in order to watch his own internal picture show. Maybe a combination of all of these factors contributed to Raun's sensory selectivity. We wanted to stay keenly alert, to be responsive, and to help him regulate as well as digest his contact with the sensory world.

Two factors loomed as critical. First, questions about his perception had to be explored further. Second, he exhibited problems with recognition, retention, and recall. Raun lacked the full power of thinking; he had a cognitive problem—an inability to match new data with old, an inability to generalize from one experience to the next. He could not form a coherent entity out of his experiences. The magic was not there. No organized whole, just fragmented pieces. It was as if he maintained a primitive expectation of help but never thought to seek it from any source; maybe he was also unaware of what he wanted until it arrived in his view.

Raun Kahlil—confined to the "now" of his senses. We knew that, ultimately, language development would be crucial in helping him catalog his intake and would allow him to derive useful lessons from his experiences. Language would be his wings.

We, ourselves, had synthesized a new understanding and clarity from being with Raun. Our plunge into his world had had a dramatic impact on us; we felt like pioneers exploring a unique and exciting frontier. Through our lovely and serene little boy, we had been reawakened to the complexities of perceiving and thinking. Whether his problems had developed during his hospital stay or stemmed from brain damage, as one physician had suggested, the initial cause no longer seemed important or significant. We had begun to come to grips with his world without fear and anxiety, but with love and acceptance. We kept probing deeply into an unknown abyss in search of our child. And now so many things about him began to make sense. Now, we no longer faced a stone wall of confusion, but an approachable individual with very special problems—a living, breathing, and beautiful person who had never made any outrageous requests or demands, who simply was.

With each passing day, we came to know our son better and

better, and to know more also about the labels, the inferences, the prophecies, and the confusions surrounding his difficulties. Indeed, some professionals had speculated on causes and had designed experimental therapies, but their work was constrained by their own limiting theories and dogma. Even now, they continued to have difficulty analyzing autistic behavior and synthesizing an approach for themselves, for their "patients," and for their patients' distressed parents. Three generations of research had produced elaborate systems of judgments as well as gloom-and-doom predictions for children like my son. All the medical, psychological, and educational output had produced little that could help Raun and others like him. We knew the "road map" would have to come from him and that we could only facilitate and help.

Raun did not need another doctor or another interview; he needed a guide, a teacher, a therapist. "Ther-apon," the Greek genesis of the word *therapist,* means "assistant" or "comrade in a common struggle."

We knew that helping Raun define himself and his wants (perhaps to be with us, perhaps not) would be the only way to help him reconstruct inoperative or partially operating systems, so that he could utilize his perceptions and thought processes more effectively in dealing with the world.

As we solidified our perspective, we knew that it would take many hours — constant work and constant exposure — to intervene, to make contact humanly, and to make more data available to him. Stimulation was essential. Even overstimulation. The more he drifted and became encapsulated, the fewer possibilities there would be for him. Until he could take hold of the world by himself, we would be there each and every moment feeding it to him, redefining it for him, chopping it into digestible parts, breaking it into sections and fragments to be reassembled in the interior of his mind. We knew time would not be our friend. We had to act now — now while he was young, while he was supple and developing, now while he lived the most fertile days of his life. We had to act before Raun drifted deeper into an inner sanctum and disappeared behind an impenetrable barrier, wandering alone in the recesses of his mind and searching for a passageway out that would never appear.

But we did not want just to train Raun or robotize him or

to use force or the threat of punishment as others before us had tried to do rather unsuccessfully with other youngsters like him. We wanted to draw out the sap, to fertilize the seed, and watch it flower and bear fruit. We wanted to allow him his own personal dignity and encourage him to discover his own enriching garden. We wanted to help him reach the limits of his own possibilities, not impose on him standards from outside.

4

Living in a Self-Designed Ecstasy

We had formulated a three-pronged program. We had already begun to demonstrate the attitude of approval and acceptance that would underlie every approach, every attempted contact, and every movement we made toward our son.

Second, we would offer him a motivational/therapeutic experience. Show Raun the beautiful and exciting world that welcomed him! Show him that it would be worth his extra effort to depart from his ritualized arena. We knew that our son would have to stretch himself beyond any preset limits; he would have to climb the highest mountains just to accomplish what other children do with ease. Only the most motivated person would attempt such a journey. Our job would be to find the keys to his heart and help him unlock a deep inner passion to be with us. We had to make ourselves into the most beguiling lovers and clowns of the universe so we could excite him and entice him to walk through seemingly impenetrable walls.

Hopefully, we could open some windows to his world and provide new opportunities. But Raun would have to generate his own fuel, his own wanting. To venture outside himself into a less charted and less predictable environment would require such daring and deep, deep motivation. Bottom line: No matter how sincerely we beckoned, no matter how powerful our own yearning, we could not slip inside our son's head and rewire neurological connections that had malfunctioned. Was it even possible? Could the circuitry inside of him ever be healed or repaired? Raun, himself, would be our only hope; he was already on the inside!

The third phase would involve developing a teaching program for him that simplified every activity and every event into small and digestible parts. We would help him dissect his external environment into comprehensible portions so that he could build new pathways and construct new roads where old ones might have been damaged or broken. For us, autism was a brain or neurological disorder that short-circuited the processing of perceptions and the utilization of memory. This, in turn, precipitated an altered state of consciousness and changed patterns of thinking. Raun's current deviances simply revealed his current way of seeing and digesting. We did not want to burden him by requiring him to understand our visions or norms. We did not want to push or pull him and thus create the serious emotional problems that so often emerge as an outgrowth of autism.

We chose to make contact in an environment free of distractions. Samahria and I decided the optimum room for this was the bathroom, where we could limit interference from audio and visual bombardment. The monochromatic tile walls had no paintings or windows. The tiles on the floor formed a simple soft-tone mosaic. Apart from the sink, the toilet, and the bathtub, the room was quite sparse and undemanding. The floor area between the tub and the toilet, approximately four feet by six feet, would be the place to begin. Although I would help by working with Raun when I was home in the evenings and on weekends, Samahria would basically structure and execute the sessions. The role she played in my business, conceiving ideas and copy approaches, would have to be limited. Truly, it was the miracle of her excitement, her vivaciousness, and her optimism that fueled and permeated our program for our son.

Those first days marked the beginning of a very intimate human experiment. Samahria sat quietly with Raun for hours. Together, but separate. Raun stared at his shoes; then his eyes moved to his hands and finally fixated on the lights in the ceiling. Samahria watched, then joined his movements, searching for meaning, hoping for some ever-so-minute indication that Raun was aware of her and interested in her presence. His alert eyes seemed like mirrors that reflected instead of absorbing or sending information. His porcelainlike face betrayed no expression, exhibiting only the impassive stillness of a priest meditating. From time to time, his delicate little fingers would move aimlessly in the air as if disconnected from the rest of his body. In the mesmerizing and self-enclosed way he presented himself, Raun was a towering and awesome figure, self-contained in a universe of his own design.

Samahria watched as he picked up the plate. holding it ever so carefully on its edge. With great accuracy he twisted his tiny hand and sent the object spinning across the room. Another plate, then another. Raun rose only to retrieve them once they had finished their journeys. He sat again, repeating the pattern and delighting in the movements he created, fully absorbed in the repetitiveness of this activity. Finally he stopped. He gazed at the tile walls, then the ceiling. He became fixated on the recessed lights. An endless stare. The fluorescent fixtures created a halo of light around him. His stillness had the power of the pyramids—ageless, awesome, and mysterious. Mirroring his actions, Samahria looked directly into the lights. After several minutes, her eyes began to tear and the sharp lines where the walls meet the ceiling blurred. But she stayed with this parallel posture, searching for meaning in this bleached contemplation.

Finally, Raun shifted his eyes. He dropped his gaze to some vague spot in space directly in front of him. Then he began to rock back and forth rhythmically. An eerie humming sound echoed from his throat—two notes timed to match each forward and backward movement. Samahria rocked with him now and sang in harmony with his song. Then, she concentrated on the same empty space, finally locating a spot on the wall and focusing on it. As she leaned forward, the spot became larger; as she rocked backward, the spot became smaller. She moved to Raun's rhythm, feeling his body and hers arcing through the air in the same way. Raun lost himself in the motion.

Samahria concentrated on the spot and started to feel slightly fogged. She began to enter his world in a way she found beautiful and enriching. As she participated in repetitive movements, a hypnotic calm came over her, reminiscent of the feeling she had gotten when first hypnotized. Soothing and peaceful, it induced a meditative state that created alpha waves—those waves in the brain associated with feelings of well-being. She saw clearly that Raun's way of being had its own rewards—an elevation of mood that was often practiced by many monks in the East. He had created his own Nirvana and, perhaps, through motion, generated a limitless supply of endorphins to soothe his system—a little man cruising through his self-designed ecstasy!

Samahria's participation in Raun's movements was neither passive nor peripheral. Her genuine involvement and her sincere enthusiasm for these activities allowed her to share his world and, she hoped, communicate her love and approval. Samahria stayed fully active, but gentle — fully alive, but peaceful.

While in the bathroom, Samahria always had an ample supply of all the objects Raun loved to spin. She wanted him to know that being with her would not result in deprivation of any kind. He could have his plates and his pans. He could always have his "isms." Instead of fighting them or suppressing them, we used them as a conduit through which we hoped to communicate and express our love.

The hours became days. Most of the time Raun behaved as if he did not know that Samahria was there. And yet she knew, somewhere deep inside, that he knew she was there, that his awareness of her increased each time they came together.

Her intention was to be human and inviting, but nonthreatening. Initially, she chose to stay quiet and, at times, be as predictable as an inanimate object. If Raun had difficulty in data intake and assimilation, then we wanted to make ourselves easy to digest.

On the eleventh day, after spinning with him for over two full hours, Samahria noted a single casual sideward glance at her. She acknowledged and softly cheered his action. That night, we celebrated that first self-initiated look from our son as if it had been a gift from heaven. He became more adventuresome in the bathroom. When he entered, he would now walk quietly around, exploring the walls and the fixtures from time to time. Then he would place himself on the floor and stare at the lights. Samahria decided to introduce more stimulation, assessing him to be ready and receptive, even if only passively receptive.

She moved next to him on the floor so that her leg touched his. Slowly, she reached out her arm and stroked his shoulder lightly, then repositioned her hand and patted his arm gently over and over to an even rhythm that mimicked the rhythm of his rocking. Usually, he would pull away from such contact. But this day, after almost two weeks in the bathroom together, he appeared more receptive although visibly on high alert. He watched her hand cautiously allowing what seemed soothing but, like an animal, always ready to react to sudden change or danger. His body posture suggested his readiness to withdraw in an instant. Although he appeared absorbed in the touching at first, after a few minutes his attentiveness waned as he pulled back inside himself. Samahria was learning to "read" his body language more. Since he did not pull away physically, she decided to continue stroking his arm. Within moments, he stood up and moved away, staring at the lights again. Samahria watched and waited for about fifteen minutes, then sat down next to him again. She touched his shoulder and then stroked his arm. Again he allowed the touch, staying acutely attentive. Then, once again, his eyes glazed over. He began to rock; Samahria began to rock with him.

That evening, we discussed Raun's new responses and activities. We realized that each day, after several hours with Samahria, he became more responsive. Though he never initiated or sought contact and only once looked directly at Samahria, Raun nevertheless seemed more relaxed and more daring in his exploration of his surroundings.

Samahria would now have breakfast and lunch with Raun in the bathroom. Meals ceased to be isolated and possibly confusing experiences at the table as they have previously been for Raun. Samahria now used them as another means of making contact with our son. She fed him with a spoon, morsel by morsel, never rushing meals—in fact, extending them by giving him modest spoonfuls. While he ate, she talked softly to him. She sang and hummed, sitting directly in front of him and hoping for a second or two of eye contact. Samahria wanted to make herself easy for Raun to see. The intention: human contact. The meal had become a vehicle to open the door for more interaction and, perhaps one day, more bonding between this loving mother and her very special child.

Throughout all of the sessions, during those first weeks, Raun hardly reacted. Samahria sat with him eight or nine hours each day. She talked with him, touched him, fed him, sang to him, and mimicked him. Eight or nine hours each day. He remained oblivious most of the time, except for a very few minutes—a few, very precious minutes.

On the weekends, I sat on the steps outside the bathroom listening to Samahria interact with Raun in their tiled world. The chatter and the songs alternated with periods of eerie silence. Then Samahria would sometimes go into her animal-farm routine. She quacked like a duck, barked like a dog, and chirped like a bird, then groaned the deep and lingering utterances of a cow. She began to intensify her attempts to stimulate him. Raun became more attentive in the Kaufmans' Theater of the Absurd. It was like a dress rehearsal before opening night, and the audience consisted of everyone you have ever loved, giving that performance its own specialness and rarefied significance.

Another discussion on Sunday. Although we noticed minor progress, a major element lacking was eye contact. Without it, we would never be able to move forward with Raun. If he did not attend to us, he would only have limited knowledge of us. Every once in a while, he gave us a sideward glance that lasted only seconds. At best, we represented vague background images, perceived at the periphery of his vision. He would never be able to imitate what he did not see. Until he took this primary and fundamental step in human socialization and learning, his development would be severely curtailed. He would have to see more of us in order to grasp even the simplest possibilities of human interaction. This would be our next major area of concentration.

We would always feed him now with our eyes at the level of his, creating more opportunities for him to look directly at us. Each time we put food into a spoon, he watched the process and followed the food as we moved it. We brought the spoon to our face and held it for a few seconds in front of our eyes. As he looked past the food at our gaze, we looked back at him and smiled, saying "eat" and then giving the food to him. We viewed these moments of contact as critical. Additionally, we wanted to demonstrate our usefulness in helping him to nourish himself. Each meal meant about thirty eye contacts—thirty opportunities for him to find us through his maze. We noticed progress immediately. He lingered now on our eyes as if surveying or investigating them as we moved the spoon or fork toward him. He became more attentive to eating, and in this activity, some of his passivity lifted.

The third week, Samahria felt that we could begin to heighten the stimulation by introducing more intervention activities. Raun's fleeting glances at us had increased in frequency. He looked more intently at the food we offered, following with his gaze the route of the spoon from the plate to his mouth. Although by most standards, this response would be deemed minimal at best, we cataloged

68

a definite change in the quality of such interaction. Yes, we wanted to expose him to more human interaction. At this stage of building contact with our son, we did not have an agenda to teach him specifics, such as, for example, washing his hands or how to use the toilet. We wanted only to bathe him in interactive sensory experiences in the hope of building bridges and bonding with him. We continued using affection and food to encourage him to participate, but we always allowed him the freedom to back away. We never forced him. We never pleaded or pushed. We never disapproved when he was unavailable and unreachable.

Samahria grew more assertive in approaching our son. She used more physical contact—hugging, stroking, tickling, tumbling, throwing him into the air. She utilized pieces of fruit and pretzels to engage him in games of peekaboo and hide-and-seek. She rolled tennis balls between his legs and put them into his hands. She developed other games—for example, making a pool of water in the sink and dipping his hands into cold water, warm water, then soapy water. She turned the water on and off, letting it drip and then surge from the spigot. At this point, we could not assess what Raun absorbed though he appeared fascinated with some of his mother's theatrical and playful antics.

Suddenly, for us, simple everyday activities became laden with meaning. The oh-so-taken-for-granted act of turning a faucet on and off required complex computations and involved vision, memory, motivation (desire to undertake this action), sequential futurizing (if I turn the handle, then water will flow), and sophisticated intrabody communication (idea activating neurons, which send impulses to arm muscles, resulting in a calculated hand movement). Both our daughters learned to master such a process in seconds as we once had. To Raun, the faucet and the water appeared mysterious and alien. We had jumped into a different universe with him, where human mechanics did not gel so predictably or easily with the surrounding environment. That developing insight deepened our appreciation for every aspect of life. When we watched Bryn write us a note, we stopped, awed by this accomplishment. When Thea drew a landscape with her ever-handy crayons, then proposed a short narrative to go along with her picture, we listened with amazement and fascination. What a delight that we could even understand one another.

In a very short period of time, Samahria and I grew immeasurably. Our work teaching people how to explore their beliefs, let go of judgments, change their visions, and develop a more loving and accepting attitude had provided us with an indispensable new vision to live by. What had been initially a powerful therapeutic and educational process became a true blessing. We felt privileged to have Raun. We felt honored to parent Bryn and Thea. We discovered we had opened our hearts and minds as never before! Miracles had always been all around us, but now we could see them and appreciate them. And our son Raun was definitely one of them. He could breathe and he could smile, especially when he spun those plates across the floor. He demonstrated unusual skills and great joy. Although he would not, by any stretch of the imagination, be most parents' dream child, we could see the miracle and wonder of this child. By dropping all judgments and expectations, we had freed ourselves to behold what "is"—another child of God—different, singular, yet as amazing and worthy as any other little person among us.

We continued our program of sensory enrichment and stimulation with Raun. We expanded the time frame, working with him every waking hour (about twelve hours each day). Every morning, Samahria entered the bathroom, giving our son continual input and exposure to gentle, loving, yet energetic and playful human interaction. In the evenings, before our nightly analysis of each day's process, I would sit alone with one or both of our daughters on the stairs that faced the closed bathroom door. We would listen to the chatter of a very special mom trying to reach her very special son. We heard soft talk, laughter, clapping, singing, and silence. We had brought the best of the world into that tiny room and made of it an amazing human laboratory. On weekends, I joined with my son. Our program ran seven days a week. Rather than draining our vitality, it dramatically energized our spirits. Additionally, we created special times with Bryn and Thea in the park and at the ice-skating rink each week. We wanted them to know and experience our love even as we tried to help their younger brother.

Raun appeared more attentive to our presence. We showered him lavishly with input, trying to get through with more for him to see, feel, and internalize. Yet, we maintained an acute sensitivity to what he wanted and allowed him full freedom in his choices to respond or pull away.

70

Even though still mute and without gestures (he never pointed), Raun began to understand and recognize some words and expressions. When he heard the word *food*, he became alert immediately. When we told him we intended to spin plates with him, he would flap his hands excitedly. We had simplified our use of speech purposely, trying to make our words and their meanings more digestible. We named aloud every object and activity. In fact, we talked incessantly as a way to familiarize him with more humanistic and socialized interaction, which allowed us to give a more cognitive dimension to our presence.

On several different occasions, we took Raun to the park. There, two hundred ducks wallowed in the brown-grey water of a lyrical lake. The metallic swings, each one molded into the shape of an animal, glistened in the sunshine. Children bounced up and down on the slides. Given we had developed some contact with our son in the bathroom, we wanted to explore using other environments for the same purpose. I cataloged his every glance and movement as he strolled erratically beside Samahria. He appeared stiffer than usual, almost mechanical in his body movements. He surveyed the trees, grass, and people briefly, then disconnected, running in circles and flapping his hands wildly, distinctly unavailable for even minimal interaction with us. Had the complex and random stimulus of ducks, cars, people, and noises overbombarded a hypersensitive little boy? We began to question the usefulness of such excursions.

*   *   *

Summertime. Late afternoon. We held Raun as he floated in our pool, moving up and down so his body broke the surface of the water in playful rhythms. By positioning ourselves directly in front of him, we gained many opportunities for eye contact. In this very controlled and predictable environment, he appeared much more at ease.

Later, we pushed him in the hammock, then walked with him in our backyard, bringing flowers and leaves to his hands to give him varied tactile experiences. We tried to help him those first minutes while he experimented with walking barefoot on the grass. Raun stood onto his tiptoes, then fell. We lifted him to his feet and watched him repeat the procedure. Finally, we left him to his own resources. After crawling for a short time, he stood up again. This time, he touched the bottom of his feet fully to the ground and took a step cautiously. As he made himself more comfortable on this new surface, he maintained his balance more easily even as he took additional steps. Eventually, he walked on tiptoes again, no longer touching his heels to the ground. We had become accustomed to this peculiar way of moving, which we called, playfully, Raun's ballet.

Samahria mixed earth with water and brought him barefoot into the mud. She watched him smile in delight as he wiggled his toes. Then his face became fixed and expressionless. Taking his hand, Samahria moved on to games of touching and stroking. Each time he withdrew, she initiated a new activity to reengage his contact, unless he pulled away from her. When that happened, she let him be, giving him his own space. Every waking hour was filled with attempts to interact with Raun. Samahria alone put in seventy-five intense and concentrated hours per week with Raun.

In the evenings, while he slept, we discussed his progress, examining every action and reaction. Although each individual day seemed uneventful, new subtleties continually appeared. He now allowed himself to be held for ten seconds instead of five. On isolated occasions, he would hold my hand or make unexpected eye contact. Smiling when his feet sank into the mud certainly was a new response. Animated and excited, Samahria found something very personal and meaningful in this dramatic pursuit of her son.

Now we introduced music into the sessions. Beethoven and Mahler. Brahms and Bach. Seals and Crofts. Herbie Mann. The Modern Jazz Quartet. Piano concertos by Van Cliburn and the improvisations of Chick Corea. Raun was immediately attentive to the sounds and melodies. Each day, he displayed more and more fascination with music. We had found another special pathway into his world and, with it, achieved another small thrust forward.

One morning, this little noncommunicative and enigmatic human being came quietly into the bathroom and went directly over to the tape recorder. Although he did not gesture or speak, he turned and looked directly into Samahria's eyes. In the silence and intensity of his glance, she heard him. She jumped up and put music on immediately. He turned his face toward the machine and lost himself in the soft serenade. Samahria picked him up into her arms and rocked him back and forth to the tempo of the music. Fifteen minutes later, when he pulled away and began to rock back and forth on the tile floor, Samahria slid beside him and joined her own body movement to his.

The food, the music, and Samahria's eyes began to have substantial, growing meaning for Raun. Although he persisted in his rocking, spinning, and staring, he had extended his repertoire of behaviors by engaging in interaction with us. His initiation of eye contact with Samahria in front of the tape recorder marked his first real attempt to communicate with another human being. What a gift! Certainly, these were "days of miracles and wonder!"

We continued to imitate him and join him wholeheartedly in his self-stimulating "isms," trying to be receptive to any cues that he might give us. We wanted to show him that, with minimal efforts, he could move the world outside him, effect change, and have control. We wanted to show him that he could manipulate people to get more of what he wanted — show him that wanting, in itself, could be productive and fun.

Imitating his actions yielded real dividends. He would watch us more and more when we involved ourselves intensely in his ritualized games. Additionally, he spent less total time each day absorbed in his "isms." Clearly, if we rocked with him, spun plates with him, flapped our fingers with him, Raun demonstrated awareness of our parallel involvement. And, through that awareness and involvement, he attended to us sometimes for two or three minutes. Although we acknowledged that he looked at us out of the side of his eyes, not directly (side-glancing), we, nevertheless, believed in the significance of each tiny step he took toward us.

Yet, we recognized, simultaneously, that Raun remained significantly more interested in objects than people. He still played often in the room as if we did not exist. When we went to pick him up, he never lifted his arms or made any other anticipatory gestures whatsoever. In our embrace, his body remained limp; his arms and legs dangled as if he did not want to hold on or know how. But at least he allowed us now to hold him for short periods of time before pushing away. Admittedly, our solitary little guy still preferred his aloneness and the world of self-stimulation.

However, constant contact with us and the stimulation we

offered had made a real difference. Our program of intervention had facilitated notable change; our being with him every minute and reawakening his awareness with touch, sound, food, and play had enabled us to break through the walls others viewed as impenetrable. However, building this new route required a vast expenditure of energy and time. Raun Kahlil slid often behind an invisible veil; though only inches separated us, he seemed a thousand miles away. And still no prelinguistic language—no pointing or gesturing to indicate desires—developed.

Moving on. We found an article in the *New York Times* about a California hospital's highly successful experiments with hyperactive and hyperkinetic children in utilizing special diets and controlling food intake. The experimenters had discovered that removing artificial ingredients and additives from the food enabled many of these children to improve dramatically. Although Raun's problems were certainly very different from those of these children, we reverberated to something in what we read. We had researched biochemical approaches and megavitamin theories and decided they did not apply. But what about diet? What about his food intake?

Samahria and I rummaged through our cupboards and read the labels on all our foods: artificial this, artificial that, chemical dyes for coloring and additives for food preservation. Unbelievable. Some of the so-called food products contained very few natural food elements. Their labels read like a *Who's Who* list in chemistry; xunthan gum for consistency, artificial coloring and flavoring, calcium disodium EDTA to preserve freshness, propylene glycol alginate, monosodium glutamate, and so on. My stomach belched out its acid as I continued to read the list. We had thoughtlessly and calmly consumed all these products. Quick readings of Adelle Davis and others led us to create a better plan for Raun's consumption of food as well as our own.

Certainly a diet free of these chemicals and artificial additives could only be a positive factor in his life. We did not want to leave any stone unturned. We emptied all of the cabinets, loaded our chemicalized foods into brown paper bags, and distributed them among our friends. And, although we told them what we were doing—and why—they still easily accepted all of the unopened bottles and cartons of food. A neighbor called our little adventure comic and insane while smiling with delight to receive all the free goodies. When we returned to our kitchen, we found the cupboards almost empty. Our giveaways had cost us hundreds of dollars. We laughed, feeling mischievous and liberated. Bryn, however, responded differently. Some of her favorite chips and snacks had disappeared. We assured her we would find suitable replacements.

The health food store had such a different ambience from the supermarket. Grains and dried fruit filled bins displayed in racks on the wall. Organically grown vegetables and fruits, free from chemical dyes and preservatives, lay in carefully stacked piles on teak counters. We began to acquire a new food vocabulary that day, purchasing such unfamiliar items as tamari, sesame seeds, tofu, soybean oil, fresh ground peanut butter, brown rice, bean sprouts, natural yogurt, six-grain stone-ground bread, sugar-free cookies, and three kinds of granola.

Although our taste buds screamed for the old spices and sweets, we stayed the course, believing we had faced squarely and dealt productively with an arena formerly hidden from our view. We wanted to love our bodies with the same consciousness, care, and concern with which we had honored our thoughts and feelings. We decided to remove meat from our menu since we knew the animals also had been injected with hormones and steroids and sprayed with chemical preservatives. In their place, we substituted fresh-caught fish and high-protein vegetables. In the end, we knew at least that Raun, indeed all of us, would no longer be taking in questionable chemicals and artifically synthesized foods.

*   *   *

Slowly but steadily, Raun grew more responsive and alert to music, to food, and to eye contact. We started to introduce additional materials and teaching games. We bought a large plastic insertion box in which he could match three-dimensional shapes with appropriate holes, which helped him to develop hand-eye coordination and figure-ground perspective. There were red circular shapes, green triangles, blue squares, white diamonds, yellow rectangles, and black hexagons. This tool also helped him differentiate colors. We brought in wooden building blocks of different sizes and shapes. We found elementary Simplex puzzles we could use

75

to help him identify shapes and objects. We focused on increasing his small motor coordination, developing his ability to analyze forms, and increasing meaningful interaction with the environment. However, our intention to maintain and deepen his interaction and bonding with people remained our highest goal.

The different animals and household items depicted in the puzzles allowed us to expose Raun to more of that random, unpredictable world, but still in a controlled environment. We carefully integrated all of these toys into the program, not as cold, flat objects, but as functions of interpersonal games. Above all, we tried to foster eye contact, physical touching, and verbal communication. These toys and tools we hoped would form bridges across the valleys of silence.

Sitting on the floor beside his mother, Raun appeared withdrawn and aloof. Samahria removed the little cat from its wooden slot, held it up to Raun, identified it, and then made the sound of a cat. Even her face furrowed like the animal's, as she meowed playfully by Raun's face, nuzzling into his ears and belly. Then, she lovingly handed the piece to Raun and identified it once again, allowing him time to investigate it or reject it if he wanted. But he held it, and instead of looking at the colorful creature hand painted on the wood, turned the piece over and surveyed the blank side, exploring its outer edge with intense concentration.

Later, he tried to put the cat back in place upside down. Samahria cheered him for approximating the gesture, gave him a soft organic cookie, and hugged him. Then, taking his tiny fingers, she showed him how to replace the piece properly. As he tried to duplicate her action, she applauded him again. Finally, after taking a series of small steps, Raun began to comprehend the procedure. Samahria stroked his hair and spoke softly to him.

This activity, as well as all the others in our program, was not simply performed as a mechanical process. We humanized all our interactions at every level and used every game and toy as a means of expressing love and acceptance and joy. Teaching him specifics, at this point, seemed relatively unimportant. Showing him the value and beauty of dealing with others was our primary goal.

As his skill and level of participation increased, we encouraged Raun to initiate and guide his own sessions. We would place a selection of toys and games on the floor before him. He could choose any items he wanted and determine the activity we did together. We tried to shift increasing responsibility to him. Oftentimes, he did not respond. However, when he did, we noticed increased motivation and passion in his participation. We trusted him to be his own best teacher. Our role had become clearer—to go with him, to be sensitive to his wants, and to allow him to set the direction and the pace of the sessions. We responded to his cues and inclinations. We rocked if he wanted to, did a puzzle if that interested him. We fed him if he chose food. We became students of Raun's unfolding, encouraging him to find the energy and movement from within himself.

The first month passed by swiftly. We had definitely broken through to Raun in many areas with our program, although progress remained embryonic. Raun could now make some eye contact, could accept being touched for short periods of time, and had developed some interest in games, puzzles, and music. His involvement with people, though growing, still remained minimal. We knew we had to deepen our contact with him.

We invited Bryn and Thea to join the program for their own sake as well as their brother's. If they stayed on the outside, they might become strangers to this drama evolving right in their own home, feeling deprived or alienated as a result. The girls responded with immediate enthusiasm, wanting to become part of the team. We explained the nitty-gritty details of the program to them, outlining the intention underlying every interaction with Raun. To our surprise, they adopted the posture of students, wanting to learn and be helpful. We knew, without question, that their presence would enhance the program and increase the diversity of human contact our son experienced. Both Bryn and Thea asked to be assigned times to work with Raun and specific responsibilities. Additionally, they expressed strongly their desire to keep having "special times" with us each week. Laughingly, we concurred, loving the way they worked as a team and negotiated clearly with us. Even Thea, at three and a half, had learned to bargain in the most disarmingly mature way. No unhappiness. Just determination! Ultimately, we hoped our daughters would feel as much a part of Raun's journey as we did. We told them over and over again how important and crucial their involvement would be, and we meant every word.

The fabric of the program had changed. We pulled together as an entire family now, bound with a common love in a committed endeavor to help one of us. We told the girls that we did not know whether Raun would ever change substantially or be like other little boys, but we knew that all of us would grow bigger hearts by holding hands together and at least try to make a difference.

Both daughters received their own assigned times to be with Raun, as they had requested. But, before entering the program, they spent several days watching their mother facilitate their brother's rebirth in what had become a continuum of high-energy intervention. Bryn, who exhibited real skill at puzzles and insert toys, believed she would be a very effective teacher. Thea loved movement and considered herself an excellent candidate for teaching ball bouncing to her brother. Could she teach him how to use crayons and draw houses, people, and animals? We assured her that if Raun showed interest, she would be the perfect person to develop his artistry.

Although they wanted to plunge into their brother's world with great enthusiasm, using the agenda they had set up, we guided them in a different direction, asking them to build on the momentum already established. Their activities with their brother would revolve around his cues and inclinations. We told them just to be with him, to love him, approve of him, and reinforce any social contact he made. If they wanted, they could certainly touch him, but if he pushed away we requested that they leave him alone. If he spun or rocked or flipped his fingers in front of his eyes, we instructed them not to stop him, but rather to imitate him, really join him in the activity, until he chose to focus on something else.

Their eagerness to participate really touched us. However, I reminded them that if either of them wanted to stop working with Raun for any period of time or completely, it was certainly all right with us. While grateful for their involvement, we wanted them always to choose what felt good inside. No obligations! No shoulds! We called this our journey of choice—ours and theirs.

Later one evening, as I sat listening at the bathroom door, taking notes, jotting down new ideas we could implement, I heard the sound of a spinning plate on the kitchen floor. Impossible. Samahria had just engaged Raun in a gentle movement exercise in the bathroom. I jumped to my feet and walked quickly through the living room toward the sound. I stopped short at the doorway to the kitchen. Bryn had set one spinning plate into motion and now attempted to spin a second.

When she noticed me, she stopped and said, "Hi, Daddy. I'm practicing. It's not easy. Raun's really good."

"He sure is," I agreed. "But I practiced, too, and, Bryn, you're already better at it than me."

"Do you really think so, Daddy. Really?"

"Really!" I declared, smiling.

Thea sat on the sidelines, fascinated by Bryn's antics. Her own little fingers just couldn't get those plates spinning. But she proceeded to demonstrate how she could spin her body in circles. After about ten turns, she fell to the floor dizzy.

"How come Raun can do it so many times without falling?"

"That's a great question, honey. You see how you and Bryn and Mommy and I can talk. Well, Raun can't do that, so I guess he developed other talents and skills. Your brother spins because he probably loves the feeling he gets inside; it helps him to be comfortable. You know, it's like that good feeling you have when you draw those amazing pictures."

Thea smiled and nodded. "Maybe that's Raun's way of drawing pictures in his head."

"Maybe," I laughed. She laughed, too, contemplating the novelty of her unique theory.

How amazing to watch the girls during their first sessions with Raun! He appeared keenly alert to their presence as if he knew them to be children like himself. Every time he rolled the ball to them or inserted a puzzle piece, even upside down, they cheered and giggled with delight. His victories, however small, had become their victories. When he withdrew and began one of his self-stimulating rituals, they joined him immediately. The excellence of their studentship increased with each unfolding moment. They mirrored his actions to perfection, although he remained far more skillful at spinning objects. Our daughters had added a new dimension to our program and made the family bond between us even stronger. Their sweet and encouraging sensibilities as well as their openheartedness made them very loving naturals as teachers.

5

Reaching Out to a Circle of Friends

What was merely a simple interaction for the normal one-and-a-half-year-old child appeared to be a confounding and complex experience for Raun. Trying to imitate us required intense effort and concentration on his part, though when he initiated behavior or activities, he performed with ease and great skill. In contrast, he had extreme difficulty digesting the unfamiliar gestures of others.

Passionately imitating Raun, joining him with love and enthusiasm in his activities, played a central role in our sessions. Clearly, our son could neither easily nor successfully negotiate our world. So, wanting not to push him or demand from him what he could not give, we took a very different path: We went to him in his world. By mirroring his movements, we entered his universe, participated with him on his terms, and, as a result, made ourselves more digestible to him.

Two psychologists and a psychiatrist, as well as their colleagues, whom we had consulted earlier, condemned our approach. Reasoning that Raun's behavior was "sick" and maladaptive, they counseled us to stop him, not reinforce his behavior. But, we asked, why would we want to judge the behavior of a nineteen-month-old child as "sick" or maladaptive? Like all of us, he did the best he could. He didn't see his unique and strange actions as unique and strange at all. Only those who judged from the outside could form such a conclusion. But we didn't want to judge him; we wanted to love him and learn more about his world in order to help him.

Our perspective did not come from heaven. We had worked hard, prior to Raun's birth, to change ourselves by changing our visions and letting go of our judgments. All that self-exploration and growth had prepared us for this moment, allowing us to find a peaceful yet energetic place inside and to greet our special son with love, acceptance, and determination.

I remembered in one of the workshops we taught, a woman had turned to her husband and pleaded, "Please, can't you just love me as I am?" And I reflected, isn't that what all of us want for ourselves? Both Samahria and I believed that making that kind of accepting love tangible for our son would make a powerful difference in his life. And mirroring as well as sincerely joining his actions gave us a way to make that love visible.

Ultimately, we decided it was not what we did that counted but the attitude with which we did it; the same actions done without a nonjudgmental attitude would not yield the same results.

Raun would know. He seemed almost telepathic in his ability to detect the discomforts and moods of those around him. He moved away from people who appeared distressed by his actions. If we wanted him to move toward us, we had to become inviting. Pantomime would not work. We had to feel accepting and loving at the deepest levels; his sisters drew these feelings from themselves in a matter of moments. For us adults, prejudices and fears can be a powerful distraction that clouds our vision. We dedicated ourselves to a simple aim: to be happy and to be loving. And although we fell far short of perfection in our endeavors and although at times stubborn old beliefs and biases muddled us, we focused passionately on our intention—for our own sake and for our son's. By choice, we had opened a doorway to accepting ourselves and to accepting fully the wonder of our little boy. That attitude had created a safe place in which Raun could explore and grow. We took one day at a time. No yesterdays. No tomorrows. Only today!

Additionally, we wanted to show Raun that with minimal effort he could effect change and exert some control over the external world. At the dinner table, when he shook his head wildly back and forth, we all did the same with him. When he smiled, we all smiled back at him. If he stuck out his tongue, we all stuck our tongues out. Each time, he watched us with fascination and delight. Sometimes he smiled. Other times he would quietly regard our behavior, becoming more and more aware that he could set the pace.

Once Raun had become confident that he was really in control, "Simon Says" became the order of the day. As we followed his movements, he continually changed, and then changed again. Many dinners would lie cold as Samahria, Bryn, Thea, I, and others banged, clicked, kicked, and tapped the table as Raun did. Once in a while, he would flash his bright eyes at us and give us a big, big smile, then refocus his attention on his moving hands. We loved this time that we had together, watching delightfully as Raun Kahlil took tiny steps and moved just a bit closer to us.

Many new accessories enriched his bathroom sessions—new insertion toys, more puzzles, brightly colored plastic blocks, cups, picture books, and miniature musical instruments, such as flutes, drums, tambourines, and chimes. We introduced clay and finger paints, then Play-Doh. We designed additional movement and touching games, choreographing interactions to music.

Since his movements appeared awkward, we had to direct precisely each step we asked him to take. We simplified tasks and shaped his responses. If he just approximated a movement or partially completed an exercise, we greeted such attempts with cheers and enthusiastic displays of physical affection. Sometimes, we handed him soft cookies, which he loved. We saw his specific accomplishments as secondary to inspiring him to *want* to learn and participate.

We used every toy and game as a vehicle to foster interaction and communication. Often, we had to break apparently simple steps down into more easily digestible substeps. For Raun to understand and master inserting a puzzle piece into its appropriate space, we had to break this action down into three or four distinct steps. First, we taught him how to pick up the wooden pie piece. Then we showed him how to move his hand and the puzzle piece to the puzzle board. Next, we modeled for him the act of locating the cutout that matched the piece, and lastly, we showed him how to manipulate the piece until it fit into its spot. After he mastered each operation, we slowly combined the separate actions to form one entire sequence.

Our sensitivity to the importance of making the environment digestible for Raun was fundamental in our educational project. We reviewed, dissected, and redesigned each and every task in order to make it comprehensible.

During the fifth week of our program, Raun underwent another developmental checkup and examination. The diagnosis remained very much the same. We received no new input or information. The professionals encouraged us in our attempts to reach our son, yet expressed strong skepticism. They cautioned us about working with our son ourselves in a program design never before tried that violated all the current major hypotheses about intervening with developmentally and neurologically impaired children.

Autistic children, the most difficult and unreachable of all, they believed, required a strong behavioral approach, even such aversion conditioning techniques as slapping or incarceration in time-out boxes in order to curb some of their bizarre and inappropriate actions. At best, they insisted, the outcome would still be a severely dysfunctional human being requiring custodial care. They didn't want us to delude ourselves with unrealistic hopes. We disagreed. Hope, we knew, kept us alive and fueled our program. We knew we had no guarantees; in fact, we knew we were playing the longest of long shots.

A dance in the hallowed halls of medicine. Since the future was not our focus, we had not found the professionals' advice and concerns useful. Yet we did profit from this exercise. We could compare the results of this testing and plotting of Raun's abilities with those of former examinations. What the professionals saw as insignificant, we embraced as real progress. Those increased moments of fleeting eye contact, his welcoming us into his autistic self-stimulating rituals, and his willingness to allow minimal physical contact felt like solid accomplishments. Who could know where these small starts might lead?

Our entire summer had become consumed by our endeavor to be with Raun, to reach him and say hello. Although we hired a woman to help with the housework, the pace exhausted all of us. I had spent time mixing the hours in my office with continued research and reading. Samahria's days had been swallowed up by our gigantic, beautiful new project—our son. Friends asked how we felt about being deprived of other activities and interests. One spoke of our efforts as real "sacrifice." If painters or sculptors begin a piece and work year after year on it, we wouldn't ask them how deprived they feel. We would assume that they expended all their energy and effort because they wanted to, because they enjoyed their work. In our world, Raun was our piece of sculpture, as yet undated and incomplete. We did what we did because we wanted to and delighted in doing it every day.

The modifications we made in our life-style did not prevent us from maintaining relationships we valued and some endeavors we enjoyed. Samahria gave up her sculpture for a time but still continued in infrequent bursts with her music. Since I only slept five hours each night, I still had some time available in addition to the time I spent working in the office or evolving a program for Raun. I used these limited hours to continue spreading our life-style vision via small workshops and seminars I gave. I spent extra time with the girls and worked on my writing when everyone else slept.

Our nightly discussions about Raun's progress and his changes continued. Each day we plotted our program afresh. Each evening we evaluated the effectiveness of our actions and Raun's responsiveness to them. We devoted time also to reviewing Bryn and Thea's attitudes. We decided that although we had been sensitive to the girls — to their needs and their moods — we wanted more for them.

I set aside two afternoons each week to be with them, one at a time. Thea and I spent late afternoons at the duck pond, then had pizza and played pinball. Bryn and I went ice skating, then ate clams at McGuiness's. Loving them each individually, spending hours talking with them, and discussing their feelings were important. We solicited their advice about Raun and the program, indicating to them how very important they were to us. Thea, who looked so much like Raun, would end our days together skipping up the driveway with me. Bryn, forever bursting with energy, asked that we spend the last minute of our afternoons sitting together on the couch, holding each other's hand in silence.

Making a superhuman effort, Samahria worked tirelessly each day and still found time and energy to spend loving hours in the early evenings with our daughters. My afternoons with them only accounted for a small portion of their time. Day camp, which both Bryn and Thea actively and happily attended during the week, made the summer manageable. The pleasure of camp reduced their awareness of just how much time and energy we all devoted to Raun, although both of them were familiar with his entire curriculum.

Concerned friends assisted us by taking the girls from place to place on weekends while we worked with Raun. Others participated in working our program with Raun for short periods so Samahria could rest or go for an occasional bike ride.

There was Rhoda, always nursing her eternal diet, whose entry into the kitchen came with staccato comments and instructions for everyone, but whose soft and gentle concern touched us with her help with Thea, and at times, with Bryn. When others began to turn away, feeling too uncomfortable to enter our home or see our strange child, Rhoda moved toward us even more strongly, opening her heart wider and helping us with our other children.

Jerry J. was an eighteen-year-old version of the last Neanderthal man. His elephant imitations and soulfulness pervaded our home with special warmth, laughter, and caring. Often, he served as a loving companion to the girls and performed lifeguard duties as the two swam in the pool together. And vocal Laura, whose beautiful egocentric enthusiasm and poetry filled our rooms with light and excitement, assisted us directly with Raun. Her mellowness and her soulfulness softened many summer days. Jerry with his vibraphone and Laura with her soprano saxophone sometimes played together from the hilltop behind our home, filling our land with notes of jazz and melodic renderings of themselves. Even Raun stopped to listen to their music and hear its heartbeat.

And there was Nancy, no longer so shy that her hands assaulted and hid her face. She had first come to us at the age of thirteen as a mother's helper. As she had been living with us on and off for the past five years, we considered her part of our family. Samahria and I became her surrogate parents, while the girls adopted her as their older sister. Her baggy pants and boatlike shoes hid the blossoming of her body and camouflaged her womanhood. Her sensitivity, caring, and help during these months contributed to the stability of our home and family.

The visits of gentle Jeffrey, our yoga-styled, string-bean partner in meditation, were always welcomed. He transformed his transcendental Eastern attitude and vegetarian cleanliness into graphics painted on the ceiling of our bedroom. Samahria, Jeffrey, Bryn, Thea, and I enjoyed many silent, warm twilight evenings doing yoga together as the haunting cello of Casals filtered through the outdoor speakers.

Summer passing. We had visits from brother Steven, a steady, predictable suburbanite, directing a drug-rehab program at a university hospital while negotiating daily contracts with his liberated wife. One afternoon, his hairy body parted the waters in our swimming pool; he had dived in to pursue Raun, who, having fallen in, was taking his first, unauthorized swim.

Laurie, Steve's wife, whose love and beliefs made it difficult for her to accept Raun's autism, joined us, too. She hoped for some magical solution that would turn him into a communicative and playful little boy like her son, who was the same age.

There was also my father, Abe, whose athletic form projected the image of a man thirty years younger and whose studied mustache brought back nostalgic visions of William Powell's debonair portrayal in *The Thin Man*. He and his wife, Roz (stepmother), stayed one week at our home, supplying slices of the past as they melted into the energized framework of our lives. I used this time to renew a love and affection for my father, which had flowered in the nine years since the death of my mother. All this while Roz played lovingly and easily with our children.

We spent some lazy summer nights with Marv (or Merv, as Bryn called him affectionately) and his wife, Elise. She performed the duties of a resident astrology whiz, eating her way through her third and fourth lives and loving it. Marv, a fellow explorer who shared our vision, life-style, and philosophy, pushed playfully at the outer boundaries of his understanding, trying to support our efforts with his observations and ideas. Beneath the banter, we felt his love and unending concern for all of us, all the time.

Evenings of dialogue with Marshall and Joy. Both, with their razor-sharp intellects, entered into debating matches with me about the attitude and process we taught. We loved their challenges; they helped us further clarify our vision and realize how unshakable our conviction had become in regard to the power and usefulness of the nonjudgmental attitude underlying our program with Raun.

An occasional horseback ride with Bryn or alone ushered in the early morning hours on Saturday. Swimming each morning and evening allowed me to throw off the accumulated energy of the day. For all of us, it was an involved and exciting summer. Most remarkably, this summer marked the time when Samahria laid down her sculpture chisel to pick up a tambourine for Raun.

Eight weeks of the program had elapsed. Beautiful. Difficult.

Sometimes confusing. Always rewarding. The progress had been just fantastic. For another child, Raun's accomplishments might merely be a new lesson learned in a single day. But Raun's struggle and the risks he took to be with us and to explore the world were profoundly heroic. The little boy who had looked through people now sometimes looked at them and even occasionally smiled at them. The deaf one would be attentive, from time to time, to someone calling him. The recluse participated genuinely and actively now, though for only moments or minutes at a time. Our "special" child appeared to have more fun with himself and with us. He kept unearthing new ways to piece the world together and make sense out of his perceptions.

*   *   *

One morning, while in the kitchen, Raun walked over to the refrigerator and started to cry. Samahria asked him if he wanted juice. He started to cry even more, his body language expressing an uncommon urgency. Tears cascaded down Samahria's cheeks. She knew her son had pushed through some unknown barrier to reach out, for the very first time, and indicate something he wanted. Rather than teach him a more socially acceptable way of communicating, Samahria jumped up and immediately gave him juice. As he drank it appreciatively, she applauded him vigorously, then broke into cheers. The tears kept coming—happy tears. A child drinks the juice he requested, and for the mother watching, it's a miracle!

In the midst of making a presentation to a client at my office, I received a phone call from Samahria.

"He did it, Bears! He made his first request today. Today—he did it today. For juice—for orange juice."

Tears filled my own eyes as I heard her crying. "It's okay," I reassured her. "No, it's not okay; it's tremendous. Really! It's bigger than words."

Now her sobs turned to laughter. "I don't even know what I'm doing right now," she said. "I feel absolutely smashing. I guess I never anticipated or pictured that he'd take such a big step today— or any day."

"Do you want me to come home?"

"Yes, of course, but no! Bears, I knew you would want to know."

As I hung up the phone, looking at the photographs displayed on the wall, my staff and clients gaped at me. Suddenly, I realized tears had been flowing down my cheeks. I smiled. "Well, you see," I shared with them, "my son just asked for orange juice. And in our home, that's a big deal—a really big deal."

Any form of communication marked a shift in Raun's ability to think and express himself. We stood on the edge of new possibilities—just on the edge. Two hours later, during a second phone conversation, Samahria and I discussed the implications of what had occurred. We would honor any gesture swiftly. If he could understand, truly understand, that he could trigger desirable responses from us, then we had opened a doorway into his mind. In the afternoon, on that same day, he went over to the door to the den and began to cry. Samahria opened it immediately, and he thereupon stopped his outcry and walked into the room. Minutes later, he stood at the bottom of the stairs and repeated his act. Samahria removed the gate. Within seconds, he scooted quietly up the staircase.

He had moved into an active stage of prelinguistic communication. He wanted things external to himself and now actively tried to get them. A breakthrough! For the first time, he brought himself into our world and became an active, initiating participant in our family unit.

This week also marked his beginning to mimic words, giving us the first reward for our verbal cues and emphasis on language. Raun started to repeat words said to him, though always using the same tone, pitch, and accent. He mouthed them like a parrot. But had he digested and assimilated them? No! He used them randomly, disconnected from any object or event. Rather than verbalizing the word *light* to indicate a fixture, a lamp, or the brightness he desired, Raun babbled the word when he rocked or rolled a ball. The words had no meaning. Like many other autistic children, Raun became echolalic, repeating words exactly as he heard them rather than using them meaningfully to communicate. Yet, even though he did not communicate verbally, his parroting of words was indeed an amazing first step. Perhaps echoing sounds was his way of holding what he heard before his mind's eye in order to extract its meaning, not unlike the student who repeats the teacher's question in order to hear it again and absorb it. We believed that if further development was possible, it would not depend on rote training, but on the increased intensity of his wanting and increased awareness that others could help him to attain his goals.

Raun had made some dramatic leaps this week—like a sky diver pulling the cord for the first time or a skier suspended in the air during the first downhill race.

*   *   *

We kept notes from the inception of our program, but now, at the end of the eighth week, we decided to begin a formal journal, making entries in a log. The first entry included a summary of Raun's behavior at the outset of our program.

Log: Eighth Week—
Raun Kahlil, Nineteen Months—
Schedule: Eighty-five Hours per Week

Notes: Raun Two Months Ago:

No social contact or interaction, no eye contact; enjoyed objects more than people; no language or gestures, no anticipatory gestures when being picked up; when he is held, he goes limp and he smiles to himself. Always self-stimulating—spinning, rocking, looking at his hands, making repetitive motions with his fingers against his lips. Repeats strange movements with his hands. Pushes away from physical contact. Never cries to get out of his crib or to eat. Often appears deaf and blind. Stares constantly. Shows great desire for sameness. Throws everything and does not play.

Current: Changes up to and Including This Week:

- Much less rocking movement; mostly rocks in his crib.
- Real eye contact established when playing certain games.
- More facial expression.
- Still ignores people, but is somewhat more receptive to familiar people.

- Attentive to being called, although most often will not come on request.
- Making fewer finger motions against his lips.
- Hardly ever pushes away his mother.
- Has started to indicate wants by crying—for first time; definite efforts to communicate.
- Mimics words (echolalically).
- Reacts to some spoken words when being addressed: car, cup, bottle, come, up, water.
- For the first time, expressed strong emotion (perhaps anger) during an interaction in response to our attempt to remove something he apparently did not want to give up.
- For the first time, he gestured with his arm when he was about to be picked up.
- Has begun to drink out of a glass when someone holds it.
- Cried twice when person he played with left the room.
- Occasionally follows people.
- Has started to feed himself with his fingers.

No Changes:

- Still prefers the world of objects most of the time.
- Still spins, but will now give us an object to spin with him.
- Still pushes away from people and physical contact.
- Generally, still throws things.
- Still no gesture or verbal language development for general communications (although used crying for the first time to communicate).
- Does not cry to get out of the crib or cry to indicate desire to eat.

General Observations:

- Has difficulty chewing and chokes on solid foods.
- Special desire for liquids—much more than for solid foods. Seems to be rejuvenated after drinking, as if water, juices, and milk were stimulants.
- Puts absolutely everything in his mouth.

- Often reacts to familiar words or objects as if he had never heard or seen them before, as if he does not retain them in his memory.

*   *   *

It had been an amazing two months! Our intervention had clearly made a difference, although, at the moment, limited in scope.

I began to notice Samahria growing more and more tired with the passing weeks. Her usually vibrant long blond hair hung limp from neglect. The soft creases in her forehead appeared deeper and more prominent. Though she was exhausted, her eyes still glistened and sparkled, especially when she talked about her children. Wanting to be with her son, she had pushed at the perimeter of her resources and expended every last drop of energy each day in order to help her son.

I knew she viewed this adventure as a pilgrimage, not a burden or hardship. But I also knew that the time and energy level required had to be so high and intense so much of the time that her body registered the wear.

On Sunday night, I approached Samahria with a new plan.

"You look happy, but wrecked," I said gently. "I have an idea. What about getting some volunteers or even hiring and training other people to help?"

Samahria eyed me cautiously. "Bears, I can do it."

"Sure you can. But I don't want us to lose you while we try to find Raun. You're the best, the very best. And you do it every day! Every day you jump into the trenches with him. More than any of us, you've made Raun's fantastic progress possible."

"But, Bears, what about attitude? You know what a key that is."

"Definitely! But we can train people, Samahria. We can teach them the attitude. Hey, if I changed from being the uncomfortable nut I used to be, then anyone can change." We both laughed. I knew she would have no disagreement with that statement. I continued. "Before we put anyone in the room with Raun, we'll train them, show them everything we know. It'll be better than before. You'll be stronger. The girls would probably adore additions to our little teaching staff. We'll have more time to brainstorm new ideas and new directions. It'll work. I know it will."

Samahria smiled. "Okay, okay, okay. I'm convinced. Maybe it would be helpful for Raun to connect with other people besides just us." She looked away for a moment, furrowing her forehead. "But, Bears, only if they're really good with him and have a loving attitude."

"Absolutely! Only if they're the best—like you."

Nancy, now seventeen years old, became our first volunteer teacher-therapist. She had overheard the conversation I had had with Samahria and excitedly offered to participate. Over the years, she had watched our growth and oftentimes listened attentively to our discussions about beliefs and judgments. She would be a natural. Her involvement with our family had spanned almost five years. She loved the children as if they were her own and had been supportive of the program from the very beginning. We asked her to think about it overnight. The very next morning, she volunteered a second time, wanting us to feel her enthusiasm and the strength of her "Yes."

We also hired another teenager, Maire, a high school senior with an abiding interest in children. Though different from Nancy, she displayed genuine sensitivity and caring. Ultimately, we spent more time working with her on attitude than showing her the tools and techniques to use in dealing with Raun. Initially, she lacked confidence. Would we judge her skill by Raun's progress or lack of progress? she wondered. We assured her that was not our intention. We always allowed Raun his interests, his contacts, and his withdrawals. She would come to understand that what he did or how he felt had nothing specifically to do with her. He made his choices, just as she made hers. She could only present things, suggest activities and interactions, and try to facilitate his participation. Flowing with him would be crucial. By developing an environment in which he could freely want and, perhaps, secure his wants, she would encourage him to relate to us. She understood. She continued to learn and grow, demonstrating deep respect for Raun's integrity. Soon Maire, too, became a critical part of our program and a valued member of our growing family group.

We reduced Samahria's involvement to a still-incredible forty-five hours per week. Nancy and Maire worked with Raun twenty to twenty-five hours a week. Bryn, Thea, and I contributed the rest, keeping the program active during his every waking hour. We never knew when he would attend to us. Every unfolding moment gave us yet another opportunity for interaction and growth. Since Raun spent only a few minutes every hour relating to others, we wanted to catch every one of those minutes. Within a few days of their active participation, Nancy and Maire's talents and capabilities became evident. These two very young nonprofessionals had more meaningful contributions and expressed more useful concern than most of the professionals we had ever contacted. They were unindoctrinated, open, alive, and, most important, loving.

Our motivational program continued in full bloom. Now we preplanned the specifics of what we wanted to teach. After initiating and instructing our new "teachers," Samahria caught up on some rest and spent extra hours with our daughters. On rare occasions, she began to sculpt again.

Both of us monitored Raun's progress carefully and helped him accept these new people in his life, introducing them much as Samahria had reintroduced herself to her son eight weeks ago. We did the process slowly and nonaggressively. During our nightly discussions at the dinner table and afterward, we talked incessantly about his echolalia. We wanted everyone to be supersensitive to all his communications and also encourage his mimicking, even though it had not as yet acquired any meaning. He spoke his words flatly, often addressed to the walls while his eyes remained vacant.

6

Raun's Choice

The crimson sun hovered just above the road in my rearview mirror as I headed home from the city. A dusty haze along the highway muted the sharp lines and distinct colors of nearby office and apartment buildings. The tires of my car hummed noisily, providing background music for my reflections. I thought about Raun, knowing he had broken through some of those invisible walls that enabled him to make more sense out of his environment than before and take some small but meaningful steps toward interacting with us. However, his continued self-stimulating behavior and his obvious inability to absorb and digest information—the enigma of some as yet undefined organic dysfunction—suggested disconnected or disassembled circuitry in his mind. The system that catalogs and retrieves information from the memory cells of the cerebral cortex seemed inoperative in him. And, if this was so, how could we correct what was already awry? It was simple: We couldn't. But maybe Raun could.

I had researched studies done of people who had suffered strokes and read of the possibility of "permanent damage." In many cases, it could be shown that specific masses of brain cells and tissue had been irrevocably destroyed. Autopsies revealed large areas permanently impaired by scarring. And yet, despite such damage, some patients found new ways to talk and new ways to move, and made new connections that allowed them to regain control over areas once paralyzed. They did not regain the functions of the destroyed cells but rather activated portions of the brain not previously utilized, expanding the potential of existing neurons.

Why did some stroke victims make these seemingly miraculous jumps while others remained crippled and handicapped? Most professionals attribute such jumps to motivation, an ingredient essential to the success of most serious operations and treatments. We knew that if we could inspire Raun to seek involvement with

94

us, he might then make new connections and open new channels. Memorizing data and submitting to simple training and behavioral conditioning could never accomplish what might evolve as a result of our activating his own desire to learn.

We needed more than his partnership; Raun had to play a leading role in his own recovery.

*   *   *

One evening, before we put Raun to bed, we sat with him in our bedroom and watched him walk around and play with our shoes. Suddenly, passing in front of the mirror, he became captivated by an image he saw there. Although he had certainly passed by the mirror many times, tonight something notably different happened. He stopped, startled by his own image. For the first time, he appeared mesmerized by a commanding form—the full-length reflection of himself.

He surveyed his image cautiously. He moved back and forth from left to right. He walked directly to the mirror and touched his reflection nose to nose. His eyes beamed like electric lights. He moved out of the path of the mirror, then slowly looked back into it. As he did, he met his own face, saw his own eyes. He moved directly forward again, touched his belly to the belly of the child in the mirror, then tipped his head to the mirror as the twin facing him duplicated his movement with absolute precision. Suddenly, he emitted a wild, unfamiliar shout—a cry of incredible excitement and joy. He began to grunt and laugh with elation. Raun Kahlil had discovered himself. I turned to Samahria, amazed and dazzled. Tears streamed down her face. I felt wetness under my own eyes and realized that I, too, was crying. The first day of creation—a new dimension. Raun had found himself, and it was a joyful experience.

Through the tears, we continued to observe our son. He played interactively with his image in a way that he had never before done with anyone or anything else. This sweet little boy made huge sweeping circles with his arms, engaged not only in his own movement but also in the motion reflected in the mirror. He stuck out his tongue, then shook his head and giggled. He jumped up and down, animated and engaged, softly babbling some primitive language as he continued to play hide-and-seek with himself.

Then he explored his hands, his feet, and his hair very carefully. As he touched different body parts, his reflected self did the same. He picked up his pajama top to expose his chest and tummy to his new partner. For twenty beautiful and gripping minutes, Raun said hello to himself. He discovered the oasis in the desert — himself. The months we spent working with him had prepared him for this very moment; he had readied himself each time he reached out for fleeting moments to touch his environment. This time, he enjoyed the encounter immensely.

Samahria and I spent a quiet and dreamy evening together. We drove to the beach and walked along the seashore as the Atlantic pounded the sand. No need to talk. We held each other's hands as we strolled. Moontides rocked the ocean back and forth, creating huge waves. Glimmers of light bounced between us as we moved through the thick mist. Ebb tide.

*   *   *

Our around-the-clock program flourished. Every minute of every day, we provided Raun with contact and bombarded him with stimulation. Our crew, including Bryn and Thea, engaged him more excitedly and more assertively. We all sensed a new dimension developing in our program. Since discovering himself in the mirror, Raun had become more purposeful in his activities and involvements, more premeditated in his actions and reactions. When he picked up a puzzle piece, he did so with more energy. When he attempted to insert it into its appropriate slot, he turned the piece more skillfully than before and demonstrated greater mastery as he matched the cutout forms to the wooden receptacles they belonged in. Had Raun opened a new neurological pathway when he took more ownership of his arms, hands, fingers, legs, belly, head, tongue, and lips in the mirror? His enhanced body awareness affected both his large and small motor skills. As I watched him and Samahria spin in circles and playfully bump into each other, I couldn't help but speculate that Raun had, additionally, found beauty and delight in strengthening his contact with himself — and with us.

The following depicts Raun's typical day. When possible, we followed this schedule seven days a week.

Daily Schedule

8:30   Raun has been awake in his crib for about half an hour. By this time, he has usually thrown his toys onto the floor. Samahria takes him out of the crib and dresses him. He glides down the stairs on his belly, feet first. Then, he eats breakfast with his mother at the kitchen table or in the bathroom, all the time being stimulated by words, sweet commentaries, or songs played on the tape recorder.

9:15   The more formal sessions begin as Raun and Samahria go into bathroom, which is filled with toys and a vast array of educational materials. They play games aimed at developing interpersonal interaction and skills, and Samahria rewards and reinforces him with smiles, cheers, stroking, and food. The toys and games include an insertion box with at least thirty different shapes, four or five wooden insertion puzzle games with hand knobs (Samahria makes sounds as she picks up each animal piece and articulates identifying nouns), a truck with seven connecting pieces, a tool game toy, musical instruments to bang and blow, insertion and building cups, clay and Play-Doh, crayons and chalk, as well as mounted photographs of family members, animals, and other objects to be displayed for possible identification. They do exercises to music. Samahria helps Raun move his arms, feet, and torso to the tempo of music and also at random. They improvise spontaneously much of the movement and dance. We've designed body parts identification games to help him develop gestures, such as pointing, and to stimulate him to speak. Touching interludes encompass stroking, massaging, and tickling as well as exploring hands, fingers, toes, noses, ears, and the like. Water games are played in both sink and bathtub. Books constitute a multidimensional resource, making it possible to turn pages, view pictures, read words, and explain the actions of vehicles, people, machines, and animals. "Smell" books (scratch the patch) and pop-up books add additional surprise to Raun's adventure and allow us to combine pointing and speaking with touch and smell.

10:30 Break from confined work area: go for a walk, play peekaboo, try to interact with some other toys, give Raun some food. All involve constant interaction aimed at strengthening eye contact, responsiveness, and bonding. Later, we abandon the breaks, finding the time spent in the room more focused and more effective.

11:00 Back into the bathroom for more structured interplay and games.

12:00 Finish morning stimulation sessions. Take another walk or a car ride, going to the park or the store, or visiting with other children. (Oftentimes, Raun withdraws and becomes frenetic in his self-stimulation during such excursions, persuading us to review the wisdom of including these adventures in his program. Eventually, we eliminate them.)

1:00 Nap.

2:00 Awake and down for lunch.

2:30 Another session in the bathroom.

3:30 End of bathroom session. Playing in the park, a bike ride. Also time for Bryn and Thea to function as playmates/teachers/therapists.

4:00 Special helper (Maire or Nancy) arrives and begins session in the bathroom.

5:30 We integrate other members of the family or teaching group—jumping on the bed, playing "Simon Says" games, and providing more physical stimulation.

6:30 Dinner with entire family along with student teacher or teachers. Now we work as a team with Raun, using all aspects of the meal to encourage eye contact and imitation games, usually with our son as leader and all of us as his students.

7:00 Additional session in the family den.

8:00–8:30 Session ends.

8:30 Raun to sleep.

* * *

Another difficulty we faced with Raun was his inability to eat solid foods. At each meal, we would attempt to teach him how to chew and, hopefully, convert his baby-food diet into a more well-rounded meal with solid foods. One night, he grabbed a handful of French fried potatoes from a bowl and shoved them into his mouth. A comic image with swollen cheeks and the amused look of a clown. Before we had a chance to dislodge the excess food from his bulging mouth, he swallowed part of it without chewing. He looked up at me, surprised, and gasped. Within seconds, he was in trouble.

The food stuck in his windpipe, cutting off his ability to breathe. He began to struggle desperately, poking his fingers into his neck. His eyes opened wide, pushing outward from his head as if he were trying to grab air through his vision. We picked up his arms and slapped his back, then shook his entire body. What we did had no impact.

He still could not get any air. He started to shake his arms, then looked at me as if pleading for help and, yet, at the same time, observing events that had slipped beyond his control. I picked him out of his chair, opened his mouth, and searched his throat for the food with my fingers. No use. I turned him upside down and began shaking him. Raun struggled more now. His body jerked spasmodically. I slapped his back, then hit his buttocks. Impossible. An every-evening occurrence had quickly assumed the proportions of an unthinkable nightmare. All present had jumped out of their seats. I could see all the rush of movement in my peripheral vision as I searched desperately for something else to do. Shock the digestive track. Send a ripple through the system that would make him vomit. I handed Raun to Samahria, telling her to keep him upside-down. With one hand, I found the soft part in his upper abdomen just below the rib cage and with the palm of my other hand slammed upward into that section of his body. He emitted a harsh grunt as the potatoes and other contents in his stomach tumbled to the floor. We had improvised a maneuver that saved our child. Years later, a physician would design a similar procedure to help choking victims.

My hands began to shake as I looked at Samahria's numb expression. She held her son close to her. Raun coughed, then recovered quickly. He looked at us with great relief. His eyes glistened as he glanced at us with an expression that seemed to say, "Thanks."

Short panting breaths dominated my body as my ribs strained under the constant and rapid pounding of my heart. Samahria and I gaped at each other through the tension in our eyes. Her face and lips had turned ghostly white, but she managed to squeeze out a smile of relief. I began to laugh. Raun was still here! He had survived. We had survived. God had given us another day—another day to try to reach our special child.

We decided in that moment to initiate immediately a crash effort to teach Raun how to consume solid foods. We would first establish eye contact, then have him watch us insert food into our mouths, chew it exaggeratedly, and then swallow it. We repeated this over and over and over again. Finally, Samahria placed soft but solid food into his mouth. For the first few moments, he just let it sit there on his tongue, then let it fall out of his mouth. We modeled a possible course of action for him by chewing the same food robustly in our own mouths. Unfortunately, he did not take our cues. Samahria talked to him as she manipulated his jaw with her hands, opening and closing his bottom set of teeth against his upper set as a way to teach him how to ready food for consumption. We repeated this exercise diligently at every meal. Samahria and I took turns working his jaw. Every so often, we could feel the muscles of his jaw work. It took forty-two meals over a period of two weeks before we noted real progress. Finally, our enigmatic son started to chew. Hurrah! Hurrah!

*   *   *

Each week, Saturdays and Sundays merged into one another as we eased into our peculiar and unique life-style. We spent many weekend afternoons building miniature indoor bonfires in the living room fireplace. Bryn, Thea, and I would gather up the stubby logs piled at the side of our house. Thea always warned me not to give her heavy ones. Bryn asked for more and more logs until, inevitably, the strain on her arms became apparent in the discomfort visible on her face. The three of us stacked the wood in and beside the brick fireplace.

By packing crumpled newspaper under the grill, we created a base for the flames. Samahria opened all the windows, sometimes even turned the air conditioning on, for our late-summer antics required immediate cooling. And then, as we all sat around, I lit the paper and ignited the many corners of our creation, always careful to have Raun break from his sessions at those moments in order to be with us and to watch, with obvious fascination, the dazzling dancing flames. Reds, purples, and white. As the fire began to roar, Bryn and Thea would cheer and clap. The stereo would belt out Bach as reinterpreted by the Modern Jazz Quartet.

Once sure of the success of our fire, we then would all clear the furniture from the center of the floor, leaving the room bare before the hearth. Bryn would bring in some beanbags while Thea grabbed pillows from the bedrooms. In two minutes, using the soft cushions for support, we were snuggling with one another in various positions on the floor, enjoying the fire and one another. Bryn's head leaned on my legs as Thea's feet draped over my stomach. Samahria lay diagonally across my chest. The Big Bear had become the big bear rug.

Within a half hour, Jerry, Laura, and Nancy joined us, all of them having become part of our evolving family. We disconnected the telephones for the remainder of the day and took turns working with Raun. He played and poked at the fire, then engaged us even more fully in the bathroom. Jerry tossed a ball to Bryn, who returned it through her giggles. Thea asked Laura to play pick-up sticks. Samahria kissed me and whispered that she was very happy.

These were beautiful times, when talking and doing became secondary to our being with and flowing with the people we loved. A time when the good feelings of each of us touched everyone else in the room. A time that included an hour-long dialogue that I did with Laura, helping her investigate the beliefs underlying the discomforts she had about school. Samahria brought Raun back into the living room for a few minutes; together, they experimented with Jerry's vibraphone, making different sounds. Bryn and Thea swayed to the rhythm of their music. Nancy stared into the flames. The voices and the music blended, creating a symphony of sounds. Mellow. A togetherness we all treasured. Poignantly aware of loving and enjoying one another.

*   *   *

As the program continued, Raun produced more varied facial expressions and communicated more with gestures. Playing in the mirror had become one of his favorite games. I was increasingly conscious of his ability to control his environment. He manipulated us now by taking our hands, pulling us toward objects he wanted, and then crying. The message was loud and clear. I want. I want.

What wonder! In the morning, he took Samahria's hand and led her to the refrigerator to show her that he wanted juice. In the evening of that same day, he pulled me to the bottom of the staircase to show me that he wanted to go upstairs. The second-floor area was Raun's private world, where he often wanted to go to be alone. We always allowed him this solitude, although we would intercede after an extended period of time.

When we put a glass of water on the table, he would go after it once he saw it. We would help him hold the glass in his tiny hands. Previously, Raun had responded only to foods and liquids placed directly in front of him. Now he extended his frontier somewhat further. He would follow us and the glass with his gaze rather than sit Buddha-like with a fixed stare. Had he solidified new connections in the synapses of his brain? Had he altered the hard wiring of his neurons as his interest in the world grew?

We had also noted his increasing attentiveness to people; he was more involved, almost caring, in his manner when playing with us. Perhaps the reasons were obvious. People had become increasingly more useful to him, helping him get more of what he wanted. And we, the people, had used every experience of contact as an opportunity to express acceptance, love, and joy. Always, we had been the ones to initiate contact and cheer his accomplishments, whether he built a tower out of blocks or looked directly into our eyes. Now Raun began to make moves toward us. He would give us a plate or the top from a jar so we could spin them. Give and take in our interactions had increased dramatically by comparison with those first weeks in which he showed little response to our imitations of him.

Another hurdle had to be jumped. Initially, Raun had used crying as a means of articulating wants and asking for things. We permitted it and reinforced it because we believed that the fact he was communicating was far more important than the specific form of communication he chose. We did not want to extinguish what had just begun by confusing him with potentially incomprehensible directions. But now Raun was much more aware of himself—of his wants and his abilities. We could build on this strength. We believed Raun could accept and deal successfully with change if we altered our own behavior slowly and respectfully. Instead of jumping to fulfill his wants every time he cried, we decided to pause, ask him what he wanted, encourage him to point or make some gesture to help us understand, and then deliver on his request. Sometimes, he appeared impatient with this strategy. Other times, he stared at us genuinely perplexed. We followed this procedure over and over again throughout the day.

Each unfolding week ushered in new accomplishments—new breakthroughs. Yet I kept reviewing an area I knew to be critically important to Raun's ability to think and ultimately talk.

Each evening, for weeks, I put him through the same test, hoping in this way to help him eventually to accomplish the near impossible. I would greet him in the kitchen and show him a cookie. When he put his hand up for it, I would slowly move it away while encouraging him to follow it with his eyes. Then I would make a great show of putting the cookie behind a piece of paper. He would lose track of it once it disappeared from sight and then stand there confused. He still could not keep an object in his memory when it was out of view. He still had a limited ability, at best, to solidify images in his mind for future reference. Developing and perfecting this area was critical; it would serve as a foundation upon which he could build language.

This would be our game—Raun's and mine. The rehearsal for perhaps another time.

Log: Ninth Week—
Same Schedule, Three Active Teachers

Changes:

- Eye contact has become excellent and sustained.
- More attentive to familiar people now, and attentive for short periods of time to new people.

- Absolutely no hand fixating or flapping this week. A real "wow!"
- More expression of wants by crying and pulling.
- Listens to requests: e.g., go here, take my hand, put it back, wait, come, go get it, eat, sit down.
- Now initiates game playing and social contact—he will give us objects for us to spin with him.
- More active interest in game-related activities, such as peekaboo, playing with insertion toys, working puzzles.
- More possessive of objects; for the first time, he will now actually fight for things and will cry if something he wants is removed.
- Starting to hold cups and glasses by himself and drinking by himself, but this is very inconsistent.
- Will follow people in and out of rooms, especially his workroom (he appears to love his workroom).
- Has started to chew solid foods without incident.
- Enjoys engaging himself in front of the mirror—goes up and down the glass with his hands, playing peekaboo with his image. Also looks at other people through the mirror.
- Now starting to solicit some physical contact, seems to enjoy it at times.
- Comes to his mother and to teachers when strangers are around.
- Starting to gesture—points and bangs some at the things he wants.
- Responds to more complex verbal suggestions: "Raun wants bottle," "Wait a minute," "Raun, stand still" (when he puts on clothes).

No Changes:

- Still prefers the inanimate world outside his work bathroom and den sessions.
- Still very absorbed by spinning objects.
- Still does not in any way indicate a wish to get out of the bed in the morning or after naps.
- Still does not use verbal language to communicate.
- Throws everything he gets his hands on.

Further Observations:

- Aware that the quality of his responses is much better in places like the bathroom, the den, or even the car, where there are few distractions.
- Imitating more of our sounds and physical acts (mouthing, cocking his head, jumping, crawling, running, hitting the tambourine as instructed, blowing, etc.).
- Stronger interaction when he initiates and controls.
- Knows the sound of the car and the doorbell; looks in the appropriate direction when he hears them.
- Curls his fingers to one side of his face if he is agitated.
- Has a peculiar behavioral pattern of turning away from people when he smiles.
- Gets notably upset when his sisters cry; tries to manipulate them to smile, by approaching them, even touching them at times.

* * *

Samahria brought Raun down from his room one Saturday morning before dressing him. As he sat on the kitchen floor while she brewed coffee, he grabbed his shoes and tried to put them on. He struggled, trying to fit his toes into the appropriate hole and caught his fingers in the laces. I sat down beside him to help. Little by little, we maneuvered the shoes on to his feet, while he directed the process. As soon as we finished, he ripped both of them off and began again. I aided him again. Once they were on his feet a second time, off they came. His tiny fingers worked busily; he was animated, excited by his accomplishment and newly attained skill. He must have put on his shoes over twenty times. Finally, he left them on, visibly exhausted.

In the afternoon, Samahria took time out to practice the saxophone, the latest endeavor undertaken only a few weeks before. Laura, an accomplished musician, had volunteered to be her teacher. Now the notes came careening out of the sensually curved bellows of the horn, invading our home with the brassy dissonance of sounds either too flat or too sharp—a beginner's shrill chorus.

Every time Samahria practiced her horn, Raun would actually run from the clamor—out of the room. Sometimes, he cried and held his ears to protest this assault. His opinion seemed loud and clear, and he expressed it lucidly and effectively. In contrast, Bryn, Thea, loving friends, and I were more accepting of Samahria's starts. We had seen many of them. Her on-again, off-again love affair with the piano. Then her lessons with the guitar, and her attempts to compose her own music and lyrics. All those free concerts with us as her captive audience. And now the sensuous saxophone. While Raun ran and hid, we rejoiced in the fact that she hadn't fallen in love with the tuba or trumpet.

* * *

We began the eleventh week in the program. As I came through the side door after a day spent working in tinsel town, I bumped right into Raun, who had been standing by the table. He peered up at me very casually, brought his right hand up from his side as if to take the oath of office, and then moved his fingers up and down against his palm. My God, he was waving hello!

Dumbfounded, I waved back. He watched me for several seconds and then looked away. What a simple and profound hello — the best I had ever had! Three months before, if I had walked through the door and thrown a hand grenade, Raun would have never so much as flinched or looked at me. Now this little man greeted me with a sweet and understandable gesture. My number was coming in. We were both the winners.

There was still enough time for Raun and me to play our favorite nongame before Samahria put him to bed. I took a cookie off the counter and showed it to him. I put it in the center of the floor, calling his attention to it. Then, as he watched, I ever so slowly placed a newspaper over it, hiding it from his view. He paused, staring at the paper for almost a minute. Then, with very little overt expression of interest, he walked over to the paper and sat beside it. He studied the photographs on the front page. His glance moved slowly across the newspaper and lingered at the edges. Samahria and I looked at each other, waiting silently. We had seen him do this before, each night, without ever going further.

But then, with a careful movement of his hands, Raun pushed the paper aside, sliding it off to the right until he had uncovered the cookie. Without ceremony, he picked it up and ate it. A random accident? We could only guess. We held our breath, reviewing the event excitedly. Try again. Take the chance.

I took another cookie and showed it clearly to Raun. I put it on the floor in another part of the room and slowly placed another piece of newspaper over it. From the corner of my eyes, I noted his primal intensity like an animal poised to pounce. My neck tightened and a flutter of energy ran through the upper part of my torso. As soon as I stepped out of the way, he followed swiftly in my tracks, lifted the newspaper, and quickly plunged the cookie into his mouth. Amazing! He seemed filled with a new sense of authority, a new confidence. Had it really happened? Did this mean he could hold images now in his memory and use them?

I grabbed a handful of cookies. I put one under the base of a light chair in full view. He followed, quickly lifted the chair, and took the cookie. I put another on the counter out of sight. He again followed, lifted his hand, and felt around on the top of the counter, his little fingers walking across the formica until finding their mark. He grabbed the cookie and rewarded himself. I placed a cookie on top of the chair. Another under the pillow of the couch. Another inside my clenched fist, which he soon assaulted and forced open. Determination. He found every cookie. We applauded and cheered him. We were drenched in our exuberance. And he was, too.

He enjoyed this game immensely, excited and eager to pursue and find the food. We played for over half an hour. Had I ever really believed that he would be able to do this? What a blessing to receive so much more than I had ever envisioned! Although I had always wanted Raun to find the cookie, I never felt disappointed when he didn't. We had taught ourselves and those who helped us to play the game of "what is," not the game of what could be or what might have been. No worry about the future. No regret about the past. Only loving Raun and working with him in each unfolding moment. That was the secret.

And now, suddenly, "what is" changed, and a diamond appeared in the sand.

＊　　＊　　＊

The following day, Samahria phoned me at my office. Her voice seemed supercharged.

"Bears, something's happening. It's not in my head. I can see it. Yesterday, he could track the cookie even after you hid it. Well, you know how he could only deal with one puzzle piece at a time—and only with explicit direction. This morning, I tried something different. When I gave him the puzzle, I scrambled all the pieces into one big pile. Bears, Bears, do you know what he did? He worked it all out by himself—without any help or guidance! He matched every piece to its place, one after the other. It was awesome to watch!" She squealed, then laughed. "Do I sound like a crazy person?"

"You sound wonderful, just wonderful. I'm thinking—"

Samahria interrupted my sentence. "He can retain more and more. He's switched on like a thousand-watt light bulb! Oh God, I'm so excited for him—for me, for all of us."

All of our efforts had been dedicated to bonding with Raun in the hope of motivating him to pierce through the invisible wall of autism. His tiny steps had giant-sized implications now. The toys and games not only allowed us to join hands with him, but had become, finally, meaningful educational tools. If he could retain data and recall it, then his capacity to learn had increased tenfold. The depths of his mind had opened. In the midst of discussing possible ramifications, we both suddenly stopped speaking. In the silence, I could hear her breathe. In the silence, I could feel the intensity of our connection to each other and to the little boy we had just begun to know.

"You're doing a super job, babes—really, a super job." Samahria didn't answer, and I could hear her sobbing softly on the other end of the line. "Hey, I love you."

Another stretch of silence as she began to find her way back, gasping for composure. "Don't mind me. I'm really very, very happy and very silly. I'm just celebrating."

Although we both realized what this new milestone could mean, we encouraged each other not to form any expectations. Allow Raun to develop his own capabilities at his own rate, we agreed. We trusted that when he wanted to and could participate and learn more, he would.

The periods between those times when he appeared remote, aloof, and self-stimulating became noticeably more productive. He became increasingly willing to interact. In the park one day, he approached several children playing in the sandbox. When they offered him a shovel, he scooted away. But then, from a distance, he watched them closely. Perhaps, for the first time, those random, unpredictable events around him had begun to make sense. Several minutes later, Raun turned and looked directly at one little boy standing near the swings. He smiled at the child and then, with no apparent warning, walked right up to him and hugged him, placing his cheek gently against the little boy's face. The youngster became frightened and started to cry. Our son backed off immediately, confused and concerned. He mimicked his little friend—scrunching up his face as if he too were sad. After several minutes, when the other child stopped sobbing, Raun moved cautiously toward him again and stroked his arm. His new friend eyed Raun curiously, then smiled. With this act of communion, this sharing of affection, a very delicate and oftentimes frail human being had made his mark.

This day, the sun began to rise in Raun's eyes.

*　　*　　*

The frenetic pace of change and growth did not let up for Raun or for us. We introduced new toys and games and created more sophisticated social interaction during our sessions with him.

A new volunteer joined our program: Victoria, a very energetic young woman with enormous talent. She could express more beauty with her movements than an accomplished poet could create with words. She used sound and motion to express her feelings and thoughts, oftentimes spitting out wild ideas faster than a perpetual-motion dream machine.

She became an instant friend. Big Vic or Vikki, as we called her, had worked with handicapped and emotionally disturbed children as a music and dance therapist. She loved the accepting attitude that underlay our program and wanted passionately to work with Raun.

"Hey, take it from me, no one out there thinks about loving and honoring children. In all the schools and facilities I've ever worked in, all they want to do is change the kids—or leave them to rot. You talk about Raun like he's—he's a real person, worthy of respect and thoughtful consideration. Wow, he's like an honored guest in your lives. I wish someone would treat me that way." She paused and laughed. **"Fat** chance!"

Vikki's aggressive stance did not mask her caring. This incredibly vivacious human being had a soft and gentle side. Her blond hair capped an impressive physical presence; her blue eyes danced wildly in their sockets. We spent over a full week training her and teaching her how to internalize the attitude underlying our program.

On her first day, in the bathroom, before Raun had really had the opportunity to know her, Vikki sat quietly in the corner and watched. Immediately after her entrance into the room, Raun registered visible discomfort. Nervous. Skittish. Perhaps, even scared. He paced back and forth between the tub and the wall, flipping his fingers in front of his eyes. So unlike the way he'd been in recent weeks—a fracture in his usual passivity. He began to cry and cry until his tears turned into hysteria. He sobbed and choked at the same time.

Vikki tried to approach him, to be with him and soothe him. In response, he banged on the door, hitting the door knob over and over again with the back of his hand. He wanted out. She opened it for him. Raun threw himself through the doorway. He scrambled through the house, searching frantically. Finally, he found what he wanted—Samahria. Running to her, he wedged himself between her legs and pressed his tear-streaked face against her thighs. His little hands clutched at her blue denim jeans. Finally, he wrapped his arms tightly around her legs. Samahria stroked his hair, and he accepted her affection.

In most families, such an event might occur many times each day, part of the unsung union between a child and parent. But for Samahria and for me, this was a very special and singular event. In the nineteen months of his life, Raun had never before solicited anyone for protection or for help in soothing his anxieties. It had never been a question for him. Indeed, it had never even seemed to matter whom he was with at any given time. He seemed to lack emotional bonds. But now a binding union had become solidified. For the first time, he had ventured outside of himself to form a strong, trusting attachment to Samahria.

For her, a mother who had waited almost two years for her child to seek her, to want her warmth and loving, it was a deeply moving, very personal experience. Her son was coming home.

*　　*　　*

Vikki continued trying to work with Raun for almost a week. The first few minutes of each session, Samahria joined them until she knew that Raun was comfortable. Yet, after only three or four days, it became apparent that Vic was having difficulty. Her way of bombarding him with stimuli seemed hectic and overwhelming to him. Her finely developed talents and tools did not prove useful. Raun remained unresponsive—not participating.

Even as we continued training her, guiding her to soften her methods and develop a more accepting attitude, Raun continued to withdraw in her presence. She insisted she could modify her approach. Yet as we shared together, Vikki realized her hidden self-doubt was undercutting her effectiveness. We explained that the dance on the outside had to match the attitude inside. If not, Raun would know; any special child would know. And, apparently, Raun did.

Vikki and I spent hours together doing dialogues to unearth her concerns, doubts, and self-judgments. She had some powerful personal insights and made changes, especially in dropping her need for Raun to respond in order to feel good about her teaching. However, Raun became more and more difficult in her sessions, withdrawing and crying. We had roundtable discussions about the wisdom of expanding the program at this time. Vikki decided finally to withdraw until Raun became stronger and could handle her special brand of magic. Admittedly, she had no experience working with children so young. But most important, she wanted to work on her attitude and establish a solid nonjudgmental, self-accepting place inside. Could we wait a couple of months and then give her another opportunity? Absolutely. Both Samahria and I concurred.

This experience confirmed the validity of two of our original premises. First, attitude greased the wheels and made our program with Raun work smoothly. If we judged him or ourselves, we would divert our attention from simply accepting and loving him and undercut the ease, tenderness, and effectiveness of the program. Second, as long as we demanded measurable signs of Raun's learning as evidence of our own capabilities, we would create a pressure that subverted our basic intention. Such concerns would become

111

a trap, leading us to push him and stimulating him to push back. We had made Raun his own teacher. Although we initiated activities, all of the games and interactions took place only with his permission. If he expressed a different interest, we followed and assisted, ever-present midwives to his unfolding. We had evolved a child-centered teaching process. In contrast, Vikki, as a result of all her training, had communicated implicitly an underlying pressure, a "must" or "should" that Raun resisted. The lesson had been for all of us.

Bryn, at dinner, expressed her growing excitement about her brother and their developing relationship. She loved the times when he responded. Chattering enthusiastically about his ease with puzzles and games, she said that she believed that he cared now. What a proud teacher—proud of herself and her pupil, as well as sensitive to his wants and relaxed whenever he withdrew into his repetitive "isms." Bryn had learned as much as Raun in their loving interchange. This beautifully attentive and compassionate youngster demonstrated power, perseverance, and a new womanliness. Her insightfulness was rapidly deepening. She read more and explored more of her talents.

Her energy expressed itself in inventiveness and a tendency to grab the limelight. She had taken violin lessons, and now her practicing had given birth to nightly performances at mealtime. Although we did not protest, the strings of her instrument whined mercilessly as they sounded their sour notes. Bryn had become an enthusiastic pianist as well, though she tended to pound the keyboard of the piano. Her acting and dance lessons resulted also in nightly performances. Sometimes, she would stand on a chair in the kitchen and recite a monologue that she had recently memorized. Bryn's facial expressions and theatrical arm gestures accented the emotions underlying her material. On other occasions, she would show us modern dance routines choreographed to music. Her vitality seemed irrepressible. Additionally, she treated us to expert comic imitations of family members and friends. Her quick character studies delighted all of us. Often, our applause encouraged her to do encores.

Thea talked less than Bryn about Raun's growth and more about having fun with him. She had a lovely capacity to meet him on his level, to play with him as a peer, and to engage him in carefree physical interaction. Her relationship was less verbal, more intuitive. Sometimes, out of her own enthusiasm, or perhaps jealousy, Thea pushed him to respond. Either Samahria or I would then gently intercede and show her alternative ways to play with him. We would see her impish grin below her bangs and deep-set eyes. Although always open to understand more, she resisted direction, hedging her responses to our suggestions. She loved working with Raun and, by her own admission, wanted to be the best teacher possible. However, she moved to the sound of her own drum, using intuition as her guide.

Additionally, Thea still spent long hours by herself drawing and painting, producing fanciful renderings of her family, her friends, and her daydreams. Often, she drew beautiful, expressionistic pictures and presented them to us as gifts. Statements of her affection. Descriptions of her feelings. Her stylized figures, captured in movement, filled drawing pads with life and unexpected color. Blue hair. Red faces. Yellow noses. Green feet. Even the small clay people she sculpted stretched their arms and kicked their legs in unorthodox movements. All of her artistic creations reinvented the familiar, leaving the viewer to delight not simply in what is but in what could be.

*   *   *

Raun sat on the back seat of my bicycle during an early-morning ride. As we pedaled through the neighborhood, Bryn rode alongside on her five-speed racer. Raun sat quietly, staring at the trees and houses as they flew by. The motion captivated his attention completely. He slid into a peaceful and meditative state. We arrived at the park, the very same one where the word *autism* had sprung to life in my head.

The previous two and a half months seemed centuries away from that time. Yet, as I put my son on the swing and looked intently into his eyes, I realized that, although his progress had been dramatic, sometimes spectacular, Raun's normal operating capacity remained far below that of other children his age. In language and sociability, this nineteen-month-old boy continued to function at an eight- or nine-month level. Only his large motor skills and some small motor activities were appropriate to his chronological age. His development of motor skills and reflexes had far outpaced his development in all other areas.

As I reviewed our journey with Raun, many delightful images flooded my mind. No matter how the world might label my son different, handicapped, or retarded, I wanted to stay in touch with his beauty, his singularity, his daring, and his accomplishments. When physicians, family, and friends deemed him terrible and tragic, Samahria and I created a different vision, seeing in him a child of beauty and wonder. I knew our son was neither terrible and tragic nor beautiful and wonderful. Those words reflected beliefs—what we chose to make up about the little boy we saw. I really liked the vision we had created; it brought us happiness and hope and freed us to try for more when others counseled us to turn away.

Initially caught in the grip of his own inertia, Raun had moved down the human river and allowed himself to float more into the mainstream. He had even learned to jump the rapids, and to use the currents to his own advantage. He had begun to make the world his, to be with others, to permit contact, and to express some of his wants. He had reconstructed his nervous system, opening the door to memory by learning to retain objects in his mind. For a severely autistic and functionally retarded little person, he had performed mind-boggling mental gymnastics, all of which would serve as foundations for future expansion and growth. At the very least, these newly developed skills gave him additional know-how, additional ways to deal with himself and his environment.

If he moved no further, I would feel rewarded by our work, knowing that in touching our son we had touched what was most beautiful in ourselves. This he had given us, by being there—by being Raun.

*   *   *

Midnight. The telephone rang incessantly. A voice pierced through years of silence; our friends from California would be coming through New York in less than two days and wanted to be with us—to lift the curtain of time and renew a long and oftentimes intense relationship. We welcomed it.

Two days later, a huge, sleek, twenty-eight-foot motor home rolled into our driveway. The sound of its horn bellowed like the baritone growl of an old Santa Fe diesel whipping across an opened railroad crossing. As Bryn and Thea came charging out the front door, with Samahria and me right behind them, my friend Jesse appeared in its doorway, mellow and tired as our arms interlocked. Our usual robust bear hug softened with the mood. Jesse's wife, Suzi, jumped from the truck into Samahria's arms. The distance and time that had separated us disappeared for these frozen moments. Then Samahria turned to the parked dinosaur, grabbing our friends' children into her arms and hugging her first hello. Strange to be meeting them now for the very first time. Julie, sensitive and intense, with her piercing eyes—very outspoken at seven. Cheyenne, only four, but already a stage-stealing comic with red curly hair and baggy Chaplinesque pants. These cute little people met our cute little people, dancing their hellos and skipping their excitement into the house.

We stood with Jesse and Suzi under the clear sky, smiling at one another, touching through our eyes. I struggled to recapture the old closeness but still tasted the distance. Jesse seemed slightly removed behind a haze of hard work. Once the lead singer and writer for a rock group called the Youngbloods, he toured now on his own as Jesse Colin Young. He had come to New York to give three evening performances at the Nassau Coliseum on Long Island.

The four of us talked and reviewed our lives, exchanging the highlights and most dramatic experiences of recent years. Jesse and I reminisced about sitting on a bathroom floor in a dormitory at Ohio State in the middle of the night, writing songs, drinking watered-down beer, and singing in harmony as the Midwest slept. He played his guitar while I wrote down lyrics on my writing pad. In the brotherhood of those years, we created a deep and abiding friendship.

Jesse recalled our motorcycle escapades in Pennsylvania while I still attended college. We spent weekends together, riding side by side along the Delaware River. Samahria hugged me from behind as we cruised along country roads on our beautiful and dignified BMW. Sometimes, Jesse and I would steer our bikes across meadows and then through endless rows of cornfields. The four of us would picnic on mountain slopes, consuming wine, cheese, bread, and the summer sun. Years later, we traded in our bikes for apartments in the city and drank espresso in Cafe Figaro, where Kerouac and Ginsberg had been only a decade before. When Jesse played at Folk City, Samahria and I sat in the audience and cheered his developing talent. Then, late at night we would all walk over to Chinatown or the East Village, making lower Manhattan our personal neighborhood.

After both Samahria and Suzi fell asleep, I shared with Jesse how I had reached for the stars with a series of short stories, two plays, and a file cabinet filled with poetry. A mountain of rejection slips decorated my desk as Samahria played breadwinner during the early years of our marriage. The completion of a first novel and the on-again, off-again production of one of my plays, which never made it to the stage, became my last hurrah. I abandoned writing, turning my energy toward the more commercial world of motion pictures and marketing. Graduate school and evening seminars as well as weekend workshops in philosophy, psychology, religion, and personal growth became part of my evolving life-style.

In recounting the specific events with our Raun, I felt filled with gratitude. Jesse laughed, saying the situation with our son scared him; however, he felt his mental circuits blown by our enthusiasm and our excitement about our family circumstance.

For the six days Jesse and Suzi stayed with us, we easily integrated them into our lives and our home. Each morning, Samahria worked her normal schedule with Raun as Suzi joined to experience our enigmatic son and help him. The other children played like fast friends. Our evening conversations ebbed and flowed as we sipped wine and discussed the impact of our beliefs and attitudes on our lives.

Jesse and I reached for each other, searching to pick up the thread. The years had taken a certain toll, yet we each felt richer in our lives than ever before. I spoke of my fantasy of creating a mountaintop retreat in New England where we could share with others and start a special community based on a common vision and common pursuit. We played out our dreams, enjoying sharing our fantasies with each other.

Opening night at the Nassau Coliseum, we saw endless lines of cars creeping into huge parking lots as we sped swiftly through a special back entrance accessible only to the performers. All eight of us packed into our jeep.

No seats had been made available for us. Instead, we were to take the children and sit on stage with the performers. A packed theater-in-the-round with fifteen thousand in attendance. A hush blanketed the huge crowd as Bill Graham jumped on the stage. Memories of Fillmore East. He made an announcement, then introduced Jesse. Wild applause came from every direction. The deafening roar subsided as the crowd's attention focused on the entertainers, energizing them.

And then it began. The music ripped through the speakers, almost throwing us off the side of the stage. Not just a concert, an experience.

When Jesse sang "Get Together," a song that had become an anthem for the turbulent late sixties, the audience jumped to their feet and cheered. When he sang "Starlight," they lit candles throughout the stadium. We would come back the next evening and the next. Each time we brought Bryn and Thea to share the magic of this floodlight world—its beauty and its special brand of community. All of it unforgettable. I couldn't help thinking that maybe one day Raun could join us for such outings. Maybe one day he, too, would understand and appreciate such a musical celebration.

The Youngs stayed one final day after their last performance before going south with their tour. When they left, we expressed our gratitude for their love and for the fanfare of their visit. We appreciated the momentary diversion from Raun's silence and for the new experiences offered the girls. The opportunities to rekindle good feelings with old friends and to explore the changing tides of our lives had invigorated us.

7

A Symphony Without Notes

Our search for Raun, for his dignity and specialness, not only brought our core family closer together, but created a new and larger family unit that included his new teachers and the many others who helped us. It was as if through our program with this little man, a special kind of love had surfaced and embraced the lives of all of us. Could this be the purpose of his life? Could this be his gift to us? Reaching for Raun meant reaching for the very best in ourselves, digging deeper and deeper to find a greater awareness of our own humanity and caring. Helping him make new connections in his mind and with his surrounding environment inspired all of us in the program to rethink our relationships with ourselves and each other. We did more than just question and explore; we reinvented aspects of ourselves so that we could let go of the normal conventions and embrace the universe of a special child whom others judged or avoided.

We never sacrificed anything, never denied any part of ourselves; in fact, we grew ourselves bigger. We had transformed Raun's individuality and uniqueness, turning them into an invitation—an invitation to make our love tangible. Most significantly, we realized that love unexpressed wilts on the vine, while love transformed into action nurtures everyone it touches. I created a softer place inside that allowed me to embrace other people much more easily. Samahria grew more determined and more radiant each day. Bryn became increasingly more tolerant and accepting, Thea more animated and vocal. Nancy bubbled with energy and delight. Maire, more comfortable and confident with each succeeding week, opened her heart fully to the little boy with soft blond ringlets. And Raun— he grew in tiny, unpredictable, and amazing spurts, like a rare flower redefining its own pattern of growth and evolution in every moment.

Log: Eleventh Week—
Schedule the Same, Bathroom
Still Principal Area for Sessions

Observations:

- Expresses strong emotion, especially when objects are taken from him.
- He initiates contact to solicit assistance by taking someone's hand and leading that person to a door in order to get in or out of a room, or to get food or toys on a table.
- Plays peekaboo—he initiates. He pulls us and even chases us as well as letting us chase him.
- Enjoys other children—laughs and cries when they laugh and cry; is attentive to them and imitates them.
- Tries to get on the chair by himself at the dinner table.
- Initiates dancing when he hears music.
- Shows still more understanding of receptive language.
- Remains echolalic, but now repeats what he hears faster, shortening the time before he responds to a verbal stimulus.
- Has lost interest in some kinds of playing—rolling balls, stacking blocks.
- Plays attentively with puzzles but either turns up the blank side of pieces or flips pieces upside down. Always investigates a puzzle piece in this unorthodox manner and then, seemingly satisfied, repositions the form correctly in his hand and inserts it expertly back into the appropriate compartment.
- Drinks out of a glass, eats solid food without incident, and serves himself most of the time.
- Uses objects that we don't want him to touch (lamps, glasses, etc.) to tease us. For example, he will not open a dish cabinet when alone but will immediately do so when we enter the room (hurrah, the more sophisticated games begin!).
- Seems genuinely excited when his mother, father, teacher, or other family members enter the house.
- Still pushes away people who try to express affection but will stay longer with physical interactions with his mother.

- Holds hairbrush in hand and will attempt to groom his hair on request.

No Changes:

- When he is not approached or is not being worked in sessions, he still chooses to be alone—still chooses objects over people.
- Still spins himself and other objects, though not as much as previously.
- Still does not indicate in any way when he wants to get out of the crib or when he wants food.
- Still does not use verbal language to communicate.
- Throws things extensively, especially when left by himself even for very short periods of time.

* * *

Raun was like a symphony without notes—like a song without words. We knew how crucial language development would be for him. We knew that sounds and words, symbolizing people and activities, enable us to remember and think about the events of our lives. If Raun did not find a way to make meaningful use of symbols, he would always be glued to the now of his experiences. Language not only allows us to communicate with others, it allows us to create a set of mental notes from which we can extract meaning and create ideas. Without such a set of notes, Raun's horizons would be limited, as if he had rooms filled with thousands and thousands of files but lacked labels and an index system that might permit him to retrieve information. In such a room, locating a specific dossier would be difficult, if not impossible. In the same way, lacking language, the means by which we recall and make use of specific data, Raun might find it difficult or impossible to retrieve information from his mind, even though it contained millions and millions of memory units.

We had made progress in most areas with the exception of language. We continued our research. More endless phone calls. We talked with speech therapists and language specialists, and read books on linguistics and manuals on language development, syntax, and semantics. We reviewed detailed information about the tongue and about the coordination of muscles in the mouth. Where was the answer?

An infant walks when he can and when he wants to. He learns to talk when he can and when he wants to.

Raun did have the facility to mimic sounds and words, although at times the way he parroted words, imitating exactly the same tone and voice quality of the speaker, seemed eerie. Occasionally, he missed his mark completely when echoing our words, raising questions about his capacity to consistently control his tongue. Even so, we believed that if he wanted to speak, he could at least approximate words audibly. That he used sounds, regardless of their quality, was important now. He had demonstrated his ability to speak, but the difficult next step of using language meaningfully loomed large on the horizon. We knew any progress in this area would depend heavily on his own motivation.

Raun's echolalia continued. He never used words with meaning fully or purposefully. An enigma. Yet, since imitation was essential to his learning, his echolalia might lead to the development of meaningful speech. As we had done before, we once again simplified our speech, removing the clutter of adjectives, adverbs, and the like. We exaggerated our gestures, pointed to objects passionately, and used clearly enunciated single words to identify objects. We encouraged everyone not only to communicate with great clarity, but also to dazzle Raun with the usefulness of speech. Our intent: heighten his desire to communicate with words. If we could light the fire, we would find a way or, at least, *try* to find a way.

We decided to cash in on a token and follow up on a promise made to us by a doctor in one of the diagnostic teams that had initially seen Raun. She had told us to bring him back at the end of the summer for another evaluation and said they would place him in a special school for language development with a program designed for children with severe learning disabilities and behavioral problems.

Tuesday afternoon. Raun, twenty months of age, sat with us in the lobby waiting for the doctors. He sat limply in a chair as both Samahria and I established eye contact and began an interactive game with him. A woman in a wheelchair sat beside us. Two young boys with glazed eyes and dilated pupils leaned against a far wall. One hung his head to the side as if burdened by its weight.

An old lady stared blankly at the wall. Two teenage girls talked incessantly to each other, punctuating their conversation with bursts of laughter.

At the reception desk, an overweight attendant munched on M & M's while vacantly "yesing" all those who made inquiries. A harried executive dressed in a black suit came running through the waiting room, almost knocking over the woman in the wheelchair. I watched Raun, who seemed oblivious to the people and activity around him. Another woman walked briskly into the lobby, called out our name, and asked us to follow her. As I heard the sound of my heels clicking against the cool, almost colorless tile floor, I noticed the irony of a wall plaque with the words "The Health Center" printed on it in bold letters.

Inside, another waiting room. This one had three chairs, bare walls, and no other occupants. Two doctors entered; they both smiled. They wanted to examine Raun alone. Since our son seemed perfectly willing to off with them, we nodded our approval.

A social worker appeared and asked us to follow her into yet another room so that she could undertake a comprehensive intake interview and take notes on our family history. Although we had participated in this procedure once before for this same hospital unit, she asked us to repeat all the information again. She smiled excessively as if to set a mood—that of an amiable cocktail party.

The social worker asked all the familiar questions we had been asked over and over again. As we answered, she scribbled notes rapidly across the page, creating elaborate clinical poetry. An hour passed. The other doctors returned with Raun, who appeared somewhat irritable and uncomfortable.

"Please follow us," they requested.

We followed them down a long, dark corridor and entered another room. More blank walls, hard plastic chairs, and, something new, a conference table. The chief of Pediatric Psychiatry sat down quickly, smiled a plaster-of-Paris smile, and neatly folded his hands. His eyes darted back and forth between us and his associates. His head seemed flattened in the front and back as if it had been compressed in some giant vice. For a moment, he appeared distracted by some internal reflection; then he returned his attention to the conference at hand as if we were all about to participate in some familiar everyday routine.

His associate, a neuropsychologist, was a woman in her middle forties whose thin nose and pointed chin accented an angular face, giving her a harsh and aloof appearance. As she spoke, her eyes blinked continuously as if to punctuate her sentences. Her choppy manner affected her speech. Although she delivered her thoughts in a highly professional and authoritarian manner, her voice sounded shallow and her words dropped like jagged pieces of glass on the formica table. Nevertheless, we felt a sincere concern beneath her polished veneer.

Throughout the meeting, the chief did most of the talking, speaking to Samahria and me as if to a large, distant, anonymous audience. His speech had the cadence of a recording. He reiterated all the diagnostic jargon we had heard previously. He suggested additional examinations to determine muscle coordination, speech and tongue development, and possible neurological damage. Even while he indicated that our son had profound developmental problems, this physician still viewed Raun as too young to help. Perhaps in another year he'd be old enough. "Bring him back when he is two and a half," he said.

The old words and worn expressions danced in my head. What about the promise for help—the promise to help us now? That had been our only reason for returning, our only reason for allowing them to put Raun through more testing. They replied that they would like to help us, but that Raun's age and his current disabilities made that impossible. They did not consider it feasible to work with him at this time. Additionally, one of the clinicians indicated that, since the possibilities of educating a child like ours would be extremely limited, he saw no reason to begin now. Perhaps, he said, one day Raun might be trained to develop some minimal self-help skills like brushing his teeth or combing his hair, but he counseled us not to expect the development of any meaningful language or substantial ability to interact socially.

I couldn't understand—couldn't grasp their meaning. What were they saying? Were they telling us that Raun had failed to meet their specifications? Because of age and a lack of certain abilities? If these professionals had a mandate to help children with profound learning disabilities, why would anything they did for Raun be conditioned on performance? Had they looked at the severity of his disabilities and decided to just write him off without trying?

123

I was angry, damn angry, but I knew an outburst would not make a difference. So I held my feelings in check.

I turned to both doctors, pleading with them to be open. Wasn't early intervention important in attempts to help these children? I queried them about Lovaas, Delacato, and Kozloff, all of whom had done extensive work in this area and had written numerous books and articles. Neither one of these professionals was familiar with the works of the authors that I had mentioned. Could that be possible? Could they be unaware of current strides and techniques in the training of autistic and emotionally disturbed children? Could they not know about research and experimentation being undertaken in their own specialty?

I believed that we had been deceived. We had been had. Raun had been had. I felt irritated, saw myself as abused. Despite all we had been through before, this morning had been the most frustrating—with its pompous "half" answers to our questions and the final "No." The more I allowed my mind to reflect on our meeting, the more enraged I became.

Samahria took Raun home. In my car, I headed toward the city. I pounded the steering wheel with my fists, looking for release. Finally, my choked emotions flowed. Silent sobbing accentuated by the intrusive sound of car horns. I was furious—not depressed and not lost, just furious. The future of my child and other children like him depended on people like these. Their hollow phrases whirled through my mind over and over again. Those quiet and dignified tones of sympathy. Those rehearsed and frozen smiles. The exaggerated sincerity. They had processed us, filling a segment of their professional time as they moved us through the system.

I started asking myself questions. If we had just received the best of what these professionals could offer, why was I so upset? I guess I believed that my anger would act as a catalyst, pushing me to change the entire system. Also, I wanted to scold myself for allowing Samahria, Raun, and me to be taken in again, misled and then dismissed, even as I acknowledged that they might have had the best of intentions. Okay, I knew we would continue to reach out to Raun no matter what the professionals believed or said. So why the anger? Certainly, it did not help me or my son. In fact, I felt drained and distracted from what really mattered. I thought more about the doctors and my own judgments, which I began to let go of as I continued with this internal dialogue. Unhappiness had just brought me to my knees when I wanted to fly. I wanted Raun to fly. Done! I did what I had been teaching others to do. Drop a judgment, change a belief, or alter our vision of an event, and the world changes—significantly, irrevocably, and immediately. I could leave the clinicians to their world, knowing their views and convictions came from what they learned, what they believed. At the same time, we could respectfully choose a different way.

Back to Raun. I knew that we were the best resource that he could have. Our caring, our knowledge, and our therapeutic input had now even exceeded the apparent expertise provided by many professionals in the field. We would continue with our son, excited to explore uncharted territory and committed to happiness, love, and acceptance as the basis of our work.

Even after such a realization and rededication to our program, we wanted to remain open to any discoveries about autism and to new teaching perspectives that might help us with our son. Therefore, one week later, we decided to allow ourselves one more interview, one more examination of Raun's condition by a sympathetic young doctor whom I had talked with on the phone weeks earlier. His name came to us after we had formed a long list of people all connected with one another. Our search began at the University of California and took us back across the country to the State University of New York. One individual referred us to another, and thus we eventually unearthed this particular professional. He directed a new outpatient program at a residential facility for autistic children and seemed sympathetic and sincerely interested in our plight. I explained to him the premise on which our program was based and detailed our progress. We believed we had facilitated real changes in our son, but we felt we had reached a dead end in the area of language.

He expressed fascination with our ideas and wanted to help if he could. He knew how unusual it was to have an autistic child as young as Raun diagnosed so early and then placed immediately in an intense stimulation program. I explained that as a result of our work, Raun's most extreme autistic symptoms had subsided dramatically. However, he now seemed to be growing very slowly, and he continued to evidence patterns of withdrawal. He suggested that we bring our son to his facility so that his developmental workup team could examine him and, perhaps, make a contribution to our program.

The building housing this residential treatment center was extremely modern, with huge windows and wood ceilings. This time, we waited alone in a lobby with soft chairs and carpeted floors. A receptionist ushered us into a room with six occupants, all members of their intake team. The people introduced themselves warmly, cordially, and informally. One woman took Raun outside and tried to play with him. The interview began with questions that by now seemed awesomely stale. Feeling numbed by the routine, we tried to stay present — to be fresh and alive with our answers and observations. We gave our history and Raun's history, provided medical information we'd received, and detailed the progress we'd made. These doctors appeared astute and focused as well as articulate.

After talking with us, they put Raun through a series of developmental tests (in which blocks, imitation exercises, eye-contact games, concentration dynamics, and social interactions all played a part). They recorded their findings on a Gesell developmental chart, measuring Raun's abilities against those of a group of statistically normal children his age.

After the testing, we heard the clinicians' diagnosis and general commentary. Raun, they said, at twenty months functioned at the age level of approximately eight months, or just slightly above, with regard to language and socialization. In large motor activity, he functioned nearly at age level. In his play, he showed a range of capabilities: from those of an eight-month-old to those of a child of fourteen months. During the testing, Raun explored the toys lethargically and, at times, sent some of them spinning across the table. After observing Raun stare intermittently, the clinicians introduced a novel hypothesis: that Raun possibly suffered from some form of abortive or incomplete series of epileptic seizures in addition to his autism and functional retardation.

Given this grim diagnosis, the supervising physician grimaced in the face of our steadfast enthusiasm about Raun's growth and progress. Had it not been for the reports detailing Raun's behavior at the outset of our home program and the changes that had occurred, he would definitely have predicted a future of global retardation for our son and anticipated as well the probability that Raun

would acquire no language whatsoever. Since many of his self-stimulating behaviors—his excessive spinning and rocking for example—
had abated, the doctors hesitated to make a final diagnosis or formal prognosis.

Also, one of the physicians on the intake team indicated that
he was not convinced that intervention really had made a difference, speculating that Raun might have simply developed in the
same way whether we had worked with him or not. In fact, he expressed his laissez-faire attitude quite emphatically. Leave Raun
alone, he said, or at least let up on the intensity of our program.
He did not seem to understand that Raun had come this far only
because of our intervention. We had allowed ourselves to want more
than all the experts deemed possible. His advice contradicted what
we had learned and knew to be true. He could afford to speculate
that perhaps Raun might have developed anyway; he could even
experiment with his supposition, as many institutions did, and ride
his hypothesis right out the window. But we couldn't. Raun was
not just another patient, another statistic; he was our son.

The clinicians itemized other services they provided. The
younger doctor, the one I had spoken to on the phone, noted that
the sophistication and intensity of our program greatly exceeded
those of almost any program their facility could offer.

He scheduled the "home interview" component of the developmental examination for the following Monday. They would
come with a videotape camera. Although we understood this facility's input would be of limited value, we felt thankful to have
met a professional who seemed really involved and concerned with
his work and the families he encountered. He had understood our
focus on the "now" of our program rather than with prognosis or
predictions of the future. Like us, he believed in early intervention. However, for him early intervention meant dealing with a child
at least three years old. To find an intervention program being used
with a child only slightly more than one and a half years old was
more than just novel—it presented a unique opportunity. They
wanted to observe us, our methods, and the responses we could
try to get from our son.

The program director and an assistant arrived at our home
on the scheduled morning. Their request: Do whatever we would
normally do that day. If Samahria worked with Raun in the bath-

room, then they wanted her to do just that. In the presence of these observers and their equipment, Samahria seemed unusually frenzied as she took Raun's hand and guided him into the bathroom. The two of them sat together on the floor in front of piles of puzzles and toys. The doctor followed enthusiastically, carrying his camera and tape recorder. His assistant also came into the room and immediately found a spot for herself against the door, which was closed once everyone was inside. The doctor surveyed the tiny room curiously, looking for a place to set up his equipment until it became clear to him that the only unoccupied place large enough to accommodate him and his paraphernalia was the cold and uninviting bathtub.

Without a moment's hesitation, the doctor lifted his robust form over the edge of the tub and slid into the cast-iron womb, ignoring his pressed pants, his well-tailored sports jacket, and his dangling tie. As he lay in the tub, he quietly set up the camera. Though he must have suffered the tortures of the rack, he treated this singular experience like a casual, everyday event.

Raun noticed the intrusion immediately. For a period of time, he just stared silently into the lens of the camera, perhaps catching a fleeting glimpse of his own image reflected on the glass. Then, as if satisfied and sated with the experience, he turned away from the video equipment and began to respond to Samahria. The young doctor pressed the trigger of his camera.

Samahria engaged Raun in a series of interactive exercises. First, they explored each other's fingertips; then they played a clapping game with their hands. Afterward, Raun pulled a puzzle toward him, which Samahria encouraged him to pursue. In fact, they did three complete puzzles together, with Samahria using each puzzle piece as an opportunity for increased eye contact and social interaction. Ten minutes later, she assisted Raun as he built a high tower out of blocks and engineered a ledge from this structure to project out onto the toilet seat. Samahria applauded his outrageous accomplishment and hugged him gently for the few fleeting moments he permitted her embrace. She introduced farm animals and did her hysterical circuslike routine, mimicking the sounds of all these creatures. Raun smiled broadly and tried to make some of the sounds himself. Then, both mother and child picked up a musical instrument and, as they sat facing each other on the floor, created a singular symphony for drum and harmonica. Then Samahria put Beethoven's Ninth Symphony on the tape recorder and danced with her son.

Once aware that Raun's attention seemed to wane, she grabbed a jar from behind the sink, dipped a special plastic instrument into the thick liquid, then brought it up to her lips and began blowing bubbles. He grabbed at the first few bubbles as they floated down gracefully toward the floor. When he caught one, Samahria cheered him like a loving and enthusiastic coach. She talked incessantly to him, trying always to draw his attention with her words, her touch, or the endless repertoire of interactive games. Sensitive to the camera, she compressed some of the activities into short periods of time so that many of the games could be recorded on tape.

The captive physician remained stoically in the bathtub as beads of sweat gathered on his forehead. He presented a humorous, slightly self-mocking image—like some comic character in an unrehearsed scene from some incomprehensible film. The air in the bathroom grew stale. The temperature rose, and the overhead floodlights began to cook the four occupants of this tiny space. An hour passed. Finally, the door opened, expelling the exhausted participants. Both observers were overwhelmed with the performance.

The doctor composed himself. He smiled and shook his head— amused and visibly excited. After taking some time for quiet reflection, he spoke, exclaiming, "An unbelievable experience! Like nothing I have ever seen before. Samahria, your attitude, your energy level, and continual nonstop stimulation were incredible. Marvelous for Raun, but also fascinating for us to watch."

Raun's apparent happiness and our sensitivity to our son's peacefulness impressed him immensely. In Raun, he had not seen the usual anger and anxieties often present in other children with similar diagnoses and disabilities. Even though Raun remained essentially unresponsive, the doctor observed that his fleeting interactions with Samahria seemed meaningful. He encouraged us to continue with our work and discussed the merits of our methods and techniques, awed by the originality of our perspective and the vitality of our program. He said that he had never before entered a home in which the parents of an autistic child had embraced their youngster's profound neurological and developmental disability as a gift and an opportunity. At first, after the initial interview, he had wanted to dismiss our enthusiasm and optimism as not credible. But now, after seeing our attitude in action, he felt genuinely beguiled and excited. "It's not simply what you are doing," he commented. "It's how you do it that has such impact." He followed his comments with one suggestion, counseling us not to ask Raun to do more than one chore at a time so as not to confuse him. In the end, he reiterated that the sophistication of our program far exceeded the scope of services offered at the children's center. In fact, he believed he had more to learn from us than we did from him. He marveled at the intensity and thoroughness of our approach, expressing great interest in the novelty of our concepts, especially since our approach differed profoundly from the behavioral approach taken by his staff and taught by psychologists and special education teachers. We joined our son's world; they tried to stop children from engaging in "inappropriate" self-stimulating and repetitive behavior. We followed our son's cues and encouraged him to initiate interactive games; as therapists and teachers, they created a program design for every session and forced children to perform to that design, even resorting to strong aversion techniques, such as time-out boxes and the like, in order to make their young patients comply. He shook his head. If he tried to institute such methods as ours at his facility, he had no doubt that he would be removed from his job immediately. Additionally, our perspectives contradicted everything he had learned in this field. Nevertheless, he wanted to keep in touch. Departing, he left behind books on developing basic skills and basic language. But in our reading and our program, we had already gone beyond the limits of these texts.

The doctor had also suggested that we have a routine EEG (neurological brain scan) done on Raun just to touch all bases, even though he believed it would not really tell us anything new.

Our evening brain-picking sessions still revolved around the subject of language acquisition. It became our primary focus. Although we all talked incessantly when we interacted with Raun, we knew we had to create additional ways of demonstrating to Raun the use and efficacy of language. We resolved to make an even more intense commitment to teaching speech. Find that new direction. Enable him to take the next step. Our conclusion: Design a shorthand system of speaking. Instead of using simple sentences to refer to events, body parts, or objects in our environment, we would develop one-word descriptions—a simple clear utterance for everything we wanted to identify. Then we honed the concept further by simplifying every word into a single, digestible, and easy-to-repeat syllable. "Ba" for bottle. "Wa" for water. "Ju" for juice.

An additional next step: Convert his crying into the use of words. Crying had become his primary language, but the sounds of crying were too unspecific and vague to serve as speech. Our new strategy: When Raun cried, we would be attentive but act somewhat confused. We would speculate on what he wanted but miss the target. We would appear perplexed so that he did not feel we wished to deprive him of what he wanted. As he cried in front of the refrigerator or whined in front of a closed door, we would say the names of everything in sight that he might be wanting. If we guessed his desire in advance, we would not identify it until we had first made a host of other suggestions. When we articulated what he did want, he reacted quickly and stopped his crying. Then we reinforced this behavior by saying the name of the object in question several times and by congratulating him on his achievement. This crude method did facilitate some communication, and we were thankful for this development. However, if Raun could see that the use of the spoken word was even more effective, he might choose it. Play dumb, we counseled ourselves, but be helpful—be loving.

Using this new approach, none of us had an easy week. Raun cried more and more, pushing us to search until we located what he wanted. One evening, when we had guests, Raun came into the living room, grabbed my hand, and started to pull. I asked him what he wanted. He began to cry and pull even harder. I told him I would come if he told me what he wanted. His crying increased. As I sat on the floor, he pulled at me with a growing intensity. I saw such confusion in his eyes. My first impulse was to get up and go with him, but I realized such a response would defeat both of us. He would have to find his crying less and less effective in order to precipitate a move toward talking. He released my hand and stood there—a solitary figure, crying hysterically. Then he moved his body close to mine and while still sobbing, leaned his head on my shoulder. I put my arm around him and stroked him. His crying subsided finally. Everyone in the room watched in silence. Raun

131

quieted his breathing, continuing to lean against me for another few minutes. His arms hung limply by his sides as if disconnected from his torso.

Finally he moved away from me and pulled at my sleeve with his hand. He began to cry again. I asked him once again what he wanted and explained that if he told me I would gladly help him. He cried more furiously and continued tugging at me. Somehow, I knew that he understood me but was unwilling to speak. He became hysterical again. Then he dropped my hand, looked at me through the rain falling from his eyes, and leaned his body once again against my chest. I comforted him as he stood there limply.

His crying slowed. He disengaged himself, stood up tall, and began to repeat the entire sequence he'd just been through. He tested me. He tested himself. The strength of his crying and tugging increased with each episode. I began suggesting items he might want or actions I could take. This time, I tried genuinely to guess what he desired but could not. We reached a stalemate. Many times I felt impelled to jump up and run around wildly to help him, but each time I talked to myself. Raun had grown stronger in his desire to be with us and interact with us. Rather than retreat, he pushed himself further. I didn't want to short-circuit the growing power he showed as he asked more of me and the world. For the next thirty minutes, this sweet little soul repeated his routine no less than five full times. Finally, he lay down on the floor, inched himself right up against my leg, and fell asleep.

I felt like a boxer who had just gone fifteen rounds . . . drained and fogged. I wanted to go with him, but I knew to stay seated. The pulling and pushing inside befuddled my emotional circuitry. I had watched someone I loved dearly go through a very private hell in helping him break through the invisible barriers that still imprisoned him.

Log: Thirteenth Week—
Same Schedule

Observations:

- Often engages in more social interactions with family members and friends.

- Uses crying continually to communicate.
- Often initiates contact by taking someone's hand and showing that person what he wants (to go out, to go upstairs, to get water, etc.).
- Plays more with toys instead of throwing them; pushes cars, rolls tinker toys, investigates objects with more patience and concentration.
- Now seems at times actually to prefer people to objects. Often leaves an empty room to be in one filled with people.
- Repeats words much more, although still doesn't use language effectively. Receptive language increasing. Understands: down, wa (for water), ma-ma, da-da, don't do that, no, more, moo (for cow), ba (for bottle), come here, Bryn, Thea, Nancy, Maire, doggie, nose, head, ear, eye, upstairs, diaper.
- For the first time, cried to eat and to get water.
- Takes our hand and sometimes throws it at what he wants.
- We have locked certain cabinets in the kitchen so that he cannot take things out and hurt himself. When we forget to close a cabinet door, he takes us over to it and shows that we left it open.

No Changes:

- Still spins objects.
- Still does not cry to get out of the crib.
- Still withdraws, although in a limited way.

* * *

We had dinner this evening with Vikki, who had just been interviewed for a job as resident therapist at a progressive hospital for "emotionally disturbed" and "brain-damaged" children. She was bursting at the seams, wanting to spit out all that she had heard and seen. Excited, confused, and angry, Vikki spoke in a rambling manner, slurring her words—just wanting to blurt out her thoughts.

"And then the supervisor of the school program interviewed me—and, Bears, you can't imagine what she said. I mean, this woman was responsible for everything—the program, the input, hiring—everything. You know what I mean? You're not going to believe this. Oh God, I asked her what she thought about autistic children, what they do with them and all, you know, because of Raun. I wanted to know more and—it's just outrageous! She said, 'Autistic children, well, they're really crazy. There's not much you can do with them.' Wait, wait—that's not all. Then the guidance counselor said, 'What we do with them is just try to train them to be good patients, so they aren't any trouble to the institutions they go on to when they leave here at fourteen. We try to get them to maybe wash themselves, feed themselves, and use the toilet. If we accomplish that, we're happy. Other than that, there's nothing to be done with them.' Oh God—I couldn't believe it. The counselor talked about them like they were animals—useless, hopeless animals. And no matter what I said, he just kept citing case after case to prove his point. Oh, it's so sad; they're all just rotting away there. I wanted to scream at him, 'You don't understand.' Look at Raun—look at what he can do now and how great he is. Jesus, I could never work there."

She panted and fumed, raging like a great rhinoceros who had just watched her habitat destroyed. Samahria and I watched her with deep concern, knowing from all our own research that her description of what she had experienced was all too accurate. Just look at what most professionals believe and what most clinicians at residential facilities do with autistic children. If they view them as essentially "incurable" (suffering from a lifelong developmental disability as the literature suggests), then why bother doing much of anything? They either warehouse them or subject them to intense behavioral conditioning in order to suppress their ritualistic behaviors. How terribly wasteful of the lives of these little people and the gifts they offer.

Vikki caught her breath and rambled on: "Then I stayed in one of the music and dance therapy classes to watch this lady I would supposedly be working for. There were all kinds of kids there with all different problems. I didn't see any of them doing the things autistic children usually do. But anyway, I just stood against the wall 'cause they warned me not to do anything to distract the kids— I mean, I might freak them out or something, the way they put it. Anyway, this one little boy walks up to me—I mean, he wasn't really little; he was almost as tall as I am, but only twelve years old—and, it was really wild; he said to me, 'Hey, lady, you're sexy—ya know, ya gimme a hard-on.' He didn't upset me, of course, but the teacher—wow! She started carrying on and threatening him. Totally ineffective! The entire place turned into a wild circus, a zoo for little kids. The music was blaring. The kids were pushed and pulled all around by the attendants and forced to participate. Incredible, really—I'd never do that to anyone. The kids got absolutely zero out of it; they couldn't care less, the way it was presented, the way they were treated—God, I mean, do you believe it? You had to see it. Oh, wait. After the class, I went to the supervisor and asked her if they taught any of the autistic children music—you know, using music and movement. She said, 'Oh no; they're excluded from the music program because they love it too much.' I said, 'What do you mean?' And she said, 'Well, you know, when autistic children hear music, they get very involved and start rocking and flapping their arms. And since that's their problem and since we want to break them of this kind of behavior and stop them from acting out their repetitive symptoms, of course we exclude them from the music program. After all, you have to understand, we try to get them to act more normal, not reinforce wild behavior.' It was really hard to control myself, you know? It took everything in me to stay cool. I asked her why she couldn't use the music in some way to reach them and teach them since they loved it so much. 'Oh,' she said, 'I've heard that one before, but it doesn't work. Take it from me, the way we're doing it is the only way.'"

A heavy silence in the room followed Vikki's last words. We had all been mesmerized by her monologue. Even Bryn and Thea, who had been very attentive to what Vikki said, appeared disturbed. Bryn's eyes glazed over. I asked Vikki if I could write down what she had experienced and what these people had said to her. I told her that maybe one day I might want to share her experience with others.

Raun banged his fork on the table and began to hum. Samahria and Bryn joined him by banging their forks and humming with him. Thea and Vikki also sounded their participation. I watched for a while, mute and fascinated. The mood changed quickly and everyone settled comfortably into their communal embrace. Then, as if drawn by an irresistible urge, I began to sing with them. Harmonies developed. A cadence was established. Our hands banged a primitive hypnotic beat on the table as the volume grew. And grew. I could feel the intensity of my breathing increase as I hummed louder. The pitch heightened as the chorus grew more rambunctious. Soon, we were all shouting at the top of our lungs. Raun stayed with us, as he looked, alert and dazzled, from one face to another. The raging earth music went on until, without anyone apparently giving a signal, we all suddenly stopped, except for Raun. Left singing alone at an incredible volume, he smiled so broadly that his eyes disappeared. Then he, too, suddenly stopped. After a ten-second silence, we all began to laugh. With this nightcap of softer and less regimented music, we ended our eventful day.

*　　*　　*

Samahria and I felt that all of us could use a break from our elaborate and demanding schedule. We arranged with Nancy to be with Raun all day Saturday. We planned to spend that day with Bryn and Thea at the home of Samahria's sculpture teacher.

As we drove up a long, curving driveway through the woods, we came upon a startling three-story structure. An architectonic metaphor composed of various forms cast in cement—a lighthearted and playful, alien, yet majestic, creation. Poking their heads out of the convertible, Bryn and Thea gaped at this huge abstraction that somewhat resembled an elephant. Further along into the parking area, the girls spotted another elephantlike creature—smaller than the first but with a wooden nose designed to be a swing. They both lunged from the car to interact with this piece of living sculpture. Off to our right, Samahria and I noticed two reclining figures carved in marble. Just in front of them, an enormous mystical and godlike face, carved out of rare, prehistoric stone, stared at us.

Through the entrance to a series of barnlike studios, we could see another rare piece: Alfred Van Loen, the creator of all this abundance. History and time had left their mark in the deep crevices that stretched across his forehead and descended to his mouth. A large, prominent nose separated his dancing luminous eyes. He struck me as a tall, lean, and bearded pre-Christian figure standing in a dramatic landscape of his own creation. A survivor of the Nazi concentration camps, Alfred rose from the dead to be with us now, to express and recreate in wood and stone, in lucite and metal, all the fantastic forms and creatures his imagination produced.

As he spoke, I heard the echoes of a thousand years in his voice. His large hands grasped mine as he smiled at us and yelled his greeting to the children. He obviously enjoyed their giggles and their delight in the forms around them.

Alfred gave us and the girls a very personal tour into the bountiful world of his sculpture and private treasures. His art had developed through several distinct periods, all of which merged to create an amazing visual experience for us. He had turned from the production of classical, lyrical works to a more impressionistic and abstract exploration of form. He believed that each uncut or uncarved piece of wood or marble or onyx had inherent qualities suggestive of its ultimate form and content. Using his sculpting tools expertly, he tried to find within the stone or rock an essence already there. He had the utmost respect for the inner life and integrity of his raw materials. His approach to art paralleled our approach with Raun, and his sculpture reflected the same sensitivity and love.

Passing from one studio area to another, he described the how and why of his passion. He opened himself to us like a dear and old friend, allowing us to see and experience the deep and haunting ravines within him that had found expression in his art. Samahria was excited and touched by the warmth of his greeting, his caring, and his willingness to spend time with us. I found myself intoxicated, almost overloaded, by the dazzling display of his art and the multifaceted stories he told. And yet, at the same time, I missed Raun, wanting him to be here—daydreaming about returning with him one day to share all this abundance. We departed carrying with us a special gift born directly from his fingertips—a pen and ink drawing. We decided to save it, hoping that one day, perhaps, we could re-present it to Raun. The increased appreciation we felt for the inherent integrity of the stone, metal, and wood reminded us, over and over again, of the inherent integrity, beauty, and soulfulness of our son.

That evening, at home, still high on the day's excitement, we built another fire and ate dinner together on the floor in front of the flames. Raun and Nancy joined us. Together, in loving silence, we listened to the music of John Coltrane and Keith Jarrett. More than ever before, I could feel God's presence in our lives.

8

Words Like Water

Suddenly one week, without warning, Raun stopped working in his sessions. He refused to participate; he would not do the puzzles or turn the pages in the books. He began to throw everything in the bathroom again and cry for no apparent reason. He also stopped paying attention when spoken to; he would even turn his back on Samahria, Nancy, Maire, and me when we spoke to him. He ignored us and made sure we took notice by shouting his defiance.

Even outside the sessions, Raun changed, and what we had viewed initially as a momentary withdrawal began to persist from one day to the next. By the third morning, we noted some loss of eye contact and a mild return to spinning and rocking. Also, Raun no longer solicited physical interaction. Often, although not all the time, he refused now to be touched. Yet he maintained some contact; when he wanted something, he would still take our hands to direct us.

He became moody. Erratic. And very unpredictable. One minute he rejected us; the next minute he played with us.

What was happening? What was our son trying to tell us with his behavior? He could have been protesting our perplexing and sluggish responses to his crying. Or perhaps, having expended all his energy for the moment, he had withdrawn to rest. Maybe he had decided, for the first time, that he wanted a change—wanted to slow down—and was doing his best to let us know.

Okay, we wanted to be responsive. We reduced his formal structured sessions from twelve to six to two hours a day. We used the time remaining for random stimulation and play, encouraging him to direct our interaction. After several more days, he began to respond again. He appeared stronger and more capable, happier and more excited.

We kept the sessions to a minimum for another week but began challenging him more rigorously. We made our requests for his participation more emphatic. He accepted our assertiveness outside of the workroom while still maintaining control over what we did. At every juncture, we allowed him to direct activities and choose the games we played. Since I believed Raun might have felt that he had lost some control over his environment, this gave him a clear way to reestablish his personal autonomy. Perhaps, his protest had allowed him to manipulate the program and precipitate a change in direction. The way we dealt with Raun's enigmatic behavior helped us to leap forward—together.

Nevertheless it remained a difficult week for Raun. He cried a lot to communicate, creating what seemed to have become a fixed pattern. When he did not get what he wanted quickly, he acted confused, frustrated, even angry. We stayed our course, and, not surprisingly, he stayed his. We trusted that he would go on, though we knew that each major step he took could prove as difficult as any step he had taken before. He was propelled, not by us, but by his own desire for a more responsive environment. His stormy crying, almost at a tantrum level, filled our house constantly with its shrill dissonance. We stayed soft, helpful, and caring. For all of us—a difficult and exhausting interlude.

Raun stood by the sink crying. Samahria talked to him. She showed him the spoon, then a fork, then the sponge, and finally an empty glass. Raun, each time, reacted by crying more intensely. Finally, she filled the glass with water and gave it to him. As he settled down, Samahria said, "Water, Raun. Here's 'wa.' Say 'wa,' Raun. Here it is, 'wa.'"

Raun gulped it down. Later in the day, he returned to the same spot and started the same procedure once again. Samahria acted out her usual confusion. Raun persisted. The intensity of his crying grew. Samahria knelt beside her son, loving him as she watched him contort his face and press his fingers to his lips.

"What do you want, Raun? C'mon honey, tell me. What do you want?"

Suddenly, twitching his eyes as if he were harnessing all the strength and the power in him, Raun blasted a word through his vocal chords and filled the room with his clear and loud voice. The little boy, who the experts said would never talk in a meaningful way, shouted: "WA."

Samahria jumped to her feet, filled the glass with water, and gave it to him quickly. Her hands trembled as she said, "Yes, Raun. Wa. You did it. Yes, you did. Wa, Raun. Wa! Wa! You're such a good boy."

A stunned little man—even he seemed surprised. As he gulped down the water, he peered up at his mother with his huge brown eyes. Samahria stroked his hair gently, marveling at his momentous accomplishment.

Hurrah! Raun had done it. He had said a word. Precisely. Deliberately. With meaning. Like wildfire, the news about "WA" spread. Samahria called me at the office, then called Nancy, then Maire and Marv and Vikki and Rhoda. None of us could contain our excitement. When Bryn heard the news, she jumped up and down, cheering her brother. Thea giggled and ran to Raun with open arms. The ice had melted, freeing the voice that had once been frozen and unavailable for real communication.

Later in the day, Raun repeated the same process at the sink. He started by crying, then became jittery as Samahria tried to help him by suggesting alternate things he might be wanting. After a short period of time, he said it again: "WA."

Samahria immediately responded with water. Raun's staccato first word suggested a whole new series of possibilities; he had made a quantum leap in his own development.

At dinner, after Raun had finished eating, he looked directly at Samahria and surprised us all by saying, "Down."

Beautiful and clear. Spoken with such authority. The word that he had heard thousands of times when we lifted him down from his chair now came freely from his lips. We grabbed him immediately and put him on the floor. Later, after Samahria had given him some juice, he held the empty glass up to her and said, "More."

The words gushed from him like water bursting through the cracks in a broken dam. It was as if he had been pregnant with those words for so many weeks, and finally, today, he gave birth to language. On the way upstairs to bed, he said his fourth word for the day, "Ba," indicating the verbal shortcut that identified his bottle.

That day ended with four giant steps—four words, all new to his throat and to our receptive ears.

The next morning, we took Bryn, Thea, and Raun to an amusement park to celebrate. Everyone, including Raun, was in excellent spirits and very excited. Our mood was rich and high this champagne and caviar day. The girls began their excursion with a past-faced ride on the roller coaster.

Samahria and I decided to put Raun on a more conservative and docile ride. We seated him in a miniature van that moved slowly around a flat, circular track. He loved the journey and grinned from ear to ear as the car traveled in circles. The girls asked permission to take their brother on the Ferris wheel. Since it moved predictably and slowly, we agreed. An attendant put the three of them into the protective wire cage. Up, up, and up. Around and down. Both Samahria and I stood on the pavement and waved to our children. They seemed so happy. Thea took Raun's hand and waved it each time they passed us. Raun smiled broadly. And Bryn, always the teacher, kept saying, "Say 'hi.' Say it, Raun. Say 'hi.'"

On to the merry-go-round. We strapped each of the girls on top of a moving horse. These wooden figures, carved half a century ago, displayed bulging eyes and garish paint. Old nickelodeon music poured out from an ancient music box. We stood next to Raun, holding him even after we had strapped him onto his horse. We wanted him to feel secure as the platform went 'round and 'round. It started to move slowly. As it gathered speed, Raun looked around wide-eyed and began to laugh. He loved the merry-go-round. The girls shouted their hellos to him as they bounced up and down on their wooden saddles.

When the ride ended, Bryn and Thea wanted to go back on the roller coaster. This time, they wanted to take their brother. Samahria and I debated for several minutes. After reviewing Raun's reaction to the other rides, we decided to allow this stretch. We tucked the three of them under the bar in the first car. Slowly, the small train moved up the ramp and then sped down the first dramatic incline. We positioned ourselves at the spot on the ground where the cars come rushing by and waited.

I chewed on my lips to distract myself. Finally, the children came into view. Bryn and Thea both had their arms around their brother. Raun was wide-eyed again. Although he did not appear frightened, we weren't quite sure he was enjoying himself. As the train sped past us, Bryn and Thea waved frantically. Then, the train continued up the ramp and made its way back down the worn tracks, its circuit complete with short and furious drops as well as sharp and twisting curves. Again the train of cars came into view. This time, Raun laughed loudly with the girls.

A cotton-candy image of children enjoying being alive, loving their experiences, and sharing their companionship. Our children touched one another with their common excitement, joined together in a carnival world of metallic dreams and playland fantasies. For Raun, specifically, this was a special treat—to experience the circular as well as the up and down movements he himself so often precipitated with his self-stimulating rituals. This mechanized whirlpool satiated, at least for now, his fascination with mesmerizing repetitive movements.

*   *   *

Another week passed. Raun seemed in great spirits. From time to time, he used his three or four words, though inconsistently. Bryn and Thea enjoyed him more. Instead of being only teachers, they were becoming true playmates. Friends. Another family might judge Raun's interaction minimal and distant. We, however, had traveled light-years since the day we began. Raun had become an involving and evolving person.

Following his increased capacity to concentrate, we decided to venture out of the bathroom and into the larger area of the den. Since he had become sufficiently proficient in playing games and participating in other exercises, we believed he could now tolerate more distractions. A room with windows! Walls with paintings and photographs! Shelves with books and records! A floor covered by a rug! This move initiated his slow reintroduction into a more realistic home environment.

We bought him a little chair and turned a hassock from the living room into his table. He appeared perfectly content in this new environment. In fact, he did not seem distracted at all. He spent several minutes investigating the room upon entering it, then turned his attention to Samahria and their interactive games.

We began another phase of the program. As Raun's participation became stronger, the sophistication of his studentship increased. It seemed centuries ago that we had first crossed the bridge into his world. Now we wanted to help him take that same bridge back into our world. With that intention, we, the teachers, assumed more leadership in guiding portions of the sessions with him. Rather than leave the total leadership role in his hands, we took some back, suggesting the games we might play together. We experimented to see if he would be responsive to our cues as we had been to his for so many months.

"Raun, touch your nose. Clap your hands now. Super! Can you point to your eyes? Eyes. Yes, eyes! Great, you did it! Okay, shake your head. Hey, watch me do it! Head. Shakes. Yes, that's it. You're the best!"

He followed gladly. Although he appeared confused sometimes, once we modeled our request, he showed us how well he could now mimic us. We knew the more he watched and participated, the more he would learn and grow.

He worked well with photographs and could now point to pictures of various people on request. However, when his interest in puzzles seemed to wane, we increased our demonstrations of affection, cheered him, and used food as a stimulant and reward in order to induce him to work with the puzzles. We also interjected more physical rolling and tumbling play, back into the program. This physical contact soon became a secondary reward for him. He loved to jump, to be tickled, and to be thrown in the air. His smiles and laughs came with greater frequency. With each day that passed, he showed an increasing openness to being loved and having fun.

Fun—somehow that was the key. He enjoyed himself more, enjoyed the games and personal interaction more. He expressed affection much more freely. Even his eyes seemed to talk, to communicate subtleties of feelings. His interest in being with other children in the park also increased. He solicited more play time with his sisters and responded more joyfully to them. This greater expressiveness characterized only a portion of his behavior, but this portion grew bigger each day.

The self-stimulating activities continued, yet on a more limited basis. Raun still spun and did so, at times, for extended periods. He still drifted off by himself and became locked in the remoteness of his self-encapsulated world. Although often in contact, he still spent a total of three to four hours out of touch—staring, rocking, spinning. During the other nine hours, we maintained a fairly continuous and rich interactive process.

Log: *The Fourteenth Week*

Observations:

- Remains in contact with family members for periods of ten to fifteen minutes at a time—making quality eye contact and engaging in an excellent way in physical interaction.
- Shows more interest in push and pull toys.
- Responds more quickly to calls and requests; more alert and receptive to words.
- Babbles incoherently now when he seems puzzled or frustrated. When unable to move something easily, mumbles continuously to himself.
- Points more to photographs; now even seems to have noticed paintings and photographs on the walls around the house.
- Still speaks those four words he began to use last week; shows no new acquisition of language.
- Sings a very specific and repetitive tune to himself over and over again.

No Changes:

- Still spins, rocks, and flaps his hands.
- Still chooses to be by himself for long periods of time. At times goes off and sits in one spot as if meditating but usually responds to our intervention and interacts with us.

Notes:

- Shows an increasing interest in music; not only likes the tapes played on the recorder, but now spends time with Samahria exploring the piano keyboard and producing sounds. Also displays increased interest in the drums, tambourines, and flute used in his sessions.
- We noted that if we say a word to him in a loud voice or low voice, he matches our volume precisely. Also noted that he often moves his mouth and tongue in a disjointed and irregular manner as if they were not fully under his control or as if he did not know how to utilize them correctly.

*　　*　　*

The pervasive nature of our program with Raun and its many amplifications, from research to hospital visits, reduced the time I spent with my horse and the pleasures of horseback riding. Aware of wanting more involvement with this sport, I decided to spend an entire Saturday in the saddle, riding from sunrise to sunset, instead of taking my usual limited three-hour outing. I longed to be with nature, with the wind, and with my horse, Kahlil.

In an ironic twist, I had given my horse and my son a common name — a poet's name. Both of these creatures had unique characteristics. Set apart and different. A year before Raun's birth, I had purchased Kahlil, a four-year-old Appaloosa gelding with a high spirit and dramatic appearance. His ancestors, painted on the walls of the pharaohs' tombs in the recesses of the pyramids, were considered by some to belong to the oldest breed of horse on the planet. In this country, the Appaloosa traced its lineage back to days before the appearance of the Nez Perce Indians. The horse, known for its athletic build, driving spirit, and sensitive swiftness, had been a favorite among many tribes.

To me, Kahlil was not just another horse. This very large, imposing animal had a rare "watch eye." His left eye was that of a normal horse, brown and deep. His right eye, the watch eye, had a light blue iris set in a wide field of white — a duplication of a human eye. Eerie, Mystical. The Indians considered a horse with a watch eye to be possessed by the gods. Our more modern society viewed the watch eye as an imperfection which often indicated a skittish and unpredictable animal. In some stables, an imperfect horse such as Kahlil would be destroyed to maintain the purity and quality of the breed. However, this beautiful sign of Kahlil's difference did not diminish Kahlil's value in my eyes, but made him unique and special.

Once he was harnessed, I found in Kahlil more than I had ever imagined — a lightning spirit and old soul character with the freedom and daring to live energetically in the springtime of his life. Consistent with nature. And now, how odd to find much of this horse in my special son. Like this statuesque animal, Raun too had a profound beauty that others judged problematic and wanted to discard. Parallels.

When I bought him, Kahlil was barely saddle broken. His only obvious talent was his capacity to go forward at great speeds. Although not an accomplished rider, I trained him myself. I wanted us to learn together. After I had read about eighteen books on the subject, we began slowly and with great difficulty. Even the stable owner and his wife, who helped me, felt Kahlil was a different and difficult animal, not easily controlled. But when he looked at me with his exotic eye, I saw his beauty and sensitivity. Echoes of the future. One day, when my special son would look at me, instead of noticing what others call different and difficult, I would see the beauty and sensitivity I had learned to see in Kahlil.

Many times, as I sat in the saddle atop this horse, it took all my strength just to keep him from bolting ahead. Often, because of his erratic and unpredictable behavior, I found myself thrown to the ground. On one occasion, he tossed me over his head at a full gallop. I fell in front of his legs, but he jumped high into the air carefully and avoided trampling me. An enigmatic but caring relationship formed between us.

We had both survived each other during this initial training period, and together we graduated from walking and galloping to jumping. At first, we took leaps over very small logs, then over larger ones. Finally, we soared over the hood of an old red Volkswagen. However, before we perfected our leaps to this degree, Kahlil threw me off him at least fourteen times during our joint attempts to master the jumps. At times, he would stop abruptly without warning, in front of a fence—and send me rolling head over heels, to the ground. Often, he made sharp, unsolicited turns as his front legs hit the ground after taking a jump. Usually, this threw me off balance and off his back.

A year had passed and we were still together. An odd couple. We both had more daring and stamina than style. We had learned to move as one, to respect each other. By six in the morning, we were on the trails, moving swiftly across the grass still bathed in the slick and sparkle of the morning dew. Kahlil's legs danced nervously on the ground. My hands already felt the strain of continuously holding him back.

As we reached an open field where the ground had been dried by the dawning sun, I relaxed my grip on the reins, knowing Kahlil would have better footing ahead. In response, he lunged for-

ward into a dead run, almost flying across the expanse of tall grass
Our bodies moved together, gliding over the surface of the earth.
I cheered him as he raced across several meadows, expending his
passion for speed. Gradually we eased back into a slow canter, then
a trot, finally relaxing into an easy walk through the tall grass alongside a majestic pine forest. In the afternoon, I stopped by the neglected ruins of the old estate, eating a sandwich in the saddle and
talking aloud to my horse. He answered my chatter with snorts.
Yet, singular as our joint adventure was, I felt a sincere and solid
affection between us. I dismounted and walked through a field.
Kahlil followed, grinding grass with his teeth as he eyed me and
pushed his head occasionally against my back.

As the sun began to disappear behind the trees, we headed
back toward the stable. He pulled on the reins again, wanting to
be let loose before returning. I obliged.

For fifteen minutes he flew through the woods, across nar-
row, winding trails and over stone fences built in another century.
His body produced a soft white lather as his lungs throatily drew
in gallons of air. The winds, their pitch rising, caressed my torso;
my limbs felt connected with all that was alive.

Later, I slowed him down for the leisurely walk back to the
stable. To cool him, to rest him, to be with him and myself. Kahlil
had given me the gift of his energy all day. The click of his shoes
on the hard earth, the soft panting of his breath, and the sounds
of the winds, like surf lapping the shore, created a quiet harmony.
My horse and I. Primitive. Pure. Our relationship elemental. Out
of what initially had appeared to be difficult and problematic had
emerged a profound mutual respect and attachment. Again: echoes
of Raun.

9

Moment-to-Moment Mastery

Now that our little boy could absorb more and more information with each passing day, we varied the content of the program further by introducing new games and interactive exercises. Since the motivational aspect of the program had provided a solid foundation for Raun's development, we wanted to introduce more sophisticated educational and skill-teaching exercises into our sessions with him.

Raun propelled himself forward, motivated from within. He initiated a major portion of his contact with us in all his sessions. During the times when he withdrew or became preoccupied, we reverted to using food as a stimulus. However, in many instances, we used secondary pleasures as a lure to involve him. Often, noting that he loved to jump on our home trampoline, to be tickled, and to go on excursions outside the session room, we would suggest the possibility of doing one of these activities as a trade for his participation in a learning sequence with words, numbers, or colors. He could then decide whether he wanted to involve himself in the activity we proposed. Most often, he participated immediately. Occasionally, he remained aloof.

His ability to close the doors to outside stimuli and find a peaceful, meditative state in the seclusion of his own mind still dazzled us. Although still learning what most children his age had absorbed much earlier and although not fully functional by most behavioral standards, Raun displayed an uncanny ability to demonstrate a moment-to-moment mastery over his senses and state of mind. When he joined us, the room came alive with his energy and expressed delight. When he withdrew, an eerie quiet enveloped him. The playroom suddenly became a cathedral. Loving interaction between our sweet son and us came to an abrupt halt, and space opened in which we could all pause. The silence became a prayer. An act of reverence.

Samahria and Nancy decided to hold their sessions with Raun in a new arena. They both agreed that water served as an excellent tool for developing increased sensory awareness and for promoting fun-filled physical contact. Their conclusion—the novelty of sessions in the bathtub.

Nancy set aside periods of time each week for this project. After a few initial exposures, Raun began to settle easily into a tub filled with water. He and Nancy became two explorers searching for the meaning of life. They ran their fingertips on the surface of the water, then plunged them down to the depths of the tub. They cupped water in their hands and splashed each other. Nancy created a controlled waterfall over Raun's head by emptying the contents of a large plastic pitcher. Giggling with delight, he tried to catch the falling water with his tongue. Within seconds, he became a splashing machine, drenching Nancy, the walls, and the curtains. After a few minutes, he rested, then made circles with his fingers on the surface of the water. Both of them watched the ripples radiate to the far reaches of the bathtub. The plastic toys floated on the surface, bobbling up and down. They spent hours finding new ways to investigate this user-friendly liquid, enjoying each other immensely in the process.

Most children are continually draped in diapers, clothing, and shoes. They never have much opportunity to come to know their bodies at an early age. However, this type of exploration of his body helped Raun solidify a more specific and definite concept of "me." Although he didn't articulate this gain verbally, he seemed to sense the boundaries of his body better and to explore the space around him with more confidence. Truly, he had discovered a new toy— himself. Sometimes, for ten or fifteen minutes, he would glide his fingers slowly and gently across his belly. Alert and inquisitive.

Raun not only continued using those few words he had already acquired, but started to learn new ones. We progressed very slowly. After tremendous prodding and encouragement, he finally began to use the words "Mommy," "Da-da," and "hot." This brought his vocabulary to an amazing seven words. He now used words he had initially learned, including "ba," "wa," "out," and "down," with greater frequency and regularity. He incorporated them easily into his repertoire of behavior. They became wheels for him, providing him with increased mobility and control.

This morning Raun ran from his crib directly to the piano, just outside his bedroom. While Samahria sat with him on the bench in front of the old upright, he touched the piano keys at random. At first, he tapped the white keys softly. Then, bursting with energy, he slammed them down with great bravado. He then suddenly stopped, noting the black keys—an area of the keyboard he had always neglected. Cautiously, he touched one of them, running his index finger across the top and exploring the side that rose above the sea of white keys. He smiled as if he had come to some internal realization.

Samahria found herself smiling, too. She knew to sit back and allow him space to explore further. He continued to make contact with her and showed his awareness of her, banging a few keys, cocking his head to the side, and looking directly into Samahria's eyes. She nodded her head and smiled at him; he smiled back.

A full half hour passed before he lost interest and moved sluggishly. Samahria decided to intervene. She played a sequence of three notes—the first three notes of "Three Blind Mice." Raun watched and listened. She played the sequence again. And again. And again. He watched her, sitting very still. Samahria picked up one of his fingers with her hand, then touched it to each key, maintaining the rhythm she had just demonstrated. She repeated this activity several times. Raun remained passive. Then Samahria resumed playing the notes by herself. Raun looked at her again, paused, and very cautiously placed his own fingers on the keyboard. One, two, three. A note for each of the mice. He did it in the exact way he had heard it. Then he played the sequence again. She responded to each of his efforts, again and again, playing with a flourish the first three notes of "Three Blind Mice." He duplicated the notes exactly as she played them. Hands moving across the keyboard. A mother and her child—experimenting, imitating, enjoying. Loving each other. They were like the wind moving through the air—so much a part of each other.

*   *   *

One warm Sunday morning, we gathered our family into the car and headed for the seashore, taking blankets, towels, bathing suits, balls, shovels, pails, and a kite.

Raun walked, crawled, and fell in the sand at the beach. Alert and comical, he played easily with Bryn and Thea as they built their castles in the sand. His feet marched over their fantasy skyscrapers, destroying their bridges, and collapsing the streets of their make-believe cities. Laughingly, the girls made a game of rebuilding the structures while pretending Raun was their Godzilla.

I took his shoes off. For several minutes, he seemed hesitant to take a step. Walking on a sandy surface in bare feet was a new experience for him. He began, as always, on his tiptoes in an effort to balance and secure himself. Despite his efforts, he landed on his face. I helped him to his feet and guided him through the motions of walking barefoot. After a bit of practice, he moved about by himself. Then we walked together down to the surf, watching the small waves from a distance. I picked him up and held him securely on my hip so he could dangle his feet into the water. In response to the bite of its cool surface, he shimmied up my body. After holding his feet high for a few seconds, he dipped them back in the water by himself. He stayed with this game for almost an hour.

The sun began to wane, and we gathered our crew back to the blanket to watch the sunset. Samahria, Bryn, Thea, and I cuddled together. I got up and brought Raun back to the blanket. He stayed only for a few seconds and then walked off, intermittently joining us and wandering away. Testing. Coming and going in a further exploration of his freedom and space—and our acceptance.

At home, over the next three days, he seemed to become bored. His behavior patterns appeared slightly more infantile. The little achievements that used to occur each day ceased to be obvious. He treaded water, biding his time.

We responded, once again, by easing the formality of our program—exchanging hours of his work sessions for more random, unstructured play. We also noticed a loss in the joy and playfulness that he used to exhibit in physical-contact games. He chose to be by himself more and more. Raun was moving away from us. Everyone became sensitive to his withdrawal. Something had changed. A diminution of the spark. A loss of motivation. A new sluggishness. Most significantly, an obvious movement away from people—away from us.

Samahria, Maire, Nancy, and I joined together in lengthy conferences every night. We shared our observations. We brainstormed, trying to find reasons for Raun's current behavior. Sometimes, at two or three o'clock in the morning, Samahria or I would wake the other so we could continue analyzing every aspect of our program, searching for some clue that might help us reconnect with our son. We dedicated ourselves to staying hyper-alert to any messages implicit in his actions.

Raun's outbursts increased in number and intensity. He started to throw over the furniture in the house. We allowed it, thinking it would probably pass, and decided, at least initially, not to restrain him. Unfortunately, he escalated his attacks on the chairs and the couch, causing damage. We introduced verbal disapproval for the very first time. Each time he threw something over, we responded decisively, saying, "NO!" It didn't seem to help. In fact, our scolding actually fueled the flames. It brought more attention to his actions. Raun controlled the situation and, I guess, got what he wanted. But we felt cast aside.

Our responses, ironically, reinforced his behavior. We had hardly ever used a reprimand as an educational tool, and each time we did, it slapped us in the face like a backfiring rifle. We experienced this backfiring in many ways. Raun would continue to do his routine as we scolded him. We would also catch him smiling as he completed his disruptive act. He had set in motion a series of actions designed to control us, and we had been sucked in. Compatriots and partners.

For the sake of ourselves, the furniture, and Raun, we removed all the light pieces of furniture he could easily overturn and stored them in the garage. By doing this, we accomplished two things: We saved our furniture, and we ceased feeling any inclination to use disapproval as a way to communicate. Raun appeared very concerned about the missing items for almost a week. He did not welcome this change in his environment. Although we tried to explain what had happened, he peered at the empty spaces in the living room, looking more like a little boy in search of his lost dog than a marauding youngster bent on finding tables and chairs to overturn.

Now he became even more unruly and unwilling to cooperate in his sessions. He refused to participate in activities he had cherished just weeks earlier. We slowed down the program even more. We expanded the time period allowed for unstructured play, watching Raun for cues.

Log: Sixteenth Week

Observations:

- Raun withdrawing; uncooperative, unruly, pushing over furniture.
- Still uses very few words, such as "water," "bottle," "down," "hot," "out," "Mommy." Will no longer use words if asked to do so.
- Still very involved in music. Hums to himself; moves his body rhythmically without being told or requested to do so. Sat with Samahria for ten minutes and listened to Beethoven's Fifth Piano Concerto.
- Laughs when he does something he believes we don't want him to do.
- Bathtub sessions with Nancy and Raun continue productively.
- Relates easily to photographs and illustrations; points to people and things when asked.

No Changes:

- Spinning and rocking continue.
- Still aloof and socially withdrawn.

*　　*　　*

Raun's moods became more erratic, his behavior often punctuated with periods of unruliness. All of this continued for weeks. We reduced his regular work sessions to about three and a half hours each day, less than half as long as they had been on our modified schedule. We spent the remainder of the time still with him one-on-one in supervised free play, during which Raun always set the pace, designed the activity, and controlled the interaction.

The more we relaxed and altered the program, the more Raun's mood softened. He began responding again. Conceivably, his unruliness and mood swings might have been his way of reaching us—of communicating his desire to pull back and moving us to change the schedule so that he might have an opportunity to pause. The more we picked up his cues, the more he responded to us.

153

The changes we observed in him excited us. But then the gloss wore thin. He began to push against interacting, even during our abbreviated sessions. A darkness came over him that we did not understand. A full retreat. Our son seemed alienated and noticeably more distant as well as less sensitive to audio and visual stimuli. It felt as if he were falling away from us and we had no way to stop the fall.

His tendency to drool became more pronounced. His tongue seemed less in his control. His eyes stared into space, frozen and unexpressive. Was he physically ill? Were these behaviors signs of the flu or a cold? A medical checkup confirmed Raun to be a healthy physical specimen with a very minor sore throat. But perhaps a "minor" sore throat was a heavy burden on his physiology; maybe it took a lot less to short-circuit his neurological system than it would to short-circuit ours. We had noticed that whenever he had been ill previously, even slightly, he would slide into some sort of altered state or go through an "apparent regression."

Now, before putting a puzzle piece into its respective spot, he would pause, holding it in the air for several minutes, and stare at it. A deep contemplation. A little boy frozen in his own distant inertia. The lengthened delays between his movements duplicated those we had observed four months earlier. We also noticed an increasing lag between our verbal requests and his response to them. Making connections with people seemed to be difficult for him once again. However, when he did focus, he moved in an alert and determined fashion. Samahria and I suspected that he blocked his own circuitry, holding back, putting his gears in neutral so that he could buy time—to reconsider his journey and, perhaps, decide whether or not to continue making the massive extra efforts necessary to move ahead.

In some way, this twenty-two-month-old individual appeared self-reflective, not vacuous. We considered all the questions he might be asking himself, but the almost mute world he occupied precluded us from intervening or helping. Even the intensity and frequency of his crying had been stepped up once he discontinued using words. He no longer smiled. His expression seemed neutral and fixed. His body was more mechanical and rigid in its movements. Even the light we once beheld in his eyes dulled.

While I watched him, feeling confused and helpless, he began to position his fingers in front of his eyes and flap them. Then he rocked back and forth on the floor, making the same eerie humming sounds he used to make almost five months earlier. I sat down in front of him and joined in his movements. I tried to duplicate his sounds, interrupting myself at times just to talk to him. "We're here, Raun. We love you. Love you. Can you hear?" No answer. No indication he even heard me. "Hey, I'm doing your stuff." He stared at me blankly. "Hey, cute guy, can you take me in? What about it—just for a second? Can you give me a sign? I love you, Raun." No place to go. Nothing to do, but just to be there with my son. "Okay, I'll let go. I'll do it your way now." I stopped using words and made his sounds. For a moment, just a moment, I thought he acknowledged my presence with a slight nod of his head. Did I see something or just create an illusion to match my dreams? Raun had changed dramatically. And so our roller coaster life had taken another surprising turn.

Log: Eighteenth Week—
Loose Schedule

Observations:

- Much more self-stimulating again—rocking, flapping his hands, and spinning in circles.
- Uses less expressive language, although sometimes responsive to the verbal requests and suggestions of others.
- Avoids physical contact and fondling.
- More mouthing, rolling his tongue back and forth, sucking on his lips and drooling.
- Often wants to go upstairs alone.
- Some playing with toys by himself and scattered interaction with the family.

No Changes:

- His fixation on spinning objects dramatically increased.
- Moves away from social contact.

*   *   *

All of us tried to adjust to our rapidly changing circumstances. We modified our responses to Raun, trying to meet him in a manner he could digest. Yet a growing tension filled our home. Each day, his temperament became more erratic, his behavior less predictable. Sometimes he worked well, and then, at other times, he did not cooperate at all—as if he were testing us. We allowed him his space, permitting him his deviance and withdrawals.

Yet his reclusiveness grew more severe as if some spreading cancer threatened to extinguish him and all that we had accomplished. The "isms" began to reappear with increased intensity: He rocked more, spun and stared more, often avoided physical contact, and pushed away when touched. Raun's crying had expanded, penetrating almost every waking hour. We had to abandon many of the games and more sophisticated interactive exercises we had developed with him. And then the roller coaster ride delivered another surprising curve. Saturday morning, Samahria lifted Raun out of his crib, noting his continued aloofness and serious demeanor. She guided him into the kitchen, then went to fetch the other children. From the bedroom, I heard the top of a metal can hissing its way across the floor. Raun was spinning. It went on incessantly. I found myself transfixed by the sound. Waiting. Finally, in the midst of shaving and trimming my beard, I decided to interrupt myself. To see if I could join Raun or interest him in something else. Sensing that Raun might be alone, I wondered where everyone else was.

As I entered the kitchen, Samahria stood motionless against one of the cabinets, staring glassy eyed at the little boy in the center of the floor. Bryn and Thea watched silently from their seats at the table, feeling the uneasiness in the air. Raun appeared extremely busy and involved; each time he got the top going, he stood up on his tiptoes, bent over the whirling object, and flexed his hands in a strangely jerky and irregular movement. The strength of his fixation disarmed everyone. He seemed more profoundly autistic and more unavailable than ever before. The clock had not simply been turned back to the beginning. Something deeper and more perplexing played out before our hesitant eyes.

I sat next to my son and quietly called his name. No answer.

156

I said his name louder. Again, no answer. Deaf? It couldn't be. I grabbed a book from the counter and slapped it against my hand only five inches from his head. Not a single twitch in his eyelids. No evidence of having heard the noise in any part of his body. Not the slightest movement.

As he continued to spin, I waved my hand in front of his eyes. No blinking. I snapped my fingers, almost hitting his face. No response—no recognition of intake, only his fixation on the spinning object.

I rose from the floor, aware of an emptiness inside. Our son—here in our presence and yet totally gone from us. Avoiding Samahria's eyes, I suggested we all have breakfast together.

Samahria went over to Raun to pick him up, but he resisted by making his body stiff and pushing her away with his hands. She came over to the table alone. We ate our meal in a pensive silence as Raun kept up his bizarre and intricate pantomime only four feet from the table. We offered him food continually. He ignored us and kept spinning the metal top.

What to do? Go back, back to the very beginning. Intervene with food. With affection. Gently. Sit with him. Imitate him. Approve of him and his activities.

It could have been easy; we had all been through it many times. Elementary! And yet, it was not. We had first to assess our feelings and scrutinize our beliefs. Were our love and good feelings about Raun contingent on his progressing and achieving? Did we expect a guarantee that his forward movement would continue, that he would always keep improving and never return to his original autistic state? And were we now thinking that this day marked the end? That it had all been in vain? That we had lost him behind that invisible and impenetrable wall? Although neither Samahria nor I had expectations of Raun, any uneasiness inside would undercut our sessions with him. As we explored all our questions and issues, we realized that as long as any one of us judged his profound withdrawal as bad, we compromised the attitude underlying the entire program. We had seen so many people view our son and our family's situation as bad or tragic. We knew those kinds of judgments don't exist "out there," but reflect the thoughts and beliefs we hold inside. We label people and events as we choose. In fact, most of us scurry all the time trying to answer a single com-

157

pelling question: Is this bad for me or is this good for me? Had we begun to see Raun's withdrawal as bad for him and bad for us?

I knew, that no matter what our son did, we had to find a happy, peaceful, and loving place inside so we could truly extend an accepting and loving hand toward him. More than ever before, we had to solidify the heart and soul of such an attitude, root it deep inside ourselves, and then bring it powerfully to life. Our self-explorations and rededication to a nonjudgmental vision infused us with new vitality. Nevertheless, in the unfolding days, Raun did not change. In fact, we seemed to be losing him a little more each day. Still, as his temperament became less even and his behavior more erratic, we stayed the course—loving him, moving with him, making ourselves as accessible and digestible as possible.

We could really know nothing for sure. We could only love our son and keep going. Through it all, we knew that this was a time for Raun to be with himself, perhaps to return to what now had become a former way of existing, a previous life.

He seemed to be engaging in a strange and melancholy dialogue with himself, as if deciding whether to stay with his present accomplishments, go back to old behaviors, or push ahead into a world even more unknown and, perhaps, difficult.

Adjust everything. Go all the way back. First we told Nancy, then Maire. They were somewhat tense and confused, but accepting. They both wanted to do what would be best for Raun. Maire had her first afternoon since Raun's profound withdrawal. Samahria stayed close by, sitting in the living room with a friend. From the corner of her eye, she noticed Maire standing in the doorway to the den. Samahria asked her if everything was okay. Maire nodded her head. Affirmative. Minutes later, Samahria realized that Maire remained standing in the exact same position as before. But now, she held her hands cupped over her eyes. Samahria went over to her immediately. She could see the stream of tears flowing down Maire's face.

"What's the matter, Maire? What's wrong?"

"I can't stand it. I love him so much and to see him like this after all the progress just kills me."

Samahria hugged her until she had finished crying.

"Come on, Maire, let's sit down and talk about it. About Raun."

Maire felt that Raun's "regression," as she called it, was terrible—irreversible. In many ways, she had expected him to keep getting better, to keep improving. In loving him, she had found herself needing him to be healthy and involved. She understood the trap that she had created; she understood her unhappiness. It would not be okay to lose him, she insisted. And yet, precisely because it was not okay, she understood that, in some way, she was now disapproving of his behavior and, ultimately, that would lead to disapproving of him. She wanted to feel good about his withdrawal—to allow him this slide backward (or forward) into the autistic womb. She knew, as we had all come to learn, that, if we had expectations for him to fulfill, we set ourselves up for directing him toward specific goals and for creating our own disappointments.

Samahria talked with Maire about fundamentals, about the concept of working with Raun without judgments and without expectations. Together they explored the nature of the attitude "To love is to be happy with." Bottom line: Loving Raun would mean being happy with him—right now, that day, as he was! Yes, we might have our dreams for him and a vision of what he could become, but that meant putting ourselves into the future. All we really had was that day. And that was the time to love him, to be happy with him, to celebrate his life. She tried to inspire Maire to let go of the day before and begin anew. No prejudices. No sadness. No sense of loss. We still had Raun. We had ourselves and one another. We had our dreams. And we had our passion that enabled us to persist in reaching for the stars.

If this was it for Raun, the ultimate design of his world, could we feel good about this little boy and what we had shared with him?

There were no promises. Just today. Maire looked into Samahria's eyes and managed a half smile. The intensity of her dedication to Raun had clouded her vision. She was learning how to love more freely. Maire called out Raun's name and returned to her very special student.

We worked through similar issues with Nancy. With Bryn and Thea. I did a series of dialogues with everyone in the program, helping them explore the questions, concerns, disappointments, and fears raised in them by Raun's change of behavior. I knew each of us provided a pathway back to our son, and I wanted the roadway to be as clear as possible. We had to stretch ourselves further. It meant back to the trenches for us, throwing this new reality to one another until we could all field it. Again and again. There was no way to predict an outcome. There was just the wanting and the doing. Push beyond the probable. Be with Raun. Love him. Be happy with him—wherever he was. Be happy with ourselves.

* * *

The program reverted to the very first stage. We strove for intense communication of our approval and loving, trying to motivate Raun again and to tap his wanting. Each morning and afternoon were like replays of the past summer.

For over a week, we mirrored Raun in all his self-stimulating rituals. The sound of spinning plates echoed with haunting familiarity throughout our home. Bryn and Thea matched Raun's rocking. Nancy and Maire mimicked their student by flipping their fingers in front of their faces with great expertise and enthusiasm. Samahria sat with her son once again on the bathroom floor and joined him as he stared at the lights in the ceiling. As I entered Raun's twirling world by whirling in circles beside him, I felt a profound release—as if the meaning of life and love had little to do with what we did but everything to do with how we did it. In these moments, I could think of nothing more meaningful and loving than spinning and rocking.

* * *

The ninth day after Raun's withdrawal. Early morning. Samahria went to his crib to bring him to breakfast. As she entered his room, he hummed. When she appeared beside his bed, he looked directly at her. After experiencing absolutely no eye contact for over a week, she was elated and joyful. She touched his cheek with her hand, and he didn't pull away. She put her lips gently against his opened hand and kissed him. He grabbed her nose. Samahria laughed and began to tickle him as he lay down giggling. Suddenly Samahria's laughter turned into loud and heavy sobbing.

I could hear her from the den. The sounds startled me. Jumping out of the chair and flying up the steps, I fought against my mental picture of the nightmare that could have caused Samahria's crying. As I entered the room, I saw her holding Raun in her arms and walking back and forth across the room. She touched his hair and rubbed his back. He appeared incredibly alert. As I watched, he began to imitate her sad face. I knew instinctively what had happened. Raun had come back to us. Our little man had returned from his twilight land of in-between.

We brought him into our bedroom. His mood was definitely cheerful. As soon as I sat on the bed, he came over to me, seeking my hands. Smiling at him, I helped him up and then tossed him into the air. He began to laugh and say, "More. More."

His words were like music—the first words he had emitted in over a week. An incredible wow! Impossible! Raun had moved through it. This day he had recreated the world again, choosing to be with us more willfully than ever before. He allowed us to tickle him and hug him. He jumped high on the bed while holding my hands. And when I scratched my nose, he said, "Nose."

When Samahria touched her hair and asked him what it was, he answered, "Hair."

And as one of the dogs came charging through the door into the room, he announced, "Sacha."

He had never used these words before on his own. Yes, he had heard them often. And yes, he had repeated them on cue, but he had never been the originator, the first speaker. In the kitchen, Raun asked for water by distinctly saying, "Water," not just "Wa."

And then after he drank the contents in the glass, he said clearly, "More."

His performance stunned us. We could not move fast enough each time he uttered his request. He pointed casually to the steaming tea kettle on the stove and spoke another new word emphatically, "Hot."

It was as if he could not contain himself, could not restrain himself from naming and saying everything he knew. He did not confine himself to the five words that he had learned to use during the previous month. He now responded verbally to all the words we had carefully and repetitively presented to him over the past five months. At the end of this week, Samahria and I sat down to record every word that he had spoken. The list was spectacular. Raun's active vocabulary expanded in this one week from a mere seven words to an incredible seventy-five.

Later during that morning, Raun took Samahria's hand, saying, "Come."

And where did Raun take his mother? Into the den, to begin a session, to communicate his wanting. He walked over to the closet and clearly asked for a puzzle. She responded immediately. When she took out only one, he indicated that he wanted more of them—all of them. She unloaded the contents of the closet onto the floor. He sat down directly in front of her and waited to begin. Before Samahria had a chance to separate the puzzles, he grabbed the form of the cow and quickly moaned in a fashion familiar to him. "Mooooo. Mooooo."

Raun gave us his message loud and clear. He wanted to work again, to learn, to interact, to talk. In many ways, his desire and apparent enthusiasm had grown much stronger. He exhibited a new forcefulness. A new lucidity about his wants and a renewed interest in relating to people bubbled provocatively to the surface.

10

Loving Life

Log: Twentieth Week—
Schedule Resumed in Full

Note:

This week has been like a roller coaster ride. First, Raun is supercooperative and in contact; then he is detached and unpredictable. Shows irritation and annoyance often. Much fluctuation in moods and behavior patterns.

Observations:

- Makes more of an attempt to use language.
- Seems to really enjoy working sessions and actively indicates a desire to go into his workroom so that his sessions can begin.
- Has begun to bring strangers into his workroom to show them his puzzles and games; he will engage new people to assist him in putting puzzles together.
- Effective use of language; uses words on his own, articulating them with varying degrees of clarity, to express wants. He uses some words to express wants, others to name appropriate objects. Active vocabulary: hair, nose, ears, eyes, teeth, neck, arm, hand, finger, shoe, leg, head, penis, come, yes, out, no, more, flower, water, bottle, light, hot, up, down, chair, don't do that, pillow, music, rug, ball, crow, doggie, duck, piggie, lamb, goat, cow, hen, horse, boy, penguin, deer, cat, bunny, donkey, carriage, closet, baby, dolly, drum, book, barrel, fish, clock, Daddy, Mommy, Thea, Bryn, Maire, Sacha, Nancy, clap hands, piano, door, belly, pretty, juice, Bonnie, stop, banana, go, upstairs.

- Receptive vocabulary is much larger; can also follow complex demands, i.e., "Raun, please pick up the bat and give it to me."
- Initiates play with members of the family.
- Shows more interest in going outside and taking walks.
- Has become fascinated with license plates on cars and letters in general.
- This week has started eating by himself with a spoon.
- Will take puzzles and play with them by himself with obvious enjoyment.
- Still hypnotically fascinated with music.
- Climbs on a chair in order to hop on my back for a piggyback ride.
- Plays ring-around-a-rosy.

Additional Notes:

- Still drools excessively and allows his tongue to hang out of his mouth. He does respond cooperatively when asked to pull his tongue back into his mouth.

*　　*　　*

What happened? What did it mean? His withdrawing and then returning. Had he pulled back into his autistic world and, perhaps, compared it with his evolving new feelings and experiences? Had he realized that he had unearthed within himself the power to choose between a secluded autistic womb and the stimulating, loving, and interactive world we tried to present? No matter how difficult and confusing the last six months had been for all of us, they had been filled with such exciting and enriching experiences. Raun had come to discover the richness of our lives and participated actively in them. He had learned to sort and digest his perceptions—to be a participant and to break through the invisible walls that once confined him.

*　　*　　*

Log: Twenty-Second Week—
Same Schedule

Note:

Raun still works well, although inconsistently. At twenty-two months, he exhibits a new mischievousness and tests our authority constantly, challenging us, his siblings, and his other teachers. We note a great willingness to interact socially, but he still wants to be in control. Teachers show him how effective, exciting, and useful his participation can be for him. Imitation exercises resumed with full force. When we mimic his clapping hands or the way he shakes his head, he becomes animated and joyful. However, when we try to initiate similar movements, he will only follow upon specific and direct request.

Observations:

- Increased propensity to engage in the same activities—over and over again.
- Since he showed interest in letters (on license plates, for example), we have introduced letters into his interactive exercises (carved letters on blocks and magnetic letters on boards); we have started to teach him the four letters of his first name.
- Now when we ask him who wants the water or juice, he will say "me" and indicate further by banging his hands on his chest.
- Can now distinguish between hard and soft; can demonstrate comparisons.
- Actively initiates his sessions (brings us into the room).
- Shows greater facility in learning new words; absorbs and retains information faster.
- We're starting to teach him self-help skills, such as taking off his own clothes.
- More involved and playful interaction with our dogs.
- Aggressive game playing with Bryn and Thea; excellent peer playing with Thea.

*　　*　　*

Today, we celebrated our son's twenty-second month of life. As previously arranged (in our effort to explore every possibility), we took Raun back to one of the hospitals we had visited earlier for an electroencephalogram. We were ushered into a special wing of the hospital, where we met five staff members, each of whom played a different role in Raun's examination. Two of them actually administered the test. The others took supportive roles in the process. I explained that before we could allow the procedure, we wanted to be shown exactly where and how the examination was to be performed. We remained alert, cautious, and cheerful throughout our tour, not wanting to frighten Raun or do anything that would diminish his sense of safety and trust in people.

The technician took me into a computer data processing room. A two-way monitor, covering almost one full wall, would allow us to observe Raun and the actual testing procedure. The clinicians intended to perform the tests with our son fully awake. However, because of his youth, if he squirmed or moved around too much, they would eventually have to sedate him mildly. Once on the table, he would have twenty-two electrodes taped to various parts of his head: one on each of his temples, one in the center of his forehead, and the remainder spread out over his head. Seven electronic readings would be taken simultaneously, with one additional track monitoring any movements that might distort the readings. Breaks or irregularities in patterns of electrical impulses would indicate certain types of organic or functional brain damage.

In this antiseptic environment, Raun became unusually hyperactive. In an effort to relax him, the nurses played with him first in the lobby, then in the testing area. Through the two-way mirror in the adjoining room, we watched the doctors finally administer tiny doses of sedative orally to Raun over a period of three hours until he fell asleep. Then, after all the electrodes were taped carefully to his head and the technicians began the tests, Raun suddenly awoke for only ten seconds—long enough to look around and pull all the wires from his head. As soon as Raun settled back into a quiet sleep, they retaped the electrodes and resumed the procedure.

The harmless sedative left Raun dizzy and disoriented for over two days. The results of the tests—normal readings for a child his age.

* * *

Log: Twenty-Fourth Week—
Same Schedule

Observations:

- Joins us easily and fully in the games that we initiate.
- Exposed him to four new puzzles (each with thirteen pieces); he did them quickly and with notable skill.
- Drooling less and less each day.
- Starting to put words together, i.e., "thank you," and "I wanna."
- Acquiring more words and participating verbally more often.
- In the park, more inquisitive about other children in general, but most interested in more passive children—will approach them with great zest, touching them, hugging them, or gently pinching their cheeks.
- Learning to identify colors—red, white, blue, green, yellow, black, orange, and purple; demonstrates how he can generalize this conceptualization by organizing different objects of the same color on the table.
- Stacks blocks very well now; can build towers and simple buildings.
- Manipulates a six-sided insertion toy box easily and locates the right hole for a specific form (the box has a total of thirty differently shaped holes).
- Waves to people and says hello as well as good-bye.
- Moved a chair across an entire room and climbed on it so that he could reach a cup on the counter.

* * *

The next week, Nancy made a dramatic and unexpected announcement: She had decided to leave the program in order to pursue other activities at school. Obviously, her making such a choice after having been so much a part of our world and Raun's world had a profound impact on all of us. She avoided looking directly into our eyes when she told us her news. Her voice quivered. We could feel her tension and hesitancy. Did she believe that she "should" continue or that she would be unhappy if she did not? Her words of good-bye seemed rehearsed. Later, she shared with us that she had repeated her pronouncement over and over again in her head until she had made it palatable. She wanted to remain our friend and continue to be part of our family while withdrawing from the program. Finally, her eyes filled with tears. Would her decision result in a loss of relationships that she had treasured over the past five years?

Nancy slumped down into the chair; her long dark hair hid part of her face. She folded her arms across her chest. Although she had resolved to stay with her decision, her voice became thin and trailed off into a whisper. Samahria and I loved Nancy very much. We assured her that our relationship was not contingent on her remaining active in the program.

"Nancy, you'll always be part of this family—for as long as you want to," Samahria said smiling. "And you'll always be part of Raun and his journey."

Samahria and I hugged her for a long, long time. None of us spoke. We used our arms to communicate our caring. And then I said to Nancy, "We can never thank you enough for helping us. No one can ever take away what you did. I want you to remember it always, honey—just as we will. We jumped off a cliff with that little guy, and you dared to come along with us. We don't know where all this will end, but you made a real difference." I could feel my throat choked with emotion. I drew a deep breath. "Nancy, we think of this time together as a blessing. And you are part of the blessing. Thank you so much."

Nancy started to cry. Samahria, fighting back her own tears, took Nancy's hand and kissed it. "Hey, you've been like a friend and a daughter and a big sister to the kids. It's okay. You're growing up and moving on. We'll miss you, but we're not going to focus on missing you. We're going to focus on being so grateful for all you gave us and all you gave Raun."

"Me, too," I shared. "I can barely remember anything other than these six months." We all laughed. The gravity of her announcement had lifted. We experienced only sweetness between us now.

We sat together for about an hour. As Nancy talked more,

she gained increased comfort with her decision. Her most powerful impression and reflection: She had grown up quickly and learned so much during these past six months.

*   *   *

Our next immediate concern was the impact of Nancy's departure on Raun. What would this mean for him? Although we valued Nancy's contribution and involvement tremendously, we chose to concentrate on promptly filling the gap rather than lingering with the loss. Nancy had been with us for so many months, and this juncture marked an inevitable reshuffling of our teaching team.

Although we had worked alone as an extended family group, awareness of our program with Raun had spread throughout the local high school and several neighboring universities. So we called guidance counselors and deans to solicit their help in finding students in psychology and special education who might want to involve themselves in our unique and intense home-based program. Many responded. To our surprise, we received an avalanche of phone calls within several days. After numerous interviews, we began training another teacher-facilitator, whom we introduced to Raun slowly while simultaneously phasing out Nancy's participation.

Raun greeted his new teacher, Louise, with visible caution. At first, he walked in wide circles around her. Although he approached other people outside of his workroom easily, he held himself at a distance when this new person intruded upon him, entering his sacred space. In response, Louise talked softly to him, introducing herself with ease and obvious concern. To facilitate the transition, we had her team-teach with each of us. Afterward, we gave her solo sessions with Raun. He withdrew noticeably, escalating his modest protest while concurrently developing a sore throat. Whenever he became ill, his participation in the program always diminished. We lost some ground in interactive games. He became noticeably inconsistent. He used language sporadically again. He began to rock again, especially during his segments with Louise.

To help her maintain a self-accepting attitude, both Samahria and I did dialogue sessions with Louise. She had begun to question her teaching style and doubt her abilities. However, after exploring these issues, Louise decided not to take Raun's avoidance

169

of her personally. Instead, she wanted to champion the nonjudgmental attitude we had taught her to uphold with Raun. Even when he moved away from her, we cheered her obvious warmth and softness with him, reminding her that Raun still made his own choices, no matter what she did. We couldn't dictate his responses; we could only encourage and inspire him to participate. He made his choices just as we made ours.

Louise had real heart, and we wanted to help her grow it bigger. If Raun had difficulty with Nancy's leaving, we wanted to help him through it. Be open. Be sensitive to his cues. Catch every message. Our maintaining a happy and loving attitude could provide the stability and safety net required to help him reestablish his footing in a changing world.

During this period of readjustment, Raun developed a fetish for the garbage pails in the kitchen and bathroom. For two days, he asked for them continually. On the third day, we went to a store and purchased every pail in sight. Large ones and small ones. Pails of different shapes and colors. Fifteen rubber containers. His delight was immediate and overwhelming. He laughed and yelled when we presented the pails to him. He jumped up and down and actually clapped. Pails everywhere. Stacked in tall towers against the wall. Inserted neatly into each other on the floor. He adopted a yellow pail as his hat. The large red one became a hideout. The small blue one served as a reservoir, always filled with water. He honed his architectural and engineering skills with these containers. By the force of his imagination and creativity, he had transformed simple household items into toys and learning tools. All of us loved this new garbage pail universe.

Occasionally, Nancy returned to visit us and Raun. He appeared glad to see her, but, by now, he had come to accept fully her departure from the program.

More solid in his interactions than ever before, Raun continued to build his strength and power, demonstrating a new independence. I felt the time had come for Samahria and me to take a short leave of absence. After pressing Samahria for weeks, I finally persuaded her to take an extended weekend off from our intense schedule. We believed that Raun could adjust to further changes — and grow in the process.

Once we made that decision, dramatic preparations got underway. Elaborate schedules were designed for both Bryn and Thea, not only in terms of their participation in the program, but in terms of activities and get-togethers with friends that we planned in advance. My brother and his wife offered to take the girls for a day. Beautiful. Then Samahria revised Raun's daily schedules to accommodate her absence as well as my own. Maire agreed to live at our house over the weekend and to work with Raun as usual. Louise would simply continue doing her sessions. Nancy agreed to help. And then Victoria—Big Vic—who for months now had become close to us and the program, also wanted to participate and try again. Although she and Raun had had difficulty during the summer, she believed that she had since learned a great deal from us and could be much more effective in the program now. After long and intense discussions, we decided to have her replace Samahria in the weekend morning sessions. We had arranged for a total of six people to cover our absence and comfort these three children. Secure, but with a sense of daring, we departed.

The next morning, Vikki arrived to find Raun more verbal and communicative than usual. He was affectionate and worked well in his session. The hours whizzed by as the two of them glided through the games and the toys. Nancy and Maire handled the afternoon and evening sessions with Bryn and Thea taking half-hour shifts. Toward the end of that first day, something in Raun's demeanor changed. On several occasions, he called for us. Even though less than a full day had passed, this time represented the longest single period during which he had not seen or interacted with his mother since the inception of our program. Raun sensed the difference. His glow dimmed; his early excitement turned into dullness. Maire and Nancy watched him behave in a most unusual way—he began to cling to them physically. He held their hands very tightly. He wrapped his arms around their legs and squeezed, sometimes refusing to let go. He buried his head in their laps. This little boy grabbed for physical contact with a new force. And yet, despite this effort, he seemed to be losing his own equilibrium.

"Can I help, Raun? Do you want something?" Maire asked over and over again.

They all questioned him gently. No reaction. He slid farther into the well of his own thoughts and feelings. Even Bryn and Thea noticed the change and tried to intercede. Bryn wanted Maire to call us; she believed that our absence had made her brother sad. Their concern mounted, and his melancholy mood deepened.

Vikki returned the following morning and brought Raun downstairs. He appeared alert. Enthusiastic. Very cooperative. A noticeable improvement over his twilight malaise. This time, before reaching the den, he stopped in the hallway to look at the photographs of his mother and me hanging on the wall. He stared at the pictures for a long time. He approached them carefully, like a hunter stalking his prey. Deliberate. Determined. Then, in a great burst of excitement and joy, he pointed to my photograph and yelled, "Daddy! Daddy!"

As he continued to repeat my name, his voice trailed off into a whisper. His face registered an intense longing. Over and over again, he called to me through the photograph. Each utterance bounced off the glass unanswered. I was lost to him, and somehow he knew it. Confused, perhaps even fearful, he pivoted quickly and faced Samahria's portrait. With the same incredible enthusiasm, he shouted, "Mommy! Mommy! Mommy!"

Then, as before, the words started to fall limply from his lips until again they became almost inaudible. He went on repeating his chant, not wanting to give up. Daring to come closer to Samahria's photo, he touched her nose, moving his fingers up and down the photograph of her face, caressing her hair in its one-dimensional world. Trying to make sense out of it—trying to make love. He pulled his fingers back and stared at them, cheated by the illusion. Then he refocused his eyes, concentrating on Samahria's baby blues as if trying to bring her back. A willful reincarnation. Finally, he dropped his hands limply to his sides. He sighed, lost in his own gaze. Several minutes passed in silence, then he turned to Vikki suddenly and said, "Puzzle, Bikki. Come. Wanna puzzle."

Vikki smiled warmly at the little man as she took his hands in hers, stroking them tenderly. Raun was searching not just for his parents, but for himself.

Vikki began the day's session in the den. Although Raun did cooperate, he seemed lifeless and distracted. Every time he heard a sound from another part of the house, he would stop precisely on that cue and listen intently. Then, aloud but as if to himself, he queried, "Mommy? Mommy?"

Vikki began to speak to him as he stared at the doorway,

"Mommy gone away, but Mommy coming back. A few days, that's all. Mommy and Daddy will be back soon."

Raun looked at her and posed the same question, "Mommy?"

A query or a statement? Perhaps a prayer. The absence of his mother haunting him. Riveting his attention. Raun then closed his mouth as Samahria had taught him and began to hum. He rocked from side to side, soothing himself. Like a recording on play-back, Raun began to sing the repertoire of songs that he had learned from his mother. He sang one song after another without inter-ruption. "Three Blind Mice." "Over There, Over There." "A—You're Adorable." "Splish Splash." "Tie a Yellow Ribbon." And all of the others. Notations of love. Familiar. Warm associations held dearly in his memory. Perhaps, a source of comfort as well.

Vikki sang along with him. Yet, with each passing hour, she could feel him slipping away—though differently than he had in the past. He did not resort to his elaborate system of autistic behaviors. Nevertheless, both Nancy and Maire became upset by the continu-ing strain they believed Raun felt because of our absence. Vikki tried to put aside her discomfort and stay present during her sessions.

By evening, he appeared somber, but he nevertheless con-tinued to interact although without real fire and energy.

By morning, Raun appeared more polarized attitudinally. A reversal unlike any of his previous reversals. Not withdrawn or out of touch, instead he appeared angry. After breakfast, Vikki and Raun began their session. For several minutes, he cooperated and then suddenly stopped short. He seemed to be closing a door in him-self and opening another. He peered directly into Victoria's eyes. A blast of defiance. She speculated that a complex and thought-ful dialogue was going on inside Raun's head. His facial expres-sion grew more determined. He locked his jaw and bowed his head as if committed now to some great purpose.

Another jump; Raun was changing.

Grabbing the edge of the puzzle, he threw it full force and watched it break apart as it hit the wall. Splintered pieces flew in every direction. Fireworks for the amusement of one little person. He knocked his blocks down and started throwing them into the air. Vikki smiled at him, extending her hand. No response. He pulled the leg from under one of the chairs and toppled it. He ran to the desk and pushed off all the papers and books.

"What do you want, Raun? Tell Vikki. Vikki help you."

He pushed her away and overturned another piece of furniture. Then he stopped and stared blankly at the wall. Saliva drooled from the corner of his mouth. Without warning, he pivoted on his left foot, turned around swiftly, and lunged forward. Vikki watched him charge the table like a bull fighting for his life. He toppled it, then ran toward another chair. Each time he pushed something over, he screamed out its name. "Chair! Book! Blocks! Table!"

Vikki's mind raced; her thoughts tumbling chaotically, one upon another. What to do? Do something, and do it now! Now! She pushed herself, processing and reprocessing while fumbling through the quicksand of her thoughts, looking for something to grab on to—a way out. She reviewed the hundreds of conversations she had had with Samahria and me. Images of how we made contact through intense involvement, joining his world without disapproval or expectations, filled her mind. She remembered our descriptions of the early phases of our program. Love. Intervention. Let go of the judgments. Allow him to be. And then join him.

In her mind, Vikki watched flashbacks of Samahria trying to make contact with Raun for endless hours without any visible effect. She could hear Samahria's words bouncing back to her across the threshold of time. "He knows when you're sincere or insincere," she had told her. "It's part of our attitudes that we give off like an odor, which we communicate with the tone of our voice, the texture of our body language, the quality of our gestures, eye movements, and facial expressions. When I imitate Raun, I'm not putting him on—I'm really involved. I'm caring. I want him to know that I love him, that he's okay, and I really believe it. So, when I rock, I become as much a part of that movement as he is. I'm there for him and for me, and he knows it."

The words reverberated through the membranes of her mind. An overture inviting her to act. Vikki jumped to her feet, turned all the furniture right side up, and then proceeded immediately to knock everything over again. Raun watched, amazed, formulating tactics. Within seconds, he joined in. However, she moved faster than he did. One time, he came directly up to her, shoved her aside, and said, "Go away. Go away!"

Vikki did not resist him. She moved away as he requested, then went to another chair and threw it over. As she became more and more involved, lost in the growing frenzy of her own energy, she went into other rooms and started toppling other pieces of furniture. Raun ran parallel to her, flipping everything in his path as well. A wild rampage of two gifted people producing a bizarre pantomime of love and, perhaps, anger. Raun's intensity grew until he became almost breathless. Beads of sweat decorated his face. More than a temper tantrum—a statement.

At times, he would suddenly stop all his frenetic activity to walk over to Vikki and hug her leg. Then he pushed off again continuing his rampage. After two full hours of intense activity, Raun, visibly exhausted, walked over to Vikki and put his head on her lap. She was still panting as she kissed him and stroked his head. Then she asked him if he wanted to go back into the den to work. He straightened up, took her hand, and said with great authority, "Come."

Raun sat down in the room opposite Vikki. He kept rubbing his eyes as he worked the puzzles and turned the pages of his books. From time to time, he smiled at her as she talked to him. Then, after about half an hour, he stood up and came over to her. He leaned his head on her shoulder and stroked her back for several minutes.

That evening, when Nancy tried to put him to sleep, he cried frantically. She brought him back downstairs, allowing him to move about the house in the hope he would tire. He continued to stoke his own fire, keeping himself awake. Perhaps he hypothesized that Nancy, too, might disappear as had his parents. Finally, exhaustion began to overtake him. His legs wobbled, unbalancing his body as if he were drunken. Giving in, he put his head on Nancy's lap and fell asleep, still standing.

The two of them remained together in that position for about an hour. A moment frozen in time. Like a contemporary Renoir, colors earthy and muted, all the hard edges softly rounded by the sweetness of a little boy trying to reach out in the best way he could. His actions of the day had conveyed an emphatic message: Stay with me. Love me. Help me be here.

When Samahria and I returned late the next day, Raun was already asleep. We found Nancy and Maire waiting for us in the living room. Visibly exhausted, they talked as if they had survived a hurricane. Their concern and caring for Raun touched us deeply, but we noted they had ignored somehow what appeared to us as a dramatic and beautiful milestone. Samahria and I laughed with excitement as they described the events of the previous two days. Maire, slightly outraged, threatened to leave if we did not stop smiling. A long and intense three-hour discussion followed.

It had been a learning experience for all of us teachers—and, most importantly, for Raun. Defying all the authoritative commentaries in the literature on autism and even his own immediate past, Raun had done the unexpected. He had chosen people instead of his autistic rituals. He had reached out to make contact instead of withdrawing into self-stimulating isolation. He showed emotion instead of giving up or numbing himself. This weekend Raun had, on his part, made a daring movement. Though confused and somewhat disoriented, in the end, he opted for people and the world of human contact.

In the morning, Raun gave both of us an excited welcome. When we went into his room to take him out of his crib, he jumped up and down and shouted, "Mommy. Mommy. Daddy."

He smiled brightly, saying our names again and again and again. Then he showed us his stuffed doggie and his animal book, which he kept in his bed under the covers. Raun expressed so much excitement and happiness.

He looked at Samahria and said, "Hugga. Hugga."

She threw her arms around his little body and caressed him. His hands held her gently but tightly. The two of them lingered together, enjoying each other, loving each other. After several minutes, Samahria relaxed her hug. Still beaming, he turned toward me and said, "Hugga. Hugga, Daddy."

I picked him up in my arms and pressed him to me. He leaned his head on my shoulder, then tightened the grip of his arms around my neck. Loving this little boy brought the best in me alive.

Then he received one of my famous piggyback rides down the stairs. He motioned for Samahria to take him into the den, even before his breakfast. He wanted to play his games—with all their familiarity, intensity, and richness.

The following week, we reintroduced Vikki into the program as a regular participating teacher-facilitator. In addition, we began to train two other enthusiastic college students, orienting them to our concepts, while helping them explore their attitudes and their beliefs.

Each time we shared the essential building blocks of our program, our perspective came into sharper focus. Everyone helping us counted. We were more than just people executing some original educational procedures; our attitude and our beliefs about life became the heart and soul of what we taught. Before any of us could truly accept Raun, we had to learn to accept ourselves. Before we could jettison our judgments, we had to acknowledge them first. Before we could love, really love, we had to find happiness within — for discomfort and distress distracted us from being open-hearted and present with unfolding events. Helping Raun meant challenging ourselves in the deepest places. And although Samahria and I were still finding our way and certainly not manifesting the perfection of what we had come to understand, we held a dream more beautiful than any we had ever imagined and watched it come to life in our attempt to reach our son.

*   *   *

We were all energized, even the volunteers. We put the program back into full gear. Raun worked puzzles with great rapidity. He identified objects and colors quickly and emphatically. He developed an interest in dolls, having, in fact, recently begun actively to play with a small Raggedy Ann. On many occasions, Raun would cheer himself after completing an exercise by yelling and clapping his hands. His solicitation for physical interaction and contact increased daily. More piggyback rides, jumping up and down, more tickling and rolling together on the bed. His mastery of language expanded significantly as he acquired new words and used a variety of small phrases.

In response to a close friend's specific recommendation, we decided to make another attempt to solicit outside input. Although all that we had developed and accomplished came from our own inventiveness, creativity, and energy, we wanted always to remain open. Perhaps there would be others who could show us additional new directions. We would go anywhere, speak to anyone, whom we believed could help us to help our son. But we found no one and, to this day, we continue to walk alone on uncharted ground.

We visited another "special" school, created specifically for children with learning dysfunctions, as well as for those with emotional and behavioral difficulties. An ambiance of efficiency pervaded the entire facility. As an experiment, we agreed to have Raun participate in one of the classes. Samahria and I observed from the back of the room.

The teachers and their aides worked from Individual Educational Plans, preset learning designs created by a committee of teachers and psychologists that determined in advance exactly what each child would do and study throughout the day. In contrast, our program had been child centered; our curriculum evolved naturally from Raun's unfolding interests and inclinations. In this setting, however, we watched one teacher pull her students by their arms in order to get them to a work table. Then she ordered them to sit. Another child, who wanted to leave his seat, was actually held by force in his chair. When he pointed to the blocks on the floor, the instructor not only ignored his cue, but pushed his hand down and directed him to face forward. A second child had a crayon and pad pulled abruptly from her hands as she began to draw a bird. The children's natural curiosity and desire to explore were suppressed systematically and replaced with prescribed agendas. Additionally, physical manipulation supported most of the directives given by the teachers. Some of the teacher's aides would shout in order to be heard. Many of the children seemed completely lost in this highly controlled and yet frenzied atmosphere.

At one point, Raun started to write a letter on the blackboard. Instead of celebrating his accomplishment, a teacher smiled at him patronizingly, removed the chalk from his hand, and told him to sit at one of the tables. He grimaced, confused by the principles of interaction demonstrated in this alien environment.

Samahria and I felt as if we had just been dropped onto a strange planet. In a way, everything we observed appeared alarmingly familiar, reminding us of our own learning experiences in school when we were children. At the same time, everything we observed appeared foreign, disrespectful, and dishonoring of the students. However, when I looked into the teachers' eyes, I saw no malice. I knew they had the best of intentions. They had been trained, well trained, and, I guess, they followed the rules of their manuals without ever questioning basic principles. Attitude had no relevance in this classroom. Under the circumstances, these educators did the best they could. And yet, the chance of recovering a lost life here seemed remote, if not nonexistent.

Once again, we would move forward by ourselves. No other learning program existed that was more intense, individually appropriate, and loving than the one we had designed. We had nothing to prove and so much to gain by staying the course and trusting the vision we had adopted.

*   *   *

The thirtieth week of our intervention program. Raun was twenty-four months old and still moving ahead at a rapid pace. We continued the program twelve hours a day, seven days a week. Some people might have viewed us as possessed, but we felt extraordinarily blessed. We followed our passion and our joy in helping Raun. No burden. No sacrifices. I have heard it said that God lives in details. So often we turn our eyes toward the heavens in search of peace, understanding, wisdom, and eternity. I turned my eyes toward the hand of a two-year-old boy and watched him write a word on a piece of paper. All the experts predicted this could never occur. In those tiny fingers and in the mark upon the paper, I saw all that I would ever hope to see in looking toward the heavens. Indeed, God does live in tiny, amazing details. We had helped Raun acquire language and taught him to communicate in useful and meaningful ways. This little guy had moved through the barrier of his own encapsulation. Having blazed new pathways and opened new frontiers in his mind, he now addressed the world. In seven months, we had experienced a lifetime of change.

We decided on another developmental workup at the same diagnostic facility, the one that had seen our son four months before when Raun was twenty months old. We returned to the same reception room and greeted some of the same clinicians.

In the lobby, Raun was lively, articulate, and interactive. As we waited for our appointment, one of the staff members who had participated in testing Raun during the previous examination came over to greet us. As she observed Raun, she appeared visibly startled. Her mouth dropped open. Raun crisscrossed the room, moving from the couch to the chair to the lamp and naming each item that he touched.

"I can't believe it!" the woman exclaimed. "I can't believe this is the same child we saw four months ago. I'd never have believed it was possible. Oh, this is just wonderful!"

She led us back down the long dark corridors. Pale green walls enveloped us like some mysterious womb. Occasionally, windows broke the monotony, allowing glimpses of sunshine and trees. Raun ran ahead of us, almost as if he had anticipated this meeting and examination and wanted to get there as soon as possible. Other members of the diagnostic team, all of whom we had met during the previous developmental study, welcomed us in the examination room. Raun looked at each one, then said "Hi" directly to one of the doctors who addressed him. The doctors and their associates glanced at one another with obvious surprise. Their expectations did not conform to what they now observed. They verbalized their excitement as well as their confusion. Was this the same child?

Extremely active, but in complete control, Raun continued his remarkable display of his awareness and of the reservoir of knowledge he had acquired. He did this all without solicitation or reward. He walked over to the couch and said easily, "Couch. Couch. Yellow couch."

Then he stepped over to a chair and pointed at it, saying, "Chair. Blue."

Then he scrambled from one piece of furniture to another, exclaiming, "Chair. Red chair. Blue. Yellow chair."

Suddenly, he stopped as if to survey his environment, seeking reactions. He looked from face to face, studying the clinicians' expressions. Then he pointed to the ceiling and said, "Light."

He pointed authoritatively to the floor beneath his feet and shouted, "Floor."

And so he continued before the wide open, absorbed eyes of this special hospital staff. Even I was stunned by his energy and purposefulness. Although it seemed impossible, it was as if he knew exactly why he was there.

One of the doctors, who had previously shown no particular affection for Raun during the last series of tests, held him on his lap and said with great warmth, "Raun, you're a very good boy. And a smart one, too."

Then, he put him down abruptly, as if his ease and familiarity with our son had violated the rules of appropriate professional posture. He suggested we begin the evaluation immediately.

They put Raun through an intense three-hour series of examinations and interviews, using another Gesell chart to plot his capabilities. In the end, the head diagnostician and his associates faced us once again across the conference table. They explained to us that all of them had fully expected us to return, at this juncture, with a child who would, at best, be functioning at half his age level and who would be mentally retarded and withdrawn. Only four months earlier, when they had seen Raun at twenty months of age, he had functioned on the limited level of an eight-month-old in language and socialization.

Now the tests and scoring showed a child who, at twenty-four months, was functioning in every way at his appropriate age level. Even better! In over half the tests. Raun functioned at the thirty- to thirty-six-month age level. These four months had marked an incredible and real developmental surge of sixteen to twenty-six months. The dull, encapsulated, and unreachable little boy was now articulate and obviously very intelligent.

The doctors indicated again how their findings impressed and surprised them. Raun's accomplishments went beyond anything they had witnessed in their previous professional experiences. They would have expected such development to be highly improbable, if not impossible.

The senior physician reviewed the results, together with our attitude, the beliefs we articulated, and our concept of endless possibilities. He and his staff members suggested that we develop a program with them to try to help other children. Beautiful; we would consider it. Perhaps, in the near future, it could become a reality.

Our meeting ended with an ironic twist. The head diagnostician resurrected a questionable piece of advice. He thought we could ease off or, in fact, discontinue our program, since he assessed Raun to be well adjusted and, in fact, exceptionally bright. Incredible! Had they not understood?

Raun, in many ways obvious to us, still worked twice as hard as other children to perform similar tasks. He was still growing himself, experimenting with his perception and developing his cognitive apparatus. Still volatile and vulnerable. We knew that a severe cold, an injury, some new pressure, or an unpredictable and uncontrollable sensory bombardment could trigger his retreat, and that any one of those retreats could be forever.

We never lived in fear of the future. All we had was this day—and the next day when it arrived. We did agree with the supervising doctor that Raun had made wonderful adjustments to our world and demonstrated an exceptionally bright intellect. But, clearly, he had more of the mountain to climb. Although the autistic symptoms had faded, they had not disappeared entirely. He still preserved a few autistic characteristics he wanted to be able to access. And yet, at the same time, he seemed to reach out to us, wanting and asking for more. We knew to continue our program. Let him anchor his experiences even more deeply. Allow him to fine-tune the neurons and synaptic connections in his brain so they might serve him better.

One of the neuropsychologists had asked us to outline the components of our intensive stimulation and education program with our son. When I said, "Attitude, attitude, attitude," she laughed. I shared with her an experience we had waiting in the hospital lobby just prior to the examination. Samahria, Raun, and I sat together on the couch. A little girl and her mother came walking past. The child broke away from her mother's grasp and ran directly to Samahria, who smiled and opened her arms to her. The girl had teal blue eyes. Razor sharp! Samahria stroked the child's face gently and began talking to her in a whisper. The little girl just gazed into Samahria's eyes and then touched her head to Samahria's. They were like two old friends saying hello in the most intimate way. Finally, the child's mother came over. Without saying a word, she took the child's hand and directed her toward the door. All this time, the little girl kept looking back at us.

Later, we inquired about this child. We were told that she was autistic and had always avoided human contact. Hmmm. Perhaps this little girl knew. Perhaps, when a loving and accepting attitude is expressed tangibly in a smile or in the gentle touch of a hand, the invitation might inspire even the most dysfunctional little person. Perhaps, in the face of such safety and encouragement, this child stretched herself beyond her normal limits.

A little girl blue. Like a soul sister to Raun Kahlil. So young and so adrift. Professionals and educators deal with these special children en masse. They push them and pull them instead of following. The heartache. The lifetime incarceration. The fortune expended for custodial care. The wasted energy. Raun, perhaps, had moved beyond all that now; for him there would be continually evolving horizons.

*   *   *

Six more months had elapsed. We continued our program, working happily with our son during his every waking hour.

Raun, at two and a half years old, continued to soar. He demonstrated affection, curiosity, creativity—and happiness. Each day he gave birth to a new sunrise. Raun loved life and life loved him right back.

His enjoyment of people remained intense; he learned to speak in sentences of up to fourteen words. He created fantasy characters from his imagination and role-played members of our teaching crew, imitating their voices and personality traits. As the magic of music wove throughout the activities of his day, Raun explored the piano by duplicating songs he had been taught. He made this instrument his own, composing two songs, complete with melody and words. Numbers filled his world. Among his favored games: adding and subtracting. Raun Kahlil explored the alphabet and learned to spell over fifty words.

Raun's energy matched his visible delight. His curiosity, his joy, his wisdom, and his tranquillity touched us all and moved us all to places we'd always wanted to be. For each of us, Raun became a doorway into the quick of who we were and what we could be for each other.

One week, Maire announced her departure from our program in order to begin college. Tears ran down her cheeks during her final farewell. As she watched Raun construct a small city out of wooden blocks, she addressed us as if she were talking aloud to herself, "I can't get used to the thought of leaving him—he's taught me so very much; you've taught me so much. You've all become such an important part in my life. I feel so changed, so loved. But somehow, I guess I know it's okay to leave. Raun's really doing it for himself now. He's on his own."

PART TWO
The Years That Followed

1

Raun's Life Continues to Blossom

We continued to work with our son for over two more years. The unfolding weeks and months gave us boundless opportunities to enhance and fine-tune his progress. By his third birthday, Raun proved to be a most excited and cooperative student. Oftentimes, in the morning, he would take our hands, chattering vivaciously, and lead us into the den, pointing to the shelves filled with educational toys, games, books, and the like. We had made our teaching room the most wondrous and energetic place in the universe. Previously, all of our interactions had depended upon his response to our invitations. Now, he invited us to join him. Clearly, he enjoyed learning even more than our daughters did. Our program awakened in him a passionate desire to explore and understand himself and the environment around him.

Additionally, he demonstrated extraordinary abilities. He could hear sounds barely audible to us. For instance, once during a boisterous discussion about a book illustrating internal body mechanics, he put his hand up to stop the flow of our words. Then he smiled, explaining how he could hear his heartbeat. When I asked him how he managed to do that, he said, "Just listen." Later, he stood next to me as I sat on the floor and asserted he could hear my heartbeat as well. I monitored my own pulse by placing my fingers on the artery in my neck. To my surprise, he tapped out its rhythm exactly. When my heart skipped a beat, which it does from time to time, his tapping paused in the silence and then continued as my beat resumed.

Another special skill. Raun's ability to balance seemed amazing. He could walk on the edge of a low railing like a trained tightrope walker, never once looking down. Sometimes, he would stand or hop around on one foot, delighting in the challenge of mastering his own body. He could also assess balance in objects separate from himself. He could build huge towers, placing one wooden block upon the next without toppling his massive structures. Neither Samahria, Bryn, Thea, any of our volunteers in the program, nor I could match his expertise. Periodically Raun and I would race to complete our separate buildings, eyeing each other in the process. On one occasion, Raun looked over at me and shook his head playfully. He suggested that I move the top block just slightly to the left. Immediately, my tower stabilized. I smiled, acknowledging the subtlety of his engineering capabilities.

However, of all Raun's developing attributes and personality traits, his incredible gentleness and sweet innocence touched us the most.

The time: early evening. We were completing dinner when Bryn and Thea argued about which one would get the extra dessert. Samahria suggested tossing a coin. They both agreed and elected Raun to do the honors. He seemed pleased to participate and threw the coin into the air. We all watched it bounce back on the table. Tails! Thea won and screeched her delight. As she reached to take the cake from the counter, the plate slipped from her hand and fell unceremoniously to the floor. It broke, and the dessert splattered among the broken pieces. Thea shrugged her shoulders and smiled. But when Bryn laughed, her expression changed immediately. Bryn escalated her antics, pointing to the floor and exaggerating her big belly laughs. When Thea protested, the girls squabbled. Raun observed the entire event without commentary. He picked up his own dessert, which he had just begun to eat, and gave the remaining portion to a surprised Thea. When she smiled at him and refused his offering, he took her hand, held it tightly, and stood beside her. He didn't say anything. Bryn stopped laughing and looked at her brother thoughtfully. Then, to everyone's surprise, she offered to help Thea clean the floor. No one spoke for a few seconds until Raun asked if he could help, too. The mood in the kitchen had changed. A simple, sincere gesture made by a delicate and loving little boy had an impact on all of us.

As I watched my three children assist one another, I could not help but wonder about the unexpected magic in human behavior. I remembered a friend who taught college students, having cautioned us about the perspective underlying our program with Raun. "That's not the way of the world," he insisted. "It's all well and good to come from an accepting and nonjudgmental attitude, but people don't usually treat each other that way. People get angry. People yell and scream at each other. People hurt each other. You've got to teach Raun about that part of life, too." As I observed my son and his disarmingly sweet interactions with his sisters, I wondered why anyone would believe it important to teach children the ways of anger and aggression—as if acting from love and respect would not, in itself, be powerful.

✳   ✳   ✳

Every aspect of our lives had been transformed by our work with our son. We had learned to draw on our own humanity. We pulled closer together as a family. Our daughters, although still young, became our dearest friends and coworkers. Samahria and I grew ourselves stronger to meet Raun's challenge and we both felt blessed by the opportunity.

Finally, one night, I suggested what I thought might be perceived as the "unthinkable." My business in the city no longer seemed relevant. Our work with Raun felt so meaningful. Although I could not even guess where the road might lead eventually, I wanted to change the direction of my life and devote all my efforts to our son's program. That meant closing my business down. Samahria smiled.

"Why are you smiling?" I asked.

"I've been wondering for a long time when you'd come to this."

"You're okay with it?" She nodded affirmatively. "But wait, do you fully understand what I'm saying? I'll close down my business and let it all go. We'll have to make it on savings for a while, but when that runs out—well, we'll have nothing. We could even lose the house, the car, everything."

"Bears, I know what it means," Samahria reassured me. "And I'll be totally behind whatever decision you make. Okay?"

Barely hearing her words, I continued babbling. "I feel like I've spent so many years searching for answers, and now, with Raun, something at the core of my life finally feels solid, knowable, amazing. Helping him has been the best, the very best! I want to do

189

even more. It's a jump off the cliff, but I think we can survive. I realize it's not practical, but—"

"Who are you trying to convince?" Samahria interrupted. "Me? Or you?"

I knew the truth of it in that moment. I had wanted her to protest—to argue for a more reasoned and reasonable course of action. "It's me. I'm trying to convince me."

"Bears, I know what kind of decision this is for you. But I trust you so much. More than anything, I want you to be happy. To do what you want! If this is it, then I'm behind it all the way." She smiled again and touched my arm. "I mean it. No big deal. We'll handle it. Besides," she laughed, "both Raun and I will get more of you this way."

I held my breath, feeling like a parachutist about to take the first leap out of an airplane. I sighed. My whole body let go and eased into the decision. "I'll do it. I'm done with my company. I'm done with the city. This will be my life now."

The very next day, I met with my accountants and lawyers. No one could quite digest the finality of my decision. Even my father lobbied for maintaining my business.

Steve, our accountant, who had worked with my company's finances since its inception, tried one last time to change my mind. "I know how hard you've worked to make this place happen, Bears. How could you walk away from something that's so successful?"

"I'm not walking away, Steve. Really! I'm walking toward . . . my son and something I believe in so deeply. It's okay."

"Do you realize the risk you're taking?"

"We'll be fine. Even if everything I have goes down the drain, at least I tried. And that's what I want to tell my kids when they're old enough to understand. Follow your dreams. Maybe the biggest risk is not listening to that voice inside."

"You sure you want to do this?" Steve asked again.

"Sure."

"I can't believe what you're willing to do for your son."

"It's for me, Steve. I'm doing this for me. Do you understand?"

"No. Not really. But I wish you the best." He shook his head and turned to leave my office. Then he pivoted to face me, shook his head a second time, and, in a very uncharacteristic gesture, hugged me.

"Hey, sweet guy," I whispered, "thanks for caring."

*   *   *

Two months later, I wrote an article for *New York Magazine* entitled, "Reaching the Unreachable Child." Although I had stopped writing almost a decade before, I returned to my typewriter in the late evening hours, after our nightly review of Raun's progress for the day, and recorded in words what we had come to experience as a blessing. The notoriety from that article resulted in a book contract with Harper & Row. Immediately after the publication of *Son-Rise* (in its original form), we were overwhelmed with requests from parents worldwide, seeking assistance with their children, who, like Raun, had been diagnosed as unreachable, incurable, and hopeless. Even as we answered the hundreds of phone calls and started assisting families, we remained dedicated to our program with Raun.

During the next twelve months, as the fundamentals of our program became more and more sophisticated, Raun's learning curve skyrocketed. Not only did he communicate with us in complex sentences, but his level of understanding far outstripped that of his appropriate age group. We introduced first- and second-grade reading texts, which he mastered effortlessly at the age of three and a half years old. We presented books on geography, mathematics, and art. Although Raun never again withdrew back into his autistic world, we did notice that without our energetic stimulation he would become less interactive with people and less curious about his surrounding environment.

We had to help him take another giant step. Once again, we altered the direction of the program by instituting imagination games. Rather than using books, puzzles, and toys as the basis for our interactions, we tried to stimulate Raun to fantasize, to pull images and ideas from his mind and use them in joining us to design games.

For example, we utilized his interest in airplanes and rockets to create new interactive games. In an afternoon session, Bryn sat with him in the center of the room and described, in great detail, a fantasy cockpit. Raun listened intently. For a few minutes, he looked confused. But eventually he joined in her game. Ultimately, he became the pilot and Bryn the copilot. For the next twenty minutes, they flew the aircraft, making sharp turns and leaning their bodies into each curve. I had been observing and taking notes

191

for most of the session when I decided to escalate the fantasy. I lumbered noisily over toward their flying machine and became an imaginary thunderstorm. At first, Raun stared at me wide-eyed, not knowing quite what to do. But Bryn started to bounce, telling her brother they had hit choppy weather. He began to bounce up and down, laughing each time he crashed to the ground.

In another session, our friend Laura, now teaching in the program, created a fantasy sailboat and visited exotic islands with her special student. They ate coconuts from palm trees and dipped their toes into imaginary waves. Thea taught her brother a dance and then performed with him on an invisible stage. They even took bows in front of an invisible audience, which according to my daughter, gave both of them a standing ovation. Clearly, he had sharpened his wits. He could fantasize and participate in imaginary games. However, Raun still did not initiate activities of this kind. In fact, in a series of experiments, we left him alone in a room to see what he would do. If toys or puzzles or books were made available, he would become involved with them immediately. If we stripped the room of all paraphernalia, Raun would sit alone for five, ten, even fifteen minutes—seemingly content but inactive. He would stare out the window or rest his head on his hand as if awaiting the arrival of someone or something, lacking the ability to initiate his own activities.

We persisted, making fantasy a significant portion of each session for many, many months. And then, one day, Raun walked into his workroom and suggested a theme for a fantasy game—he and his volunteer teacher, Andy, could time-travel as they had read about doing in one of Raun's pop-up illustration books. Andy nodded his head but told Raun he would have to show him how to do it. What a delight! Raun asked his teacher to cuddle up next to him so they could squeeze into their tiny spherical time machine. Then our son pressed an unseen lever, made strange "time machine" sounds, and landed on a grassy savanna filled with dinosaurs. Andy looked around amazed and pointed to several creatures walking by their ship. Raun smiled and named two dinosaurs he had read about in his books. "Wow!" he said. "They're bigger than in pictures."

Soon after, we stripped the room once again and left Raun alone. To our delight, he began playing immediately with imaginary friends and decided, with their assistance, to cook an entire meal complete with invisible pots, pans, plates, spaghetti, and sauce. As Samahria and I observed, we knew Raun had broken through another barrier. He had unleashed the muse of creativity in his mind and had begun actively to use all the resources he had come to know. From that day forth, this little boy not only enjoyed and interacted with the world around him, but enjoyed and interacted with the thoughts and images he generated in his mind.

* * *

One summer afternoon, Samahria decided to do Raun's session on the outside porch beside our home. She brought with her three elaborately illustrated books on the planets, our solar system, and the stars beyond. Once seated at the table, Raun turned the pages thoughtfully, picked out words he could read, and then asked many, many questions. Why did Saturn have rings around it? Did people live on Mars? Is the sun really on fire? Samahria consulted the texts and gave Raun the best responses she could find. After about twenty minutes, Raun lost interest. Wanting to stimulate his curiosity, she decided to ask him a comical, curved-ball question.

"Hey, Raun, it's a big, big sky out there. And you're such a special guy. I just know you're from another planet. C'mon, Raun, what planet are you from?"

He looked at her quizzically, but didn't answer.

"Raun, if you could imagine the whole wide world out there, and you just thought and thought and thought about where you came from, what planet would it be? Huh? What planet are you from?"

Raun peered up into the sky. His eyes searched the heavens, and then he looked back at his mother. Without fanfare, he made his statement.

"Oh," he said. "I'm from the bathroom planet."

Samahria's mouth dropped open.

"Indeed, you are," she said with tears shimmering in her eyes.

* * *

As Raun continued to evolve, his clarity and ease with all of us filled us with awe. Additionally, he had begun to teach himself

193

unassisted, blossoming with his own inquisitiveness and spontaneity. He had become a keen observer of people and posed questions about our interactions with each other. Most notably, Raun loved to explore—the washing machine, the toaster, ants crawling in the grass, the fizz in a soda bottle, a rain puddle, whistling (wow, did he ever try to whistle, though unfortunately not with too much success), the gears inside a clock, my electric typewriter, feathers in a ripped pillow, and the telephone (he loved to hear sounds and talk back into the receiver). The list of items that fascinated this child seemed endless. We began to question whether to continue with the program since Raun had left his autism clearly behind and showed absolutely no traces whatsoever of his earlier difficulties. Our conclusion: Let Raun decide.

After his fourth birthday, we noticed that the quality of his interaction remained excellent whether we worked with him in his workroom or outside of it. We began to expand his environment with trips to a mall, the zoo, a beach, a restaurant, and finally with an adventure into New York City. At first, the noises that bombarded us in that huge metropolis shocked him. But we watched him adjust as if he turned his audio sensitivity down; rather than running from the obvious commotion of cars, buses, horns, sirens, and people, he delighted in walking, sometimes even running, through the city streets.

His keen interest in children also surfaced as we continued to explore New York. He smiled easily at passing youngsters he saw for the very first time. Sometimes, they smiled back. But mostly, they viewed our son with curiosity, as if he lacked a valuable social skill: maintaining a distance from strangers in the city. Undaunted, Raun reached out to touch children as they passed. In one instance, he hugged a little boy who had been waiting on a corner with his mother. The woman pulled the child away from Raun with obvious disapproval. We smiled at her and nodded respectfully.

Watching Raun interact in the city made it a much friendlier place for us. We all make up how we see the world. Think dragons, and we see dragons. Clearly, Raun made the city just an extension of his playground. He did not see coldness or hostility. Instead, he acted as if everyone wanted to smile at him and say hello. What a lesson! By midday, we were all following Raun's lead.

In Central Park, we said hello to everyone we passed. To our surprise, most people returned the welcome. Hmm. Truly, who was the real teacher in this family?

*   *   *

Another half year passed. I couldn't say during which month or on which exact day we finished our formal program with Raun. Each week, as he grew increasingly determined and independent, our curriculum changed. We allowed for more and more free time. Upon reflection, I could say that Raun, by his own design and self-reliance, outgrew our program. One day, we realized that the balance had shifted over time so dramatically that our son had learned to thrive completely on his own.

As I consider the next sixteen years of Raun's development, I am awed by the many opportunities and special circumstances he presented. He felt like a child from heaven. God had picked him especially for us. I know it sounds silly—like a big make-believe—but that's all we have anyway. When Samahria and I—and others we have trained—work with parents of special children, we all try to help them see the blessing, not the curse. The curse—well, that's just another make-believe, like the dragons and demons in our dreams. We see what we expect to see—what we believe we are supposed to see. But suppose, just suppose, we obliterate what we think we should see and make up the wonder and beauty. Pie-in-the-sky? Unrealistic? You bet! We'll never beat the odds and marry our dreams unless we are decidedly unrealistic.

Skeptics wondered whether Raun's spectacular growth would last. Did it last? Did Raun continue to flourish?

I will try to answer that question in several ways. It didn't just last—it kept getting better. For the nay sayers who would criticize our optimism—wow, do I have a story for you. This adventure did not end with Raun's emergence from autism. His journey became a prototype for a parent-directed, home-based program that has helped countless other children learn and grow. The key teaching: the attitude of love and acceptance. It begins with recognizing our judgments, then learning to let them go. A simple task—really! We teach it to people every day. And the benefits are enormous.

As a result of other programs parents have created based on

this model, there are now other children, like Raun, who have crossed the bridge from impairments initially viewed as unchangeable and incurable. Has everyone we have taught made it? No. No one could ever give that kind of guarantee. But it's worth taking a chance with every little person. There is a saying from the Scriptures: "To have saved one life is to have saved the whole world." We can never be diminished by trying. Never!

So why not reach for the stars! Why not go for the gold? Not the bronze. Not the silver. The gold! The criticism of such an outlook hinges on the belief that we will inevitably feel disappointment and despair if we don't succeed. How about changing that perspective and teaching people to embrace their "trying" in a new way? The glory is not in the getting there but in how we walk the path.

Psychologists and special education teachers have accused my wife and me of giving other parents false hope. These experts claim with great authority that they could know the outcome of a child's life at only two or three years old. Hogwash! That's just another make-believe. Take hope and possibility away from people, and the spirit of creativity, energy, and daring dies!

Hoping for a better day, hoping for world peace, hoping for extinguishing famine and disease on the planet drives us to be inventive and resourceful. Hope keeps us alive. If there is one thing I want to encourage in every parent of a special child, it's don't ever give up your hope! Dream your dreams! There can never be failure in loving and helping a child reach for the stars. If someone assesses your child's condition—or your condition, for that matter—as hopeless, don't believe it. Beliefs become self-fulfilling prophecies.

Each one of us is distinct—a one-of-a-kind event. We don't have to believe in the predictions of others. Raun taught me that. Hope has little to do with outcome and everything to do with an internal feeling. Hope feels good; it inspires us to help and see the possibility even amid ashes. Hope is the seed that takes root even where water and sunshine do not abound. Hope *is* the water and the sunshine!

Did it last! Did Raun continue to flourish?

More than anyone would have ever imagined. I could take you, dear reader, through all the nooks and crannies of our son's daily or weekly or even monthly development. These have been years filled with miracles and wonder. Instead, I will share a series of vignettes, documenting significant and enlightening events that footnote Raun's evolution into manhood. Be prepared to be surprised. We were!

Raun at Four and a Half Years Old

The next step would be to integrate him into a play or nursery school setting. Of all the preschool facilities in our area, one loomed as the most respected and supposedly the most progressive. We prepared Raun for the upcoming experience. He would begin this adventure by accompanying Samahria on a single visit to the school.

Samahria drove to the campus of the university housing the school. When they entered the large reception area with a high cathedral ceiling, a woman greeted both Raun and her rather formally, asking for the completion of an application as a first step. Samahria noticed that the woman, although very respectful and professional, never looked directly at Raun. No smiles. Instead, she displayed a cool professionalism. We had wanted a very human, a very warm, and a very exciting atmosphere for our son. Samahria still assumed the environment for the students would be different from the formality of this office.

After completing the forms, Samahria sat beside our son, engaged him in a game of "thumbs," and waited. Within a few minutes, another woman, who had been sitting at a far desk in the reception area, walked over and introduced herself to both my wife and my son. This administrator rattled off hard data with the precision of a computer—hours of classes, days per week, the fees charged. Also, noting Raun's longish hair, she said it would be imperative for him to get a proper haircut. In fact, it would be a definite requirement for admission. Another requirement: Before they could decide on whether to accept Raun, he would have to participate in a class. Samahria, viewing her request as reasonable, counseled our son to follow the woman into the classroom. He took the woman's hand easily and left with a giant grin. Ah, Raun's first experience in school!

When Samahria followed them, another official stopped her. No, she could not observe. They believed her presence would be disruptive to both Raun and the class. Five more minutes passed. Samahria paced the lobby, keenly aware that this was the very first time Raun had been out on his own. She knew she had to let go. "He'll do great," she assured herself.

Finally, the administrator left her desk after consulting her watch, apparently meaning to retrieve Raun. Samahria watched her walk down the long corridor and into the last classroom. Suddenly, through the opened door of that room, she heard a child screaming. Instinctively, she moved toward the sound, wanting to help. As she walked quickly down the corridor, she had a sinking feeling the screams came from our son, although she had never heard him scream before. Samahria ran to the doorway of the classroom just in time to see that same woman from the reception area dragging Raun across the floor by his arm even as he screamed his protest.

"What are you doing?" Samahria protested. "Let him go."

"This child needs discipline," the administrator said authoritatively. "He refused to let me put on his jacket and insists on carrying it."

"Let go of him right now!" Samahria demanded. The woman dropped our son's arm and shook her head disapprovingly. Raun ran into his mother's arms and hugged her tightly. "It's okay, honey. Everything's all right. You want to put on your jacket now?" He nodded through his tears. She handed him the garment and looked up at the woman, who was observing their interaction. "I don't really understand why you would treat a child like that. Your school isn't for my son. In fact, I don't think it's suitable for any child." She took Raun's hand gently and said, "Come, sweetheart, we're leaving."

Raun recovered from the incident within minutes. Later, both Samahria and I explained to him that the woman had done the best she could based on her beliefs about education and children. We knew that there was a time when we might have thought the same way as this woman—for we, too, had been taught to use force as a way to move children. We acknowledged that we thought very differently now. We wanted him to be loved—that was most important. And we wanted him to be respected and his choices honored. I asked Raun why he had screamed. He explained that another child had done just that—had screamed when the teacher took his crayons away, and she had returned them immediately. He thought the person dragging him would let go if he did the same thing. Only it hadn't worked. I laughed. Raun smiled at me. Our son had begun to learn the ways of the world.

For Raun's next preschool nursery experience, we picked a place less exotic than the first. Bryn and Thea had both attended a play group in our own neighborhood and thoroughly loved it. A former kindergarten teacher ran the program in her own home with the help of aides. No progressive philosophy. No polished professionalism. Love of children seemed to fuel the program. Yes, she exposed her students to educational toys and guided learning experiences. However, above all, she focused on interpersonal relationships between children. Perfect. More than anything we wanted and hoped for a smooth, loving, and exciting transition for Raun into the social arena of his peers.

Ruthanne welcomed us and our son. Since so many high school and college students in the neighborhood had participated as volunteers in Raun's program, she knew all about our son's journey. Additionally, she wanted to be as sensitive and responsive to us as possible. Samahria shared with her the attitude that underlay all areas of our child rearing. In addition to feeling a synergy with the principles we presented, Ruthanne delighted thoroughly in the idea of not judging, really not judging, and using questions instead as a way to understand a little person's behavior. She agreed to encourage Raun to participate but not to force him. No yelling or manipulating him physically.

"This is great," she said. "Having your son in my class will really keep me on my toes—in a good way."

Samahria also wanted to accompany Raun to the classroom each day for the first week. And then she asked to stay and observe. If Ruthanne refused this request, we had decided in advance to look elsewhere. On the contrary, observing would be fine. However, Ruthanne had no one-way viewing window through which Samahria could view Raun in the playroom. Since Samahria did not want to be in the room with Raun and, perhaps, distract him, she made another suggestion. As Ruthanne had built the playroom in the basement of her home, Samahria could watch through a window from outside the house.

A get-acquainted preview time was arranged. Raun met Ruthanne, who hugged him like a sweet grandmother. She showed him the playroom and the toys and even discussed with him who his playmates would be. Raun listened intently. He took the woman's hand and led her to the pile of blocks stacked neatly by the wall.

"Could I play with these? I love to build towers," he said.

"Sure, Raun. If you want, you can even have some of the other kids help you. Would you like that?"

Raun nodded his head affirmatively. Samahria watched the two of them. Tears came to her eyes. She felt so grateful for Ruthanne and for the little boy who had opened his heart and his mind to the world.

The first day of school. Samahria delivered our son to the classroom and stood by the door holding his hand. He released his grip within seconds and joined some of the children sitting in a circle with Ruthanne. She introduced him immediately to everyone. One little boy stood up to shake our son's hand. Raun looked toward Samahria, who encouraged him to respond by nodding her head. Raun shook the boy's hand vigorously and then surprised the child by hugging him. Ruthanne smiled. In our family, hugs had become the medium of welcome, replacing handshakes. How wonderful to watch Raun learn more about the world in a friendly and respectful environment.

Feeling secure about our son's well-being in this preschool environment, Samahria waved good-bye and left. Once outside the house, she went to the basement window to observe. A recent winter storm had covered the ground with snow. An Arctic cold front made the wind frigid. Determined to observe, Samahria lay down on her belly in the snow so she could see through the ground-level window. She saw only her child among all the other children.

Suddenly, Samahria realized she was shivering. Her toes had become numb in the snow and wind. Nevertheless, she refused to move, captivated by what she described as the most fascinating and delightful "movie" she had ever seen. Finally, she climbed stiffly to her feet and limped to the car, a wonderful easy smile plastered on her face.

Raun loved his first day at school. Samahria, based on her observations, offered Ruthanne some suggestions for helping Raun further with his integration into the class. Ruthanne listened with keen interest and a big smile, obviously enjoying their verbal exchange. Both Samahria and I cherished this woman's openness and kindness to us.

Later that week, as she lay on a blanket atop the snow, Samahria observed a very singular event. A hefty youngster, significantly larger than his playmates, grabbed a fire truck from a smaller boy and then pushed him rudely away. When the smaller child tried to grab the truck back, the other youngster shoved him again, this time more violently. Suddenly, Raun, who had been watching, stopped playing with the blocks and went over to the child bullying his classmate. Big Jimmy glared at our son. Raun appeared tiny in the face of Jimmy's impressive height and weight. For a moment, both children looked at each other. When Jimmy snarled, Raun smiled and asked him sweetly for the fire truck. At first, Jimmy looked confused by Raun's direct request; then he shrugged and handed the truck to Raun, who returned it to the other boy. Big Jimmy went back to playing with the other vehicles. And Raun walked back to the fortress he had been building with the blocks.

Samahria clapped quietly for our son. Only the trees and the snow-covered shrubs could hear her applause. Ruthanne marveled at Raun's comfort as well as his effectiveness in resolving the conflict. Jimmy had had behavior problems since his arrival in the class. Somehow, Raun had reached him with his softness and sincerity. Jimmy changed over the next few months as he became Raun's playmate and friend. In fact, Ruthanne reported later that not only Jimmy but many of the other children became visibly more loving and affectionate in Raun's presence.

Raun at Five Years Old

Raun entered kindergarten in yet another school. On the very first day of school, both Samahria, Raun, and I joined other parents and children for orientation and playtime. A vivacious, demonstrative young teacher addressed us with visible excitement. As she shared with us the scope of the curriculum and the purpose of kindergarten, the children played together in the back of the room with the teacher's assistant. Raun participated happily. In fact, he appeared more extroverted and engaged than most of his playmates.

At the end of the day, as we were about to leave, a boy ran up to Raun and asked him for the Magic Marker in his hand. Before Raun could respond, the other child punched him in the face, grabbed the marker, and ran away. Raun looked absolutely stunned. He had never been hit. He didn't cry. He just rubbed his cheek and stared at that little boy, who was now being scolded by his mother. Finally, the woman hit the child for having hit Raun. Perhaps she didn't see the connection between her own violence and her son's.

Samahria and I knelt down and looked at Raun. We knew how important our response would be to him. If we viewed this event as frightening or terrible, we would be giving him a scary or unhappy vision to adopt. Instead, we decided to ask him how he felt.

"Honey, are you okay?" Samahria questioned. Raun nodded.

"Do you want me to help you rub your cheek?" I asked. We could see the imprint of the other boy's knuckles on his reddened skin. Raun put my hand on his cheek, and I massaged it gently. The teacher came over to us and apologized for the incident.

In the car, Raun asked why the boy had hit him. We told him we didn't know for sure, although we might be able to guess. If he really wanted to know, he would have to ask that youngster himself.

"Raun," Samahria said, "people, including children, get themselves unhappy, and they express it in many different ways. Sometimes they get sad. Sometimes they get scared. Sometimes they get angry, even hit and hurt each other."

"Sometimes," I added, "they get themselves sad, scared, and angry all at the same time. When that happens, everything gets very confusing. I think that's when people hurt each other."

"Was the boy who hit me confused?" Raun asked.

"Somewhere, inside, I am sure he was," Samahria suggested.

"Why did his mother call him bad?" he asked us.

"Calling someone bad," I said, "is people's way to say what they don't want. Like—'bad boy' really means 'don't do that again.'" I paused and smiled at this sweet, young soul. "Hey, Raun, how do you feel about getting hit?"

He looked at me thoughtfully, took a deep breath, and sighed. "It hurt."

"I know. He hit you kind of hard."

"I didn't like it, Daddy. And I sure don't want him to do it again."

"I don't want him to do it again, either," I concurred. "What do you think about that little boy now?"

202

"Oh," Raun smiled. "We had fun together on the swings. I really like him."

No resentment. No grudges. No one had taught Raun to dislike or hate an adversary, so he didn't.

*   *   *

At a parent-teacher conference several weeks later, his teacher, Mrs. Jennar, shared with us a story about Raun that really tickled her. Some of the children at the desks in the back of the classroom had been disrupting the lesson by talking and throwing crayons at each other. She had asked them to stop over and over again, but they were not very responsive. Clearly, in her estimation, the ringleader was a boy named Michael. Feeling rather impatient with his behavior, she scolded him. He got very angry and shouted at her. Admitting she hadn't been as clear as she hoped to be, she recounted with uncensored honesty her words to the boy. "Michael," she had said, "stop it right now. You're being a bad boy."

About two minutes later, Raun came up to her desk and said, "Mrs. Jennar, Michael's not bad; he's just unhappy." She thought about his comment all day. "Indeed," she said to us, "Michael certainly looked unhappy as Raun had observed."

Several days later, she told us that she had been about to call another child "bad" when she stopped herself in midsentence. Pausing with her mouth open, she turned and looked at our son. He had been watching her intently from his desk. Mrs. Jennar smiled at him and said, "Yes, I remember, Raun; he's not bad—he's just unhappy."

"It's amazing," she continued. "That little remark from Raun really turned my head around. Clearly, Michael and then Jonathan, the other child, were unhappy. They weren't bad—as in a bad person. I don't think I will ever again call a child bad."

She also spoke of a drawing Raun had done in class. She had asked all the kindergarten students to make a picture of some past event that they had enjoyed. Maybe getting a new bicycle or going on a trip to the zoo. The children submitted wonderful drawings, full of color and action. One child sketched her cat playing with kittens. Another drew huge whales he had seen during a visit to the aquarium the previous summer. But Raun made a picture whose subject matter differed from that of any other child's drawing she had ever seen. In addition, he had reached further back into the past than any other child in this class or any child had done in any other class she had taught.

Mrs. Jennar, mystified by Raun's choice of subjects, pulled the picture from behind her desk and presented it to us. It depicted a childlike rendition of a pregnant woman with a huge distended stomach. Inside the abdomen, as Raun had explained, he had drawn a little boy spinning a plate. When the teacher asked Raun to identify the woman in the drawing, he said it was his mother. And he proudly identified the little boy as himself. Mrs. Jennar had not known about Raun's past, about his profound autism, and about his self-stimulating behaviors.

We pinned the drawing to a cabinet in the kitchen. We delighted in it for years, even as it turned yellow and the pencil marks began to fade.

*   *   *

Six months later. Dinnertime. The kitchen in our home. Thea had poured the last ounces of juice into her glass. Raun took the container, turned it completely upside down over his glass, and waited. When he realized the carton had been emptied by his sister, he pointed to her juice and asked her to share her portion with him. She refused. He asked a second time. She refused again. Before Samahria or I had a chance to intervene, Raun did something very strange. He made fists with his hands and scrunched his face into an angry expression.

We looked at him dumbfounded.

"Hey, Raun," I asked, "what are you doing?"

"I'm showing Thea that I'm angry."

"Oh," I blurted. His affect seemed like a performance—and not too convincing. "You don't quite look angry. Are you?"

He relaxed his fists instantly and softened the expression on his face. And then he shared what he had learned in school. Mrs. Jennar had told her students that she had placed a pillow in each corner of the room so that when someone became angry they could pound the pillows instead of hitting a person in the class. She had also explained that when people don't get what they want, they get angry, of course. "It's natural," she had told her students. So

Raun concluded that if he did not get what he wanted from Thea, he would surely get angry. What we witnessed was the anger routine he had observed his classmates engage in.

"But, Raun, are you really mad at Thea?" Samahria asked.

"No."

"Well, then," she said, "what you can learn from all this is that you don't have to get mad or angry if you don't get what you want. You can still be happy. That's your choice."

"I am happy," Raun assured us with his candid innocence.

That evening, I had a lengthy conversation with Mrs. Jennar on the telephone. Apparently, she had taken a course recently in Gestalt therapy for her master's degree. "Being in touch and expressing emotion" had become her slogan.

"Giving children an outlet to express their anger is healthy," she assured me.

I agreed. I really understood how conscientious and caring she was in trying to help her students to be in touch with their feelings. However, I tried to explain that we taught our children something a little different from the message expressed in her class. We taught them that they did not have to feel bad or get themselves angry if another person did something they didn't like or if they didn't get what they wanted. They had a choice about how to respond to what happened to them. I told Mrs. Jennar how we had taught Raun and his siblings that feeling angry was okay, but that they always had another option—feeling good even if the world didn't go their way. We wanted Raun to know that he was in charge of his own happiness and unhappiness.

"That's an interesting perspective," Mrs. Jennar said in response. "I could tell the children that I'm supplying the pillow for them *if* they decide to get angry, not *when* they get angry. Live and learn. I guess I don't have to assume everyone's going to get mad if they don't get what they want. I like that. Maybe I can remind myself as well," she laughed.

Raun at Six Years Old

A new adventure awaited Raun in this special year.

The original hardcover edition of *Son-Rise* came out in paperback form. The Book-of-the-Month Club offered it as an alternate selection. Parents, professionals, and teachers from all across the United States contacted us. The translation of the book into twelve languages then brought an avalanche of pleas for help from around the globe. As best we could, we tried to respond to everyone.

Each week, sometimes every day, families from different states and different countries came to our home. They brought their special children—many autistic, some developmentally impaired or neurologically dysfunctional. Parents with children suffering from aphasia, severe epilepsy, cerebral palsy, and a host of other difficulties we could barely pronounce asked to come as well. They shared a common bond with us; they, too, had been given no hope that their children might undergo any meaningful change. Although overwhelmed by despair, these brave people defied the nay sayers and dared to want more.

We wanted to help everyone, but we cautioned these moms and dads that no guarantees could ever be given. Even if they adopted our attitudinal perspective and developed a similar home-based teaching program for their children, the outcome could not be predicted. However, we believed such a journey, filled with love and acceptance, could only be a gift for their child and for them.

Some of the volunteers who worked originally with Raun helped us. Both Bryn and Thea participated, excited to teach other children as they had once taught their brother. The surprise volunteer: Raun himself. When he met the parents who came, he bubbled with excitement. And when he met the children, he just thoroughly enjoyed them. He found his new friends to be unpredictable, funny, and interesting.

But Raun's greatest adventure this year came as a result of working directly with one particular special child throughout the year. The most compelling growth and development of his personality came from his involvement with Francisca and Roberto Soto and their son, Robertito.

The Sotos uprooted themselves from their native Mexico, came to a foreign country where they did not speak the language, and used their life savings to rent a house within blocks of ours so that we could help them on a daily basis to establish a program for their son. Francisca and Roberto demonstrated such courage and dedication in their efforts to reach their profoundly autistic child. We not only trained them, but assembled and taught a staff of volunteers to assist. All of us, including our very energetic and committed teacher, Raun, became an extended family, now dedicated to helping Robertito.

The following accounts document a few of Raun's contributions to an adventure I wrote about later in a book entitled A *Miracle to Believe In*.

*　　*　　*

Before beginning our intensive program with five-and-a-half-year-old Robertito, we scheduled a complete neuropsychological examination.

After hours of intricate tests, the doctor eyed the little boy with great interest and compassion.

"He's very low functioning, amazingly low functioning." He stopped, shook his head, and repeated himself a third time. "Very low functioning. Tell me again, what do you hope to accomplish with this child?"

"We want to see if we can help him come to our world; but first, we go to his," I said.

"He's an amazingly beautiful child and very likable. Kind of gets to you." He muted his voice. "It's almost an embarrassment to put down the I.Q. It falls between seven and fourteen. I have been testing children all my life, and this is the lowest functioning child I've seen. Here, look," he said, pointing to the figures on two developmental scales. "The boy is over five and a half, yet his receptive and expressive language development is at a one- to two-month level. His lag in social development is just astounding. He did not listen to any requests, did not relate, and did not say any words. He did not show any indications of being able to do anything of a fine or gross motor nature. I have to say, it's very sad, because he's really a nice boy."

"We don't see it as sad," Samahria said. "We think he's the best!"

"Well," the psychologist responded, "what you did with your son was a miracle; but if you do anything, and I mean anything with this boy, there won't be words to describe it. It would be beyond miraculous."

Robertito sat by himself against the wall of his workroom. Though he flapped his hands in front of his face, he continually watched Raun out of the corner of his eye. Samahria observed from the side of the room, after speaking to Robertito in Spanish and introducing his new playmate. Under her direction, our son jumped on the mattress, did somersaults, and played flamboyantly with blocks.

"Okay, sweet boy, I want you to be with Robertito now," she said softly. "Do what he does like we showed you."

Raun grinned from ear to ear. He squatted in front of Robertito enthusiastically and flapped his hands in front of his face. After several seconds, he laughed. "This is fun," he whispered to Samahria. The two children moved as one for several minutes. Then Robertito paced around the room. Raun followed. Robertito grunted sounds. Raun imitated him.

"Mommy, can I squeeze his cheeks? You think he'd like that?"

"I don't know, Raun," she whispered. "Why don't we wait until later? Right now, why don't you concentrate on being with him?"

As the boys walked beside each other, Robertito watched Raun's feet carefully while babbling bizarre noises. With natural ease, Raun repeated his exact sounds and the cadence of his voice. He looked over at Samahria and said, "I'm talking to him in autistic talk." He paused thoughtfully for a moment, concluding, "It's different than Spanish."

Samahria laughed. As she continued to observe, the frequency of Robertito's smiles during his session with Raun amazed her.

The eyes of both children had a strikingly similar intensity. As they faced each other, Raun reached out and touched Robertito's cheeks. Samahria guided Robertito's limp hands along Raun's face. He allowed the contact, giving Raun several quick glances. Then, on his own initiative, the little boy stroked our son's face. Raun's eyes opened wide. "Look, he's doing it by himself," Raun exclaimed. "Isn't that great?" He leaned over and kissed his young friend on the cheek. Samahria saw their unstated communion.

As they left the Soto house, she questioned Raun. "Did you have fun?"

"It was great," Raun declared, rubbing his stomach as if that had been where he felt it. "He was so good that I thought he was about to talk—you know, in English." He smiled to himself. "I like rocking with him and dancing. I like everything else, too, but I like that the best."

"Raun, were you happy when you were autistic?" Samahria asked.

He thought for a moment. "Yes," he answered, "but I like it better now."

*   *   *

Samahria and I accompanied Raun during another session with Robertito weeks later. The four of us began by clapping and rocking together. Robertito kept reaching over and touching Raun. At one point, feeling the larger boy's pressure against his shoulder, Raun faked a fall and then whispered to us, "I did it so Robertito would feel strong."

Our sweet little friend from Mexico began his series of "isms," flapping his hands, jiggling string at the side of his head, and rocking in place. However, even while he "ismed," he watched Raun continuously from the corner of his eye. Our son smiled brightly and just mimicked Robertito's movement with great joy and vigor. His respect and acceptance of Robertito's behaviors were obvious.

At times, Robertito would depart from his rituals and peer directly into Raun's face. The contact lasted only a few seconds at a time. However, each time it occurred, Raun understood the meaning of the event and applauded the other boy for the direct but fleeting eye contact.

Little by little, a bridge was being built.

Later, when Robertito rolled on the floor, Raun followed along. Then Raun put his arm around his friend, spontaneously expressing his affection. To our surprise, Robertito responded in kind by placing his arm limply on Raun's shoulder. It was almost as if for Raun, Robertito would try harder and stretch himself a bit further.

I turned the music on and guided the two children in a dance together. With their arms around each other, they rocked in a simple side-to-side two-step. Finally, Robertito broke away, sat on the floor, and intensified his self-stimulating ritual of hand flapping.

Raun assumed the same Buddha-like pose and flapped his hands in perfect cadence, joining the other boy's world to make himself more digestible to him. Robertito stopped hand flapping abruptly. Raun stopped as well. Robertito looked up, faced his young mentor very purposefully, and stared directly into Raun's eyes. Our son smiled. Four seconds became ten seconds. Robertito did not turn away as was his usual custom. Twenty incredible seconds elapsed with the boys' eyes locked together. Astounded, I clocked the first half minute of sustained, direct eye contact Robertito had ever bestowed on anyone without interruption. Samahria and I held our breath. We dared not move. We had never seen Robertito do this before. Never!

Suddenly, Raun angled his head toward us. A huge, old-soul smile appeared on his face. In an unusually soft and resonant voice, Raun said, "We're telling the truth to each other. We do it with our eyes."

*   *   *

Over the next eight months, Robertito began to cross the bridge from his world into ours. He had begun to speak. He initiated interaction often and "ismed" infrequently. His comprehension of generalized concepts, such as yes versus no, same versus different, was awesome most of the time. However, we still came upon isolated hours or days where he had the appearance of not knowing or remembering what he had known the day before. Although Robertito vacillated between his internal universe and the one outside of himself, his learning process rocketed up a steeply inclined curve.

One day, Robertito was ready for a trip to the park. Samahria held Robertito's hand and I held Raun's as we crossed the street and entered the playground. I carried a two-wheel bike, equipped with training wheels, over my shoulder. As I watched our little friend, he looked like any other six-year-old in the park. Today, he had the distinct appearance of having his feet planted firmly in our world. Today.

Samahria and I lifted both boys onto the swings. They eyed each other playfully. "Push, Daddy," Raun instructed. "Robertito, we're going up-up," he said in English. 1 whispered a Spanish equivalent to him. "Robertito, I mean," Raun shouted, "uh . . . arriba!"

"Quiero arriba," Robertito grunted, confirming his own desire to go up.

With an even thrust, we sent them both gliding through the air. Raun laughed, shouting, "Higher! Higher!" as he pumped his legs. Robertito, his feet dangling, stared at the open field in front of him.

"Where's Raun?" Samahria asked her student in Spanish.

Robertito pointed emphatically and said, "¡Aquí!"

"That's right, Robertito. Fantastic! Wonderful. Now, can you look at him?" Robertito's eyes remained fixed.

"Aw, c'mon, Robertito," Raun chimed. "I'm your friend. Look at me."

The little boy turned to his smiling counterpart. Then he noticed Raun's legs with great interest and began the same movement spontaneously with his own limbs. "Look, look . . . !" Raun screamed in delight. "He's doing it—see, I told you guys he was smart."

Samahria and I maintained a low profile as Raun guided Robertito to the monkey bars and then down the slide. Later, Raun handed Robertito pieces of bread to feed the ducks, but his little friend shoved the food directly into his own mouth.

"Watch me," Raun said, tapping Robertito on the arm. In slow-motion, he threw a piece of bread to the ducks in the water. "Watch me again."

After completing his second demonstration, Raun hand-fed his young charge another slice of bread. Robertito stuffed it quickly into his mouth. "Hey, that's not fair!" Raun protested. Then he burst out laughing, patting Robertito on the shoulder and smiling back at us. "I like feeding him more than the ducks."

Five minutes later, after his own stomach had been adequately filled, Robertito threw his first piece of bread to the ducks. Raun jumped up and down, applauding. Robertito turned to our son and applauded back.

"Raun!" Samahria called. "Want to try the bicycle?" Our son nodded, took his friend's hand once again, and brought him back to us.

"Maybe you can show him first how to do it," I suggested.

"Robertito, look at me!" Raun said. "C'mon, look at me!" He hopped onto the bike and rode it in a circle. Robertito watched for several minutes, then looked away, twirling his fingers beside his head. "He's not watching," declared Raun.

"Call him again," Samahria suggested, "and say 'mira,' which means look. You remember, don't you?"

211

Raun nodded. "Robertito, mira. Here I am. Mira, Robertito." The boy stopped his "ism" and watched again.

When they traded places, Robertito appeared confused on the bicycle. Raun and I pushed him for a while, hoping the moving pedals would aid him in understanding the process. Each time we stopped, Robertito just sat there, waiting.

"Use your feet," Samahria said to him in Spanish. "Like Raun did—you can do it. I know you can."

"Maybe you can show him again," I suggested to my son. Raun whizzed around in circles, then made figure eights. When he delivered the bike back to Robertito, he stared into the other child's eyes. Robertito then picked up our son's hand and kissed it unexpectedly. Raun's face registered surprise. Without any hesitation, he picked up Robertito's little hand and kissed him back.

Raun held the handlebars tightly and smiled. I helped Robertito back onto the bike. "You're going to do it now, aren't you?" Raun said softly as he began to pull on the handlebars, propelling the bike forward. Still, Robertito did not push on the pedals. Raun persisted, then suddenly let go. The bike kept moving. Raun started to jog backward and Robertito followed him, now pushing the pedals with his feet for the first time and propelling the bicycle forward. As the bike moved faster, Raun turned around and started a slow trot. He waved to his friend, coaxing him to follow. For the next ten minutes, Raun, like a pied piper, ran around the playground with smiling Robertito Soto in hot pursuit.

* * *

At the end of another session, Raun exited the workroom with his mother. "He's so smart, Mommy," Raun gushed. "You know, *autistic* doesn't mean dumb."

"Nobody's really dumb," Samahria explained. "It's just that there are different kinds of smart."

"I think Robertito's got a special kind of smart," he said with great conviction.

The magic of Raun's and Robertito's connections, along with the growing number of people who supported Francisca and Roberto in their tremendous efforts, continued for one and a half wondrous years.

Seven months into the program, we returned to the same doctor, who had done the first examination, for an updated neuro-psychological evaluation of Robertito's progress.

Robertito entered the office, approached the doctor, and jumped into his lap when the psychologist invited him to do so.

"¡Hola! Robertito," the doctor blurted.

"¡Hola!" the child replied. "Yo quiero agua."

"Water? You people are unbelievable. You mean this boy is not only saying words, but he talks in sentences? This is fantastic."

The test results revealed essentially that "Robertito was able to understand words on a four-year-old level, and his expressive vocabulary jumped to a three-year-old level. His I.Q. had increased from under fourteen to over forty-five. He was cooperative, followed directions, and expressed his ideas. He no longer ran around the room or flapped his arms. He now looks at people, talks to them, and touches them. The boy's progress has been remarkable in all areas."

"I've never seen anything like it before," the diagnostician affirmed. "Really, folks, if this little boy never learns one more thing, what you've done here is still a miracle."

Raun at Seven Years Old

A warm summer day. We had rented a houseboat on a placid mountain lake. As city folk, neither the girls nor Raun had ever gone fishing. We anchored the boat in a cove, sat out on the rear deck, and cast our lines into the water. Bryn kept wiggling her rod, probably doing more to scare the fish than to attract them. Thea put herself into a meditative state and gazed into the distance. Raun, in contrast to his sisters, seemed focused fully on the endeavor at hand.

"If I think, 'Fish, get on my hook,' will they come sooner?" Raun asked.

"Very interesting idea," I responded. "Thoughts are actually physical events in our bodies. When we think, chemicals pop into existence inside of us. Now some people believe thoughts also can change and move things outside of us as well. I don't think anyone has the final answer about that, not just yet. But if you want to try it, why don't you? Think your thoughts, and see what happens."

"Daddy, will I get a fish on my hook if I do it, too?" Thea queried.

"Do you believe it will work?" I countered.

"No," she smiled, shrugging her shoulders.

"Well, I guess if you don't believe it will work, then it won't."

"I believe," said Raun. He leaned toward the side of the boat, concentrated keenly on the water below, and told us he was sending messages to the fish.

Twenty minutes later. No fish. However, Raun's line showed some real action. He had to bait his hook six times. Suddenly, a solid bite and his line went wild.

"Okay," I said, "now reel it in slowly. Don't jerk on the line. Easy now. Perfect. You're doing fine."

Raun's eyes glistened as he worked the fish toward the boat. Finally, the creature broke the surface of the water. Bryn stood ready with the net.

A rainbow trout. At least eighteen inches long. A great first catch for our son. Raun reeled the fish up into the air alongside the boat. It flapped wildly, hitting the side of the railing. I watched Raun's expression change as he observed the unfolding events. I saw his eyes fill with tears.

Then he started to scream. "Let it live! Let it live! Help the fish!" Raun kept screaming as he watched the trout struggle to extricate itself from the hook. I took the rod from him and guided the fish into Bryn's net.

Thea tried to comfort her brother. "Raun, the fish isn't in pain."

"How do you know?" he cried. "You're not a fish." He turned to me. "Please, Daddy, help the fish."

With Bryn's assistance, we untangled the trout carefully from the netting and released the hook from its lip.

"We'll put it back in the water. Okay?" I asked.

"Okay," Raun said tearfully. "But don't throw him back. Put him back easy."

Using another net, we lowered the creature into the lake and watched him swim away. Raun wiped the tears from his eyes.

"I don't want to fish anymore," he said firmly. "And I never want to eat fish, either. Okay?"

"Sure, Raun. If that's what you want, you got it. Okay?"

"Okay."

As I watched my son stare off at the lake, I couldn't help but think how wondrous and sacred the world must look through his eyes.

*   *   *

As a result of the publication of my second book, *To Love Is to Be Happy With,* and my third book, *Giant Steps,* more individuals, couples, and families came to us. In addition, we started to teach more workshops as a way to respond to all the requests for input. Not only did we try to help many people faced with challenges such as illness, the death of a loved one, the collapse of a marriage or financial difficulties, we also worked with many who just wanted to improve the general quality and effectiveness of their lives.

For us, unhappiness and emotional discomfort were not a question of mental health, but a function of the way we thought and the beliefs and judgments we adopted and empowered. Change the way we think, and we change our lives.

Our work took us around the world. However, not a day passed when we did not recall and appreciate what we had learned so deeply by applying the principles we used in the program to help our son. One day, after we had been working with children who had been abused and deprived and who in some cases had come close to death, we made a decision. We wanted to express concretely the gratitude we felt for our experience with Raun by adopting children other people did not want.

We presented our intention to Bryn, Thea, and Raun. They asked many questions. Raun called it a "neat idea" and gave us his full support. However, he had one request. He loved babies with big cheeks because he liked to look at them and squeeze them. Could we adopt children with big cheeks? We said we would do our best.

Months later, we returned home from South America with a little boy who had been abandoned in a jungle hospital, seriously malnourished and physically impaired His ribs flared over his distended stomach; worms filled his intestinal tract (it would take us over two years to clear his body of parasites). Surprise of surprises! This cute little guy had huge, huge cheeks. Raun embraced him as a gift from heaven, squeezing his cheeks gently and respectfully when he arrived. Thea embraced him easily. And Bryn—well, she fell in love and became the baby's second mother. We named him Tayo (for Tao—meaning the "way" to God or the universe). Although no one knew anything about his origins or the circumstances of his obvious deprivation, doctors calculated him to be about one to one and a half years old. However, unlike children that age, he could not sit up or turn himself over or crawl. But Tayo sure did have a wonderful smile.

Immediately, as is our fashion, we assessed all aspects of his development and abilities, seeing any difficulties he displayed as opportunities—for him and for us. We showered him with love and, simultaneously, designed a stimulation program for him. All his siblings helped.

Raun wanted to teach him how to sit; he identified that as his major contribution to the project of helping Tayo. After school, he would play physical games to help his brother strengthen his body as well as increase Tayo's motivation to move and interact. Several physicians suggested the possibility that such extreme deprivation of food and love in those critical, formative years would limit both his physical and intellectual development. It all sounded too familiar. We would have no limits for Tayo. Instead, we worked with him for that first year in a carefully designed but informal program. He flourished. Not only did he gain full mastery of his body, but he also developed notable intellectual powers.

Today, at fourteen, Tayo maintains high grades in school, has a most charming girlfriend, loves skiing, and is in the process of writing two novels simultaneously on our computer.

Raun at Eight Years Old

One evening at the dinner table, Raun announced that he planned to live forever. Apparently, a discussion at school about the death of a classmate's grandmother sparked his decision.

"That sounds fascinating," I said. "How come you decided that?"

"You and Mom always talk about the power of beliefs. Like

how you believed I could get better, so you helped me. So I thought that maybe the only reason people die is because they believe they'll die." He paused and looked at us thoughtfully. "Well, I like my life. So I'm gonna believe I can live forever, so then I will."

I remember thinking and thinking about what kind of response I wanted to make. Did I want to teach my children to be realistic? Galileo wasn't realistic. Louis Pasteur wasn't realistic. Alexander Graham Bell wasn't realistic. They went against commonly accepted cultural beliefs about what was possible, and, as a result, they changed the world in helpful ways. No, I did not want to limit my children to the realism of someone else's beliefs or limits. In fact, I found his idea charming. I realized that I had always assumed I would die one day. Everyone I knew held exactly the same assumption. However, more people lived on the planet today than had died over the centuries. So why assume everyone dies if the majority of all those who have ever lived are still alive? Someone might call such thoughtful meanderings just a head game. I love them, for such mental acrobatics allow us to stretch the envelope of our minds and our lives. However, every discovery and every invention has always been preceded by someone's first dreaming something new could be possible. So why not consider Raun's original idea?

At every opportunity after that initial discussion, Raun told people he would live forever. Some laughed. Some pondered his idea rather seriously. Another discussion about death at our dinner table. Raun brought the subject up again, so we probed him a bit further.

"Raun," Samahria asked, "what happens if you get to be 200 or 2,065 or 10,300 years old, and then you change your mind about living forever? What then?"

Our son became very pensive. He thought and thought and thought. Finally, a huge grin dawned on his face. "I know what I'll do. I know exactly what I'll do."

"What, Raun?" I asked.

"I'm just going to tell God that if that ever happens and I say I don't want to live forever anymore, don't believe me."

Samahria and I laughed uproariously.

*   *   *

217

Samahria and Raun took a walk together after school. Our little motor mouth babbled on about the nitty-gritty details of his day. He explained to his mother how thunderstorms happen and how the moon affects ocean tides. Not only did Raun enjoy gathering new information, but he had to tell someone about it all. Finally, having verbalized all his thoughts, he settled into a quiet time.

About five minutes later, he turned and said with strong emotion, "Mom, I love you so much!"

Samahria smiled at her son, noting the intensity of his words. "I love you very much, too." She paused for a moment, then continued, "I really appreciate that you love me a lot, but how come? Why do you love me so much?"

He considered her question as they strolled and then touched the four corners of his head to signify that he was working on the answer with his whole brain. Suddenly he stopped and looked directly into her eyes. "I love you so much because you're so useful."

His comments blew Samahria's circuits. Although many parents might recoil from such a comment, we delighted in his observation and appreciation. We could imagine nothing more wonderful than to make our love tangible by being useful to our children.

Raun at Nine Years Old

Raun decided what he wanted to do when he grew up (a nine-year-old perspective).

1) To Time-Travel

He wanted to design a time-travel machine so that he could visit not only the past, but the future. Favorite time destinations: the moment the universe first began, the time of the dinosaurs (definitely a highlight), the days of cavemen and cavewomen (as he astutely and politically correctly referred to them), ancient Greece, the Wild West, and then times one hundred years into the future, one thousand years into the future, and five thousand years into the future. On the basis of those experiences, he would choose further destinations.

218

2) To Be an Astronaut

He believed rocketing to the moon and then to other planets beyond would be a truly great adventure. He found the idea of weightlessness fascinating. Among his contemplated adventures as an astronaut: visiting other solar systems and other galaxies and then discovering a never-before-known galaxy, which would be named after him—the Raun Kaufman Galaxy.

3) To Be a Rock Star

He thought dressing crazy and wiggling onstage with dark glasses and a guitar would be great fun. Admittedly, he considered the music itself secondary. Although he had taken piano lessons, then violin lessons, and was now taking viola and vibraphone lessons, he loved the act of making music (with his arms, hands, fingers) more than the actual sound itself.

To Never Kiss a Girl

He wanted definitely to get married and have children. However, he vowed he would never kiss a girl, not even his wife.

*　　*　　*

Another major event occurred in our family life and in Raun's life—the adoption of a five-year-old little boy who had spent several years in an orphanage after almost being killed by his birth father. At two years old, his mother died. At three years old, living in extreme poverty, his father attacked him with a knife and slit his throat—twice. Miraculously, the child survived.

Although his vocal cords remained intact, he spoke rarely. At times, he would go to sleep standing up as if he guarded himself silently by remaining in an upright position. A psychologist called his behavior disturbed, though "justifiably" disturbed. We smiled on hearing his words. We saw only a sensitive and frightened little boy doing the best he could to take care of himself and make sense out of a very violent world. No labels were necessary for us.

We called him Ravi, a name meaning sun or rising sun. From

the very first moment, he addressed me as Popi, a name that ultimately replaced Dad or Daddy in our home as the other children
adopted the word he used to address me. Ravi never left my side,
always standing by me and hugging my leg. His siblings nicknamed
him playfully "the appendage." In those early days, I could never
quite decide whether he liked me or feared me, hoping I would
not do to him what his first Popi had done. Perhaps, by holding
tight, he believed he could solidify our relationship and inspire a
different outcome.

During every interaction, I reassured him that I loved him
and would never harm him. I tried not to surprise him with my
presence, keeping all my physical movements, which he monitored
intensely, predictable and gentle. My heart melted when he hugged
me; each time I could feel his arms trembling.

Everyone loved Ravi. Tayo became his mentor and protector
during his first months in our home. Bryn and Thea accepted him
easily into our family unit and treated him as if he had always been
part of us. Raun, always an extraordinarily curious person, wanted
to see Ravi's scars. We explained that we wanted to give his new
brother some time first; perhaps one day, on his own, he would
show them to Raun.

For years, Raun had been the family baby, the perennial youngest child. As the result of Tayo's and Ravi's presence, he now became a big brother to two people. He loved the role and took it
rather seriously. He volunteered to teach Ravi English, to help him
learn about the house, and to play ball with him. Clearly, as Raun
grew older, he welcomed more responsibilities and saw his expanding family as presenting exciting challenges—like big brotherhood.

Even though extraordinarily withdrawn at first, Ravi emerged
slowly from his shell with the gentle and loving help of his siblings.
At first, most of his interactions seemed cautious and tentative.
But eventually, as he grew stronger and stronger, he shared his
sweetness with us, becoming a master helper. Whether we cleared
the kitchen table, hung the bicycles on hooks in the garage, or
washed the car, Ravi jumped front and center to assist, always making a significant contribution.

In junior high school, he stretched himself with great courage,
deciding to run for class president and making a speech in front
of the entire junior high school student body. He won the elec-

tion. Over the years, Ravi developed into a fine athlete, much more secure in himself and his abilities. Today, as a high school student, Ravi can always be seen wearing his favorite Chicago Bulls cap, his head bobbing up and down as he listens to rap music on his Walkman. Athletic awards decorate his bedroom. And although still not the consummate conversationalist, his quick wit and dry humor keep us all laughing.

Raun at Ten Years Old

Raun experienced his next major transition during this year, moving from the home he had known all his life and from the citified environment he had always enjoyed.

The requests for our services from individuals, families, and groups escalated dramatically each year. In addition to working with people out of our home, we rented nearby facilities to accommodate the overflow. Samahria and I had continuous discussions about the optimum environment in which we could work with people—a pastoral retreat center in a soothing and inspiring country setting away from the hustle and bustle of the city.

In this year, 1983, after years of planning and searching, we located just such a property on a mountainside in western Massachusetts. There we founded The Option Institute and Fellowship on an old estate whose main structure had just been partially renovated after years of neglect and decay. Eventually, this eighty-five-acre campus would contain a series of buildings, designed carefully to blend with the natural setting containing soaring evergreens, mighty oaks, small ponds, a spectacular limestone ravine, and a creek that meandered through a valley after rushing down the mountain over small waterfalls and through pristine pools of clear water. In the evenings, deer grazed on the lawns, sometimes as many as twelve and fourteen at a time. For me, a city boy, moving to this property felt like having died and gone to heaven.

At first, our children, however, had compelling concerns about the move. Although we had discussed this dramatic change of lifestyle in depth and secured their support (we voted together, unanimously), they raised concerns about losing our family privacy if we lived among the people we helped. Also, even though we had showed them the local movie theaters, restaurants, playgrounds, and bowling alley in neighboring towns in both Massachusetts and Connecticut (our property sits on the border between these states), they referred to our neighbors as deer, cows, and raccoons.

We assured them that we would do everything to make their life in the country work and that, bottom line, we would never sacrifice our family's intimacy and communion. We would still have our own private home space and have our special family days every Sunday as usual. Our guests and clients would be like neighbors, living in other buildings but sharing the property with all of us.

Bryn had the greatest difficulty adjusting, spending her senior year in high school away from friends she had known most of her life. Thea adjusted easily, welcoming the new adventure. Tayo and Ravi, now fast friends, provided camaraderie for each other as they began a new phase of their lives.

And Raun—well, Raun jumped into his new life with his typical enthusiasm. First, we had to hike up to the top of the mountain behind our property and look off at the valleys and lakes in the distance. Then we had to climb on the rocks in the ravine and visit with the fish, frogs, salamanders, and other miscellaneous creatures living there. We no longer had to visit the American Museum of Natural History or the aquarium or even the zoo; Raun and his siblings played with the world of nature in their backyard.

When Raun first visited his rural school, he could not quite digest its small size. Although they had two classes per grade, the overall number of students and teachers paled in comparison with that of his former grade school in New York.

"Not to be mean or anything," he said, "but it's kind of small." When he perused the parking area, with its ten cars, he seemed even more surprised. He shook his head, shrugged his shoulders, and laughed. "Where are all the people?"

Ah, the world through Raun's eyes—curious, innocent, always amazed.

*   *   *

Later that year, Raun joined Little League, wrote his first short story, and developed a crush on a girl in his class. Above all, he showed great interest in our work with adults. He knew all about our program for families with special children; in fact, he had participated and, oftentimes, talked with parents. However, the group programs for adults mystified him.

Though we offered weekend and week-long programs, he inquired most about our eight-week summer program, "Living the Dream." Of all our workshops presented throughout the year, this course, I thought, offered the deepest and most comprehensive exposure to the heart and soul of what we taught.

Raun wanted to know what all the participants would do together for two long months. I explained the intention of the program: to explore all our beliefs about such subjects as relationships, health, sex, money, work, parenting, authenticity, aging, and death, and to have the opportunity to change the beliefs that don't serve us—the ones that cause distress and discomfort. In effect, the intention of the program was to unearth completely the very substance of who we were and to recreate ourselves in accordance with our own individual designs—as he had recreated himself in our family program in accordance with his own unique design.

"In your program, you had the opportunity to learn to be the best that you could be," I said. "Now these people, teachers, doctors, homemakers, lawyers, businesspeople, helping professionals, artists, and students—just about everybody—will have the opportunity to create the same possibility for themselves."

Raun smiled and then stared at me pensively for a moment. "Since it's during the summer and I'm off from school," he said, "can I take the program?"

His request startled me. Wow! I tried to imagine Raun, at ten years old, sitting among adults who might share their concerns and deepest fears in very open and authentic ways. Could he handle it? Could they handle him?

After much discussion, Samahria and I decided to begin the course without Raun's involvement. However, if we felt later that he could assimilate the group process, we would invite his participation on a limited basis. That time came within a few days. We asked Raun to participate as a guest in a class session on the power of beliefs and judgments. He enjoyed his experience thoroughly and, to my surprise, raised his hand to talk as much as anyone else in the group. Everyone loved him and encouraged me to have him participate even more.

About mid-summer, we began to teach the group members

what we now call Optiva Dialogues℠, a gentle and respectful process of self-exploration (part of The Option Process®) intended to help people find their own answers so they can change beliefs and as a result experience increased comfort and clarity. Raun took every one of these classes. He understood, perhaps more quickly than most, that a loving and nonjudgmental attitude was crucial to the effectiveness of these dialogues.

One afternoon, we broke the group in pairs. We gave the two people in each dyad one full hour to take turns doing these special dialogues with each other. First, one person would be the mentor who asked nonjudgmental questions to enable the other person to explore and resolve his or her own issues. Then the two would reverse roles. Raun ended up being paired with the oldest member of the group. A rather sincere but cynical seventy-one-year-old man named Charlie, a retired business executive, shook his head disapprovingly as he walked off with his little partner. When Raun took his hand, he sighed noisily, apparently further expressing displeasure that this small person selected to work with him now held his hand. They walked across an expanse of lawn and then sat together under an ancient copper beech tree. I considered substituting myself for Raun but then decided this could be a useful experience for Charlie. The man resisted new situations and seemed overwhelmed by the truckload of judgments he carried with him most of the time.

I kept a careful eye on Raun from a distance. Obviously, Charlie took the role of mentor first. Our little talking machine chatted away on some subject I am sure he wanted to explore. When he and Charlie reversed roles, Raun leaned forward and concentrated on Charlie's every word. From time to time, he asked his questions studiously, then listened again.

When everyone returned and joined into the larger group, Charlie shook his head from side to side and then raised his hand. Here it comes, I thought. However, the man surprised me and everyone else in the circle.

"I just want to say that Raun and I had a wonderful time. I can't quite believe it," he said. "This little guy asked great questions and me—well, I actually solved a problem that's been bothering me for years."

The group cheered.

"Wait," Charlie said, putting his hand up again. "Don't cheer me. Cheer Raun. I never really felt comfortable around kids. What could they offer me at this time in my life?" He paused. "You know, I was positive this practice session would be a disaster. But—it wasn't. It was very, very helpful. I'll never look at youngsters that way again."

Raun at Thirteen Years Old

Raun loved school and prided himself on maintaining an almost straight-A academic average. He had developed a tight circle of friends, including some very articulate young girls. Though Raun enjoyed tennis and volleyball, his favorite sport seemed to be talking—engaging in thoughtful discussion, asking probing questions about people, politics, and science. He always tried to figure out how it all worked.

During this same year, parents with special children who had come to our institute to learn the Son-Rise Program shared their stories about the many hurdles they had to jump in order to get accurate diagnostic evaluations and find even minimal help for their children. Additionally, and to our surprise, they had difficulty securing the phone number and address of our learning center from the Autism Society of America (then called the National Society for Autistic Children).

We had known for years that many individuals connected with that organization disapproved of our philosophy and teaching. They believed strongly that imitating a child's autistic rituals would be decidedly detrimental to the child. Also, many of these people objected to the idea of parents taking on the responsibility of designing and implementing their own home-based programs—believing that should be the job of professionals and the schools. And others scoffed at the notion that a nonjudgmental attitude had any relevance whatsoever to the teaching of autistic or developmentally impaired children.

Over the years, we had been in touch with this organization, keeping them informed of our continuing work. We had sent them copies of *Son-Rise* as well as *A Miracle to Believe In,* which recounted our journey with the courageous Soto family, who relocated here from Mexico in order to help their special child. That book also detailed Raun's continued development. In addition, on several occasions, we sent members of that organization literature about our programs.

I decided to call the national office in Washington, D.C. A man answering the phone, who identified himself as having an autistic brother, said he would be happy to help me. When I asked him about the "Son-Rise" people, he told me that Raun had been placed in an institution, still very autistic and dysfunctional, that Samahria and I had divorced, and that our children had been placed in foster homes. When I identified myself, the man excused himself for several minutes, then returned to the phone. Even after I told him that all of his information was profoundly incorrect, he insisted he had it on good authority. I asked him to cite his good authority; he refused. When I suggested that he no longer repeat this erroneous story since he now knew it was untrue, he became evasive.

As we continued the conversation, I realized his dilemma. Perhaps, if I had an autistic brother, still dysfunctional, and I held the conviction that autism was incurable, I would have easily adopted his stance and found the story of Raun's mental demise very believable. Why would he want to support data that contradicted his own experience? Not wanting to give up, I invited him to visit our institute, watch us work with families and children, and meet Raun himself. He countered by telling me about his busy schedule but, nevertheless, thanked me for the offer. I extended the invitation to all the officials of the organization.

He never visited, nor did any of his colleagues, even after I called others and made them the same proposal.

*　　*　　*

Samahria and I have always tried to use every controversial event in our lives as a learning. Although we stumble at times, like everyone else, we try to pick ourselves off the floor with a useful lesson. We called this one The Big Let Go (we've done that more than a few times in our lives). Rather than try to fight or even push those who wanted to stay with their established beliefs and visions even in the presence of new information, we decided instead to focus our energy on sharing what we learned with those who wanted to listen.

Raun at Fourteen Years Old

Another change in our family dynamics occurred that presented a real challenge for Raun.

A woman called us about a ten-year-old girl orphaned in war-torn El Salvador. She had dedicated herself to finding this child a home. Explaining how difficult it would be to place a youngster of her age, given the extreme circumstances of her traumatized childhood, she asked if we would be open to adopting her. After conversing with our children, we responded with a yes. She asked if we wanted to fly down to San Salvador, the capital city, and see if we liked her before we made our final commitment. Since we believed that loving someone was a choice, we decided, sight unseen, to love this young girl in that moment.

If I had to pinpoint the single most essential message of our seminars, it would be that happiness is a choice. For us, the natural extension of such a perspective was that liking someone, indeed loving someone, was a choice as well. We could decide at that moment—and we did—to like her, to love her.

We then supplied her with photographs and a letter translated into Spanish. Days after she received our communication, something rather fortuitous occurred. The movie *Son-Rise*, which had been made for an NBC-TV movie presentation here in the United States (Samahria and I wrote the screenplay), aired on nationwide television in El Salvador. Sage, as we later named her, watched the film and sent a message back to us—she very much wanted to become part of our family.

Within twenty-four hours of her arrival, tiny Sage, four feet, nine inches tall and weighing just eighty-two pounds, looked up at my over two-hundred-pound, six-foot, two-inch frame and delivered a surprising message in Spanish. Pointing her delicate little finger toward me, she said, "One—I'm not going to learn English. Two—I'm not going to school, ever. And three—I don't like you."

Someone overhearing her pronouncement characterized this youngster immediately as big trouble. Not so for Samahria and me. We saw only a very frightened little girl with riveting black eyes trying, as best as she could, to stake out some territory and take care of herself. Sage kept her word. She resisted learning English for many months. She ignored the elaborate tutorial program we designed for her at home. In addition, she stole and lied, a leftover from all the years spent in survival mode. Often, she expressed anger; sometimes, she expressed deep, deep sadness. The challenges she presented us daily gave us a chance to tap into the softest place inside ourselves. When she rejected us confrontationally, we met her with happiness. We met her continuous distrust with love. Although we handled her firmly, we tried to create a very safe, supportive, consistent, and caring environment for her. Perhaps, one day she would come to trust us, maybe even love us.

For the other children, especially Raun, Sage proved to be more than just another opportunity. This sweet guy, so incredibly authentic and gentle, could not quite grasp his new sister's dishonesty and aggressiveness. On one occasion, she planted something she had stolen in Raun's bureau. When we discovered the item, he could not believe she would have done such a thing. The other children shared his outrage when she similarly tried to incriminate them.

In fact, one Sunday morning, Thea, Raun, Tayo, and Ravi met in the kitchen and voted to send Sage back to El Salvador. Raun seemed apologetic about the decision, but, nevertheless, indicated that if she did not appreciate being in our family, he wanted us to find someone else who would.

We explained to him and the other children some of the difficulties Sage had experienced in her life in El Salvador, events she did not want to speak about to people. "She's really still very scared, even under all her anger. She never learned to love and trust people. You guys could help her by just being patient and loving her no matter what she does. There's a really big heart hidden behind that cute mask of hers. Give her some more time," I said.

Thea considered my words, then asked, "But, Popi, how long will it take? I'm really nice to her, but she's nasty to me."

"We know," Samahria interjected. "Maybe you could know, deep down, that Sage wants to love and be loved just like you. Only she doesn't know how."

"Will she ever?" asked Raun.

"We don't know. We hope so. Just give her a chance." I looked at all of them. They did not seem convinced, so I decided to try another tactic. "Okay, guys, we told Sage we would be her Popi and Mommy as long as she wanted. So she's here to stay. Since she's going to continue as your sister, you have a choice to make—to be happy or unhappy about it. My suggestion: Try being happy about it—that feels better."

Raun eyed me with great curiosity.

"All right, Raun, what's going on in that cute head of yours?" I asked.

"Well, I'm definitely going to be happy about having her here. I just decided," he said with great conviction. "But could I be happy and still want to send her back?"

Everyone laughed.

It took Sage almost three years to put down her armor and allow us in. What she came to reveal of herself moved us deeply. Her power to resist now became her power to participate, to give of herself, and to be a real sweetheart. Now, at seventeen, she remains a delicate flower, only four feet, ten inches and about eighty-five pounds. In her room, she has created an arboretum, filled with plants she tends with such love, gentleness, and care. She has become the environmental watchdog of our family, keeping us up to date on recycling in her efforts to safeguard the planet. This year Sage announced she wants to join the Peace Corps. Whatever her final destination, this special young woman has demonstrated that no matter how deep the hole, we can climb out of it. And no matter how brutalized and scared we might have been, we can heal ourselves and begin anew—with love and caring.

Raun at Seventeen Years Old

Raun spent many summers attending computer camp and involving himself in their extracurricular circus program offered each year. In fact, one year, he became the show's master of ceremonies. Later in his camping career, he helped the staff teach younger campers.

He graduated from grade school with an almost straight-A average and maintained the same level of scholarship in high school. In fact, since he viewed his classes in the local high school as unchallenging, we transferred him to a local preparatory school. As a developing teenager, Raun experienced the normal stresses and strains of post-puberty: infatuation with girls and the importance of coming to grips with himself as a young man about to face the world.

On his seventeenth birthday, we offered him the gift of taking The Option Institute's eight-week "Living the Dream" program—only this time as a fully matured participant. He had some sweet memories of his original, limited involvement seven years earlier and thought he could certainly use some input now. Lately, he had become more serious and, at times, seemed to feel confused by current events and questions about the future he faced as a young adult.

Since I played a major teaching role in this program, I had the honor and delight of watching Raun share his joy, insights, and fears with forty-one other adults, who assembled as a group of strangers and went on to build a powerfully loving and supportive family. Once again, Raun found himself to be the youngest, although several group members were just a few years older. He jumped into each interactive experience with a full heart. He became a lively member of discussion groups and challenged other participants with great honesty and daring—though always in his gentle way. Later in the summer, he fell in love with an "older" woman, a nineteen-year-old, and matured through exploring that relationship with her. Nevertheless, his passion for the classes and the group itself never ebbed. He used the program to fine-tune his intellect, drop some core judgments, change beliefs, and create more happiness in his daily life. As a parent, I could not have wished for more.

＊　　＊　　＊

In the fall, Raun refocused his attention back on school. He also began, once a week, to visit the parents who had come to the institute to help their own special children. Aware that the following year he would be off to college, we started to videotape his sessions with families so that future families could meet him—on tape, if not in person.

The following has been transcribed from one of those videos. It contains questions asked by the father and mother of an autistic child during an evening visit. Raun's answers reflect not only his thoughts and experiences, but also his developing personality.

Father: You've been part of a very special family all your life. How do you feel about your parents' philosophy and way of life and how has it influenced *your* life?

Raun: Well, it's funny. I never really took it in fully for most of my life. Because I was always a *really* happy kid. Everything went my way, so I was really up on life. I mean, I used to say, "I love life" all the time, but I never thought it was because of my parents. They definitely raised me in a unique way, but I think I didn't understand it totally. I was just like: "Well, that's nice. That's what they believe." And then I got a little less happy in high school. Nothing major. I just wasn't as happy as I remembered being when I was younger. Then last summer my parents offered to let me take the "Living the Dream" program at the institute. And I took it. Seriously, it was the best two months of my entire life. It was indescribable. I totally changed. See, it wasn't just two months; that's the other thing—it was the *best* two months of my life. It's altered the course of the rest of my life. That's pretty important. Now I would say I love what my parents teach. It's very important to me.

Father: Do you dialogue a lot?

Raun: Do you mean with my friends?

Mother: No, with your family or whoever you like to dialogue the most with. Do you use dialogues?

Raun: I do on occasion, but I don't regularly or often. I don't find that I even feel like doing them a lot. I just like to think my way through things.

Father: Sort of like self-dialogue?

Raun: Yes, actually. I do it when I'm alone and I'm bummed out about something. I definitely ask myself questions. It helps me figure things out and change my attitude. But, I don't normally, say, take an hour to walk with someone and dialogue in a formal way like staff here does with people who come.

Mother: Did you go through the typical teenage rebellion stage?

Raun: Actually, I thought about that recently because, over the years, I stop every so often and think about where I am. No, I never really did that. There are certain times when I'm less in the mood to hang around with my family than with my friends, but never like a teenage rebellion.

Mother: Do you think it comes from your parents being so non-judgmental and accepting of you, perhaps?

Raun: I would guess so. I never even had the urge.

Father: You go to a local high school in this area, right?

Raun: I used to go to the local public school, but it wasn't challenging at all. So now I go to prep school. That's why I'm dressed like this, by the way. This is the dress code: You have to wear a jacket and tie, except on days when it's eighty degrees, and then you don't have to wear a jacket. The girls have almost no dress code; they pretty much just have to look nice. But the guys have a strict dress code. It's pretty intense. We have school six days a week, including Saturdays.

Mother: Do you have a major that you—

Raun: Academically?

Mother: Yeah.

Raun: See, it's interesting. As far as subjects go, it keeps revolving for me. I have to say when I was younger, I tended to be more math and science oriented. As I got older, a little before high school, I switched toward being more interested in English, history, and foreign languages. The funny thing is, I'm consistent in all my subjects. My grades are very, very close, within points of each other in all my courses. So I can pretty much just pick what I want to study. But I'm not sure about a major. Right now, I don't know what I'll major in when I go to college.

Father: It's probably the number-one question seventeen-year-olds are asked besides "What are you going to do with my car tonight?" But, what are you going to do with your life?

Raun: I'm thinking about economics, but I don't know if I'll end up in the field of economics. Fifty percent of students switch their majors anyway. What I really love is writing. But I wouldn't want to major in creative writing. Although I love the subject, it's not a practical degree that I could use. But I still love doing it. Right now, actually, I'm writing a novel. Hopefully, it's going to turn out awesome. I'm hoping to publish it at some point.

Father: So I guess you have some of your father's natural talent.

Raun: Actually, that's weird you say that. I wouldn't call it "natural." When he was in high school, teachers said my Dad was not just a poor writer but a miserable one. They said he'd probably never make it through college because of his poor writing skills. He really wanted it and really worked at it. Shows you what motivation can do.

Mother: I've taken a lot of writing courses myself, and I love his writing. Have you read his books?

Raun: Most of them, yeah. I've really enjoyed them. I read *Son-Rise* for a book report in the fourth grade.

Mother: Did you get an A?

Raun: Yes, I did. [Everyone laughs.]

Father: What do you do for recreation? Do you have any interests?

Raun: Sportswise?

Father: Sportswise, or just what do you like to do with your spare time?

Raun: I play tennis. I love it. I compete on the tennis team. I also really love volleyball, but I can't play it in a serious environment because my school offers only girls' volleyball. Since I can't play on a team, I play with my friends. At the institute, we have a net, and we play a lot of volleyball all summer. I really enjoy playing. I like other sports, too—like football and baseball—but not to the extent where I would spend much time doing them.

Mother: What about music? I remember reading in one of the books something about you and music.

Raun: I was into instruments for a while: the cello, the viola, the vibraphone. I messed around, but I never ended up sticking with it. I lost interest after a while.

Mother: I think I read somewhere that you don't remember when you were autistic.

Raun: No, definitely not.

Mother: But you do remember working with Robertito and how that was?

Raun: Sure. I can remember that time with a lot of details. It's funny: I can remember certain specific things—really insignificant things—like the shape of the spoons in the Soto house. I remember being with him was a fun thing to do. For me, it wasn't like anything intensely significant at the time. I don't know if *significant* is the right word; I guess maybe the word's *serious*. It wasn't like, "Okay, I want to do something important here; better buckle down." It was more like, "Oh, I'm going to play with Robertito now. Cool." I was about six years old. I think at that age I might have had a slight recollection of being autistic, but I'm not sure. My farthest memories back are of my fourth birthday.

Mother: How about your adopted brothers and sisters? I know they had a lot of severe problems or challenges when your parents first adopted them; were you part of that process, too?

Raun: Yes. It was less intense or focused than, for instance, with Robertito. My two little brothers and my younger sister didn't have any severe disability, so we didn't sit and spend twelve hours a day working with them the way my parents worked with me. We helped them more informally. And, yes, I helped too.

Father: Are you involved in any other ways with The Option Institute? As far as programs go? I mean, this is great, coming and talking to us families the way you do, but how do you feel about the whole institute—just living in this environment and having all of these people around you?

Raun: Well, it's funny. I never really appreciated it 'til this summer. At first, it felt like: "Why are these people walking around? I don't know them very well." It was a question of my privacy, you know. But then, after a while, I didn't have a problem with it. But I didn't say, "Wow, this is a great place!" either.

Father: It's just where you live?

Raun: Yeah. "This is where I live. And I love my home." And then over this summer, after taking the eight-week program, I thought,

"God, it's too bad. I've been living here for almost eight years already; I never realized what I had here." It was a total realization. I stop a lot now, look around, and think, "This place is awesome."

Mother: Someday, you may even want to come back here. Maybe after you've made your own way in the world.

Raun: You never know. Bryn never thought she'd end up coming back.

Mother: She's great. Watching her work with our son—God, she's just right there. She's really amazing.

Raun: And she loves working with kids, too.

Mother: What's Thea doing?

Raun: Thea's a dancer. She graduated last June from NYU. She is incredible. I've never been like her, and I know very few people who are. Since she was eight or nine, she wanted to be a dancer. I've never seen such a driven person. It's been her total life's commitment. I mean, it's been her sole focus, and it's just incredible.

Mother: Is she in ballet or modern?

Raun: She's never really liked ballet. Oh, she can do it. Initially, she was really into jazz. Now, she's more into modern. She's also an awesome choreographer.

Father: When you hang out with your friends, what do you guys do? For instance, what do you guys talk about? Just normal seventeen-year-old stuff?

Raun: Yes. But it's varied. Just about everything you'd expect us to talk about.

Father: No celebrity status?

Raun: Oh no, I wouldn't want it. Oh God! No one cares, and that's great. Most of my friends know, and they don't care. It's totally irrelevant. Actually, the funniest thing just happened. My friend, just today, had to read a book and write a book report for history class. It's the policy at school, where every month you pick an outside reading book in every class and you read it and do a book report on it. It's pretty simple, right? So he decides to do Son-

235

Rise. He's one of my good friends. But he's a major procrastinator like me. He never ended up getting to it, and it was due today. So he kept saying, "Man, oh man, what do I do?" So I said, "Just get out a piece of paper," and I told him the whole story. He said, "Oh, man, that's awesome. Thanks. Hey, my buddy's a celebrity." Kind of kidding around, but it was really fun.

Mother: Do you have a girlfriend?

Raun: I had two—not at the same time. But now, no. I'm definitely going to remedy that situation as soon as possible. We have a big dance coming up.

Father: Do you do extracurricular activities—clubs or anything like that?

Raun: I write for the school newspaper. I also write for *The Dome,* which is the school's literary magazine. It publishes poetry and short stories. I love submitting my short stories. It's really, really cool. And I'm going to do that at college, too.

Mother: Do you have a favorite writer?

Raun: I have a couple. I really like Terry Brooks. And actually there are others. I don't know if you'd know them, but they are pretty well known. I like reading fantasy; that's my thing.

Mother: Do you like science fiction?

Raun: Science fiction tends to be more futuristic and technological. Fantasy is more like magic.

Mother: Like Tolkien?

Raun: Like Tolkien. I haven't read Tolkien yet. I want to save him for last. Everyone tells me once you read Tolkien, you're going to hate every other book you read after because his books are so good. I don't know if you've heard of Stephen R. Donaldson. He's great. And I like Pierce Anthony, too.

Father: What about music? Do you have any special music interests?

Raun: As far as groups I like?

Father: Groups you like. Or style or types of music.

Raun: I like rock music. I guess you'd call it pop rock. I could name some groups for you. I like Steve Winwood. He's very diverse. At the same time, I like Prince, Billy Joel, Peter Gabriel. I really like Phil Collins and Genesis a lot.

Father: I have at least one album of every one of those people you mentioned.

Mother: I have a question that you may have gotten before, but I read you have a near-genius I.Q., whatever that means. You probably never read that yourself. Do you think that autism has something to do with that quality?

Raun: Well, I have a theory. I think you *have* to be smart to be autistic. I know that sounds weird. But I don't think that's true in all cases, like, say, with Downs syndrome or something similar. I believe it takes a certain amount of intelligence to pull it off — to be autistic. So I don't know that I would say if I'm smart, it's because I was autistic. But I would say, maybe, that intelligence was there all the time. I'm not sure about that, but I've given it a lot of thought.

Mother: I like your answer because I've thought that same thing about autistic children and autistic adults. The circumstances they're under are probably very, very strange, and they're choosing this way to deal with the world. You'd have to be pretty intelligent to figure that out.

Raun: When I was very little, I figured out that I could stand a shoe box on its corner and spin it. I couldn't do that now. I don't know how I came up with such a move, but I managed it. I mean, it sounds pretty outrageous.

Mother: Maybe it's some kind of incredible way of focusing that autistic kids have that we lack in some way — because they do focus in on things.

Raun: And then they can tune out everything else.

Mother: Do you have anything to say to us as parents of an autistic child?

237

Raun: If I could say anything, and I don't know if you've heard this before or not, but if I could say anything, this is what I'd say. If you have a special child and you're going to work with the child, I think it's really important that every day—*every* day—when you're with that child, just think to yourself that you're doing it because *you* want to do it. Because *you* want to do it for you, rather than, say, for him. Like in an obligatory way. Like: "Oh yeah, he's in such a bad position. I want to help him out, so I'll work with him—for him—and maybe he'll get better"—again, all for him. I think it's better to do it for a different reason. I think it's important to do it if you're doing it for yourself.

Raun at Eighteen Years Old

Raun graduated from high school as a Cum Laude Society, High Honors student. The following fall, he entered one of the top universities in the country, his first choice among all of the colleges that accepted him.

Who would ever have imagined?

2

Our Family as Raun Nears Twenty

A year later, another challenge and learning for everyone in our family. Bryn, who had returned to the institute to teach and work with families, had been plagued for almost a decade with an increasingly debilitating heart condition. At twenty-five, she had continuous bouts of severe arrhythmia, which caused her heart to beat rapidly and ineffectively for ten, twenty, or sometimes forty hours at a time. During these periods, she experienced intense pains radiating throughout her chest and constantly felt as if she was suffocating. She could no longer walk up small hills on the property and had to climb stairs very slowly, often pausing midway to rest. Twice, in the last three years, she had almost died.

Both Samahria and I did dialogue sessions with Bryn, trying to help her cope with her condition. Sometimes, she could force the rhythm to correct itself. Most often, however, her crippling heart episodes ran their course over hours or days. Amazingly, using the sessions we did together to learn and grow, Bryn dealt with her fears and came to find peace, even happiness, while her condition worsened.

Finally, she decided to submit to an experimental operation in the hope of correcting the arrhythmia. Bryn spent days trying to negotiate with the possible complications of the procedure. The surgeon had explained that, although complications should not be expected, he had to inform her of all the risks. The three that echoed in her mind over and over again were loss of limb as a result of a blood clot, a stroke, or death by cardiac arrest. She prepared herself for life but opened herself to the possibility of not returning after the operation. In fact, we drew all the children together, including Bryn, for evening discussions so all could express concerns, feelings, and fears.

Two nights before the surgery, Bryn looked at all of us tear-fully. She wanted us to know that, while she was not afraid, she loved being alive, loved us, loving having all her brothers and sisters, loved working with families with special children, and loved William, a young man she intended to marry. While deciding to focus passionately on living, she wanted to face simultaneously the other possibility. We all decided to do a gratitude circle with her. Each of us spoke to Bryn from our hearts as she, in turn, spoke to us. And then she did something very much her style. She turned to Sage and said that if she died, Sage could have her earring collection. Ravi could have her stereo. Tayo would get her bicycle. Thea would get her clothes. William, Bryn's fiancé, would get her car. And to Raun, who had given her such inspiration, she offered her books—for they both shared a love of reading.

Before the operation, many of the institute's staff members gathered together with us in our main teaching room. They had come to support their friend, Bryn. I demystified the medical procedure for everyone by drawing diagrams of the heart and explaining the route and purpose of the many catheters which would be inserted into different arteries and then directed into the heart itself. The goal, if possible, would be to map the heart's electrophysiology and then zap the cells involved in the arrhythmia with radio waves. The time frame: up to eight hours.

Forty-five of us held hands in a giant circle that included Bryn. We did a meditation and visualization together, sharing with this very vivacious young woman all our hopes and our prayers. The group decided that, in our absence, they would come together the following day, just before the procedure began and again send their love and prayers to Bryn.

Raun, Thea, William, Samahria, and I accompanied our daughter to Boston for the operation. We waited in a small room provided by the hospital. About three hours into the operation, the surgeon came to tell us they had just aborted the procedure midway through after discovering that Bryn's condition emanated from the sinus node in her heart, an area deemed untouchable. In effect, her condition was inoperable.

Two hours later, we gathered around Bryn's bed in her hospital room. The doctor delivered the news to her sadly and apologetically. Bryn smiled at him and, though still groggy, said with her unique pizzazz, "Hey, Doc, I still have my arms and legs. I didn't have a stroke. And I am certainly not dead. Look at all the pluses." The physician smiled weakly. "Really," Bryn continued, "you don't have to be sad about this. We can always find something to be grateful for."

Samahria and I held our daughter's hands. She looked up at us and said, "God gave you an incurable son and look what you did. Now God gave me an incurable heart, and you just wait and see what I'm going to do." She paused thoughtfully, then whispered, "No guarantees, but, oh, for the joy of trying!"

We move through our life with Bryn one day at a time, grateful to have her with us. Even with limitations, she makes living a celebration. What a wonder to see her achieve a personal milestone she never thought she would live long enough to achieve: Bryn married William in a most intimate and heartfelt wedding ceremony.

*　　*　　*

Raun, at twenty, thrives in his third year at college. As he shared in the foreword of this book, he has a girlfriend, participates in his university's intercollegiate debating team, joined a coed fraternity, became politically active (working in the last presidential campaign), and chose biomedical ethics as his major area of study. Out of eight hundred applicants to undergraduate and graduate schools throughout the country, Raun was among fifty selected to design and teach courses to junior high school students in a special summer program. This year he became an exchange student at a university in Europe, where he will continue his education and pursue his interests by studying another country's health care system.

Thea, having just completed six months as a choreographer/artist-in-residence at a university, pursues dance with unending passion. Additionally, she explores her developing fascination with body mechanics and healing. Sage, Ravi, and Tayo grow older, wiser, and more loving as they, like Raun before them, move through high school and their challenging teenage years. Bryn, using attitude and willfulness, has gained more mastery over her heart-

241

beat, though she still negotiates with her arrhythmia. She continues as an Option Institute staff member and teacher; her love and insights are a powerful gift for all the families and special children she touches.

And Samahria and I—after thirty-three years, we're still madly in love

PART THREE

The Miracle Continues

1

Sharing the Vision

What began with one special child in a bathroom as a unique experiment in attitude and happiness has blossomed into a method of working with children from all over the world who face special challenges. Most important, this attitudinal and educational approach, which is profoundly accepting and respectful of each child's dignity, has facilitated deep-seated and lasting change in hundreds and hundreds of children and their families. This section will present stories of some of those parents, who, in spite of a barrage of pessimism and the dooming prognoses they encountered, challenged the universe with their love. Their courage and passionate desire to try for more for their children (and themselves) brought about changes that defied all expectations.

Both Samahria and I dedicate this section to these and many other courageous and dedicated folks and to all those inspired by their stories. For us, personally, and for all those they touch, these parents (some of whom have requested that their names be changed to protect the privacy of their child) remain a source of encouragement, inspiration, and hope—teaching us that we can build a bridge to our dreams, even if none existed previously, and cheer the children we love to walk across them.

Never, never, never could any of us be diminished for at least trying!

*   *   *

Every child is special and unique. However, some children, more unique than others, are labeled handicapped, retarded, and emotionally disturbed. Considered less than perfect in their appearance or ability to function, they become part of a vast subculture of little people viewed as more of a burden than a blessing. And yet, each one of these amazing human beings is someone's

245

beloved daughter, son, grandchild, niece, or nephew. Their difficulties might have arisen from genetic defects, birth traumas, diseases, accidents, or causes unknown. Their thinking processes and behavioral expressions can be unusual and baffling. While many specific physiological problems yield to proven medical remedies, the problems exhibited by these very special children usually defy easy resolution by means of traditional medical, psychiatric, psychological, and educational modalities.

Parents are forced to ride a confusing roller coaster of extensive diagnostic examinations and repeated intrusive testing of their innocent loved ones. Their sons and daughters will be defined by dreaded labels that are at once diverse and indistinct. As a result, many children will receive multiple diagnoses of which autism, pervasive developmental disorder, cerebral palsy, schizophrenia, severe developmental delays, retardation, aphasia, epilepsy, attention deficit disorder, hyperkinesia, and neurological anomalies are but a few. In effect, clinicians tell the parents what the parents already knew—their children are very, very different and have noticeable difficulties learning and socializing within their families and communities. However, the labels add a new ingredient to the problem— futurizing! In an effort to be helpful and realistic, diagnosticians, coming from the best of intentions, often deliver stark descriptions of children's conditions and predict dismal probable futures for them. Unfortunately, no useful gifts are given through such communications. In fact, as a result, these parents feel robbed of what they need most—hope!

Without hope, discomfort and desperation reign. As a result, these gloomy and frightening prognoses can create responses in both parents and professionals that set them adrift in a sea of contradictory treatments, sometimes leaving these children far more dysfunctional than they were originally.

A cognitively impaired toddler will be slapped in the face or sprayed repeatedly with a water gun as part of a behavioral conditioning program. A six-year-old little girl, fearful of human contact, will be further traumatized by strenuous and continuous hugging during a therapy session even as she screams to be released. An autistic adolescent will have his arms strapped tightly to the sides of a chair to prevent him from flapping his fingers harmlessly in front of his eyes, his behavior considered undesirable. A youngster with cerebral palsy, trying desperately to gain some control over her spastic arms and legs, will be forced to crawl for hours each day, held captive in a highly structured program, though she resists and makes attempts for personal autonomy.

In addition to such forced stimulation and attempts at behavioral programming, powerful medications, which impair neurological functioning, produce lethargy, and cause seizures as side effects, are all too frequently utilized. In some cases (though less commonly fashionable than in previous decades), children can be subjected to electric prods as part of aversion techniques.

Although these methods might seem extreme, major reputable hospitals and clinics, as well as residential and educational facilities worldwide, use them. These therapeutic and educational modalities do not reflect any underlying malicious intent on the part of helping professionals or participating parents. In fact, many doctors, therapists, educators, and parents have been at the mercy of prevailing conventional perspectives, which do not create effective, humane, respectful, and loving options to help special children. Only in recent years have we seen a small but growing number of professionals who have begun to acknowledge the merits of the fundamental teaching principles we have used for twenty years and to incorporate some of them (such as mirroring or imitating a child's behavior, using parents as active, participating resources, working one-on-one with the children, making aspects of programs home based, and embracing attitude as a meaningful component of the teaching/healing process) into their treatment programs. Some others have come to value and use a more gentle and loving hand in dealing with these special youngsters. Additionally, sensory training, dietary consciousness, and the like have had meaningful impact.

However, these changes, as welcomed as they may be, do not represent most of the services currently provided to children with developmental and cognitive disabilities and their families. Parents continue to share with us on a daily basis disheartening and distressing experiences they have had in trying to secure assistance for their children. They wanted so much more—hoped and prayed for so much more. Instead, these caring people found themselves lost in a sea of confusion—a confusion that claims two groups of victims: first, the children themselves; second, the parents, grandparents, concerned relatives, and friends who try with the best of intentions to make a difference, only to experience bitter disappointment and profound issues of guilt if they have subjected their special child to any one of the vast array of aversive methods. They follow the dictates of established procedures and lose part of themselves in the process.

*   *   *

Oftentimes, we have begun our work with families after the professionals and educators have turned away, leaving them with words like "hopeless," "incurable," and "irreversible," or with phrases like "You want too much," "Be realistic," or "Your child will never talk or walk or live a normal life" echoing in their ears. We feel honored always to share with them a perspective and process that has had a profound impact on our lives as well as on the lives of others we have tried to help.

For us, a loving, accepting, and nonjudgmental attitude is everything! Building on that foundation, we have watched people help themselves and their children be happier and make concrete, demonstrable changes in every aspect of their lives. Sometimes, we have watched others do what the experts had claimed to be impossible. Although medical science is just acknowledging the impact of attitude (for example, in studies of psychoneuroimmunology at major universities), we can bear witness ourselves to notable physiological improvements, startling behavioral changes, and dramatic jumps in cognitive ability brought about by programs in which a loving, accepting, and nonjudgmental attitude became the most significant facilitating vehicle. Dr. Carl Menninger of the noted Menninger Clinic once said, "Attitudes are the most important facts."

In some cases, even if dramatic healing did not come quickly to some of the adults or children we taught, a change of attitude so enhanced the quality of life for the families involved that we often did not know which benefit of the process to applaud more enthusiastically.

Happiness makes a profound difference in any healing and educational process! Love is useful in nitty-gritty, observable ways. And an accepting attitude can open our eyes to an endless array of possibilities normally hidden by the walls of our judgments.

*   *   *

I have highlighted just some of the significant perspectives that guided us in our work with our son, Raun, and that continue to guide us now in our work with others.

(1) **The special child is a rare gift for any family.** By being different, these unique little people give us a rare opportunity to access the most powerful, loving, and creative part of ourselves. If we hope to build bridges into their world and help guide them gently into our world, then we must become master architects in opening our hearts, inspiring their trust, and making our love tangible. In responding to the challenge they present, we come to experience the gift and blessing of our special children.

(2) **Parents are their children's most valuable resource!** The physician, the psychologist, and the educator no longer need dominate parents or dictate to them what treatment programs to follow. The professionals perform tests, conduct interviews, and, possibly, work with children for a few moments in time; then they move on. In contrast, the parents are committed for a lifetime, and that commitment and love make them the most valuable resource in their child's life. Parents can learn to be effective directors of any programs implemented for their children and to trust their own sensibilities and abiding dedication. The professionals can play a crucial role as assistants and helpers of families, supporting them and their children in the process.

(3) **The children become the ultimate teachers,** showing us through their actions and preferences how to help them. We follow their lead. Our children's wants and choices are *truly* respected.

(4) And, finally, **good fortune is an attitude, not an event!**

*   *   *

As I gathered data for this section of the book, I found myself touched so deeply by what moms and dads have shared with us about their special children and the Son-Rise Programs they implemented in their homes. Yes, Samahria and I, with the dedicated, enthusiastic Family Program staff of The Option Institute and Fellowship may have taught them the attitude and guided them through an educational program, but then these people took charge, went into the trenches, and made miracles an everyday event in their lives. Originally, I had intended to write about their families and children. Instead, I have chosen a very different path.

First, rather than skim the surface by presenting a hundred profiles, I have selected five from the vast reservoir I had considered presenting initially. I believe detailing these adventures in depth will give the reader a more moving and inspiring insight into the hundreds of other families represented by these portraits. Second, I enlisted the help of my daughter, Bryn, a Son-Rise Family Program teacher, for this project. As I listened to endless hours of recorded interviews she did with each family, in the evenings and over the weekends, I found myself mesmerized by what these people said. Some talked with great clarity. Others shared with disarming simplicity. All grabbed my heart and revealed the most intimate aspects of themselves—their fears, their failings, their transformations, and their triumphs. As I wiped tears from my eyes, I decided that instead of telling their stories through my words, I would let them speak directly to you, dear reader. What follows comes from those taped interviews.

2

In Tribute to Laura's Love

John, Laura, and Their Daughter, Julie

Bryn: John, tell me about Julie.

John: The first thing would be her eyes. Big, big, beautiful, almond-shaped eyes.

Bryn: Yes, they are beautiful; she is a beautiful child. When did you start to see that there was a difference in Julie?

John: Laura knew much earlier than I did, because she was with her all the time. She was the mother, and she would see other kids and how they behaved when she took Julie out anywhere. She'd say to me, "You know, Julie acts a little different. She's not talking." And I would always brush it off. "Give her time. Give her time." When I really started to become aware of the difference, Julie was over two years of age. When Julie was sixteen months old, she got some antibiotics because she was sick with a throat infection. From that point on, she was never the same.

Bryn: What do you mean?

John: Before the age of sixteen months, she was a totally, perfectly normal child. You know, she was growing up. She had started to say, "Mommy," "Daddy," "smile" and "get up" and "get down." When she was sick, she was listless and had glassy eyes. So then, when she got this heavy dose of antibiotics, I guess, in my opinion, that's what triggered this thing, even though every medical person disputes it. After she finished taking the medication, she was still listless, with that faraway look, and she never came back to normal. So we thought, "She's just still sick and getting over it." But she really never got over it. From then on, she just declined, until the second year, when it was just the bottom of the barrel.

251

Bryn: How did she act at that point?

John: Between two and three? Well, she was in one of two stages. Either she was in a constant state of motion, constantly running, running, running on tiptoes from room to room to room. Or, she was in a total deathlike state, just sitting in one spot, staring at nothing, totally oblivious.

Bryn: Did Julie have any specific ritualistic behaviors, or did she just stare?

John: Frequently, when she was running, she would hold a pencil or twig in her hand and just shake it back and forth beside her head. And watch it. Also, she kept bobbing her head to one side. Bob her head to the left and then back, to the left and back, like that. Julie kept shaking this twig or pencil or whatever she picked up. Then she'd have these ferocious, ferocious temper tantrums where she'd knock everything off the countertops and off the table. She'd start pulling things around and eventually drop to the floor in hysterics; once in a while she might even bite her arms and hands.

Bryn: That sounds very intense. How long did one of those tantrums last?

John: It would last until we practically just had to sit on her to stop her from hurting herself. As Julie drifted more and more into her own world, life became unbearable. The constant and fierce temper tantrums, the loud and endless crying and screaming, the destruction of our household possessions and—and the physical damage she did to herself. We lived on pins and needles. We became prisoners in our own home. Sometimes, on Sunday afternoons, I used to pray for Monday morning to arrive fast so that I could go back to work and breathe a sigh of relief. But, then, at work, I'd think of Laura and feel miserable and guilty. At least I had a break now. But what about her? After a weekend of horror, she now had a full week ahead of the same—and without my help.

   Let me just give you an example. One day Laura had to go to the mailbox to mail some letters. It was a beautiful, sunny day and she felt sorry for Julie just sitting in the house. She decided she would try and take her out for a walk in the sunshine. When

Laura mailed the letters and started to come home, Julie refused. She pulled and tugged and simply would not walk back. Finally, Laura had no choice but to pick her up and carry her home. Julie struggled furiously and slammed her elbow into Laura's eye, knocking out her contact lens, which fell into the dust and disappeared. Poor Laura! Her eye was in horrible pain. Julie struggled like a maniac. She put her down for a moment and looked for her contact lens. Not finding it, she picked Julie up, rushed home, and burst into tears. Laura was at her wit's end.

We both started to get really frightened. Julie was still very young, and we could barely manage her physically. What would we do in a few years when she was larger and more powerful?

Bryn: Was this the time when you first went for help?

John: We had been invited to a function at a friend's house. In fact, she's a doctor. And knowing how Julie was, as soon as we came in, I held her in my lap. I knew if I put her down, she'd go running from object to object. Run and pick up an object and drop it, run and pick up another object and do the same thing. I knew if I put her down, she would do this in my friend's house and maybe something much worse. So I just held her in my arms. People said, "Put her down." I said, "No, no, she's better off like this." They said, "Put her down. She'll be okay." I said, "I don't think so. Let me hold her." And, just as I knew she would, the moment I put her down, she ran to a table, picked something up, and threw it on the floor. I told Laura, "I'll just take her out and walk around with her. You stay and eat, and when it's time, you come out and I'll come in." So, when I took her out, Julie just ran to the gravel beside the driveway, picked up the stones, and threw them in the air. She'd run around, pick up more stones, and throw them, back and forth, back and forth. Totally oblivious of me. I'd talk to her, try to turn her. Nothing worked; she was just busy with the gravel. Finally, we brought her in, and my doctor friend took her in a room by herself. She tried to talk to her. She called her name a few times—no response. That was another thing with her hearing. She would act as if she absolutely could not hear. My friend clapped her hand, she called her name, nothing. So she started getting concerned. She said to me, "You know, it seems like she can't hear, and maybe you should take her for a hearing test."

So that's how it started. We took her to Children's Hospital. The first test with the doctors trying to put those things on Julie's ears was a total fiasco.

Bryn: She wouldn't let you?

John: Well, Laura went in the room with her; I waited outside. When they both came out, they looked as if they had been through World War III, sweating all over the place, very disheveled. It was total chaos. So we had to go back a second time, and they sedated her. And then they took the test; her hearing was normal.

So then we went to a psychologist and she said, "Yes, there's something very seriously wrong. Go for a neurological evaluation." We went for the neurological evaluation: MRIs, EEGs, whatever— you name it—skin tests, cultures, everything. And the results: Everything turned out to be normal physically. Finally the neurologists and other specialists said, "She's autistic."

Bryn: How did you and Laura feel when they said that?

John: Well, our world fell apart. From what we had read that meant she was totally, totally hopeless. That there was no hope for her. We were shattered. The psychologists said, "The best we can hope for is that maybe she will go on and learn a few minimal skills; maybe she can feed herself and maybe, one day, she'll be able to dress herself." It was very dismal. She didn't speak anymore. In fact, she had stopped talking a long time ago. She didn't understand even the simplest instructions like "come here" or "sit down." Julie was completely disconnected from her environment and from us. Everyone said, "Well, she can't fit in at home; she's got to go to a special school." So we put her in a special school. This was the worst point of our life. We felt we had no purpose in living. We were in that state for a time, until all of a sudden, just out of the clear blue sky, an event happened which opened the whole world.

Bryn: What was that?

John: We heard about The Option Institute and the Son-Rise Program. We used to go to a wonderful chiropractor, basically as a family, just on a preventive basis. We used to take the other two kids, but we never took Julie because of her condition. There was simply no way she could sit in an office. This one time, we had no baby-sitter, so we said, "Well, we have to take Julie. Let's take a chance." So we walked into the office—I was holding her in my arms—and, as soon as we entered the room, she went into an absolute panic. She started clawing me; my neck and face were bleeding. And then she started clawing herself; her face was bleeding. It was awful. Fran, the receptionist, saw what was happening and asked Laura, "What's the matter?" And at that point, all the accumulated pressure had just built up and Laura let loose and just started sobbing. Then she told her the story about Julie. And what Fran said was, "Look, Laura, bring her in. The doctor has had good luck with children like this. Just bring her in."

So we took her into his office. She paced furiously and screamed, trying to pull things off of the desk and tables. Finally, the doctor came in. He saw what she was doing, and right away he started doing something which, at that point, was incomprehensible to us. What he started doing was imitating her. She was running, he would run. She would touch something, he'd touch it. We thought, "What, he's nuts? He's crazy? What's he doing?" But it seemed to have an immediate effect. For example, she had absolutely zero eye contact; she'd never look at you. But we started seeing that out of the corner of her eye, she'd look at him for just a twinkling of a second. He had her attention in a definite but minimal way.

Finally, he went over to her, picked her up, and put her in his lap. He felt her whole spine while she struggled furiously. He said that he could start addressing the situation by at least adjusting her spine, which he felt caused a lot of pressure on her, and getting her back into alignment. We starting taking her to him three times a week. And Laura totally changed Julie's diet also; she took her off sugar and everything else like that. And we started to see her calm down just a little bit.

This went on for a few weeks. All of a sudden, one day the doctor came in and he gave this book, *Giant Steps*, to Laura, and said, "Read it. That's how I knew what to do with Julie. To imitate her actions." Laura had no time. I mean she was with the three kids, crazy at the time. So I took the book and started reading it. I found it so engrossing and beautiful that I finished the whole thing in one day. Then the doctor told us, "The book you really want to read is *Son Rise*." We got it, and we just dug into it. That was the first time that we started having hope. Up till then, we had read Bruno Bettelheim and many other books on autism and childhood developmental problems that spoke about how dismal these conditions are. This was the first thing we saw that said, "There is hope; somebody has done it."

Bryn: Is that when you decided to come to the institute?

John: When we got the book, we read it, and using the book, Laura started to do the impossible. To me, it was as if like she were climbing Mt. Everest alone. She said, "Well, Samahria has done it; I'm going to give it a shot." So using the book as a guide, she started doing what we thought the Son-Rise Method was—basically trying to be very exaggerated, following Julie all around. But we didn't have any concept of the playroom or anything; it was just, wherever Julie ran, run behind her. It was some sight. Julie would be running a hundred miles an hour. Laura would be running behind her. And Tommy was about a year old; he would be on all fours crawling behind them. From room to room.

We started doing that, and then again, we spoke to the chiropractor; and he said, "Well, you know, you can only do so much from using a book." At that point, we didn't know there was an Option Institute or anything like that. But the chiropractor said that he believed Barry and Samahria Kaufman had some kind of place somewhere and that they trained parents.

Finally, he found some Option Institute literature, and that's how it all started. One morning, very nervously, I called up The Option Institute and a wonderful voice said, "Hi, can I help you?"

What really drove us to decide was that one day while I was at work, Laura called up, hysterical. She said, "You've got to come home immediately." I said, "What's the matter?" She said, "Well, Tommy's all beaten up." So I came home, and I saw that the house was in a shambles. Laura was there with Tommy in her lap; his face was all scratched up and bleeding. Tina, our oldest child, was there crying, and Julie was on the porch with a devilish look on her face. She had done it all! Laura said, "Look, at this point, I don't care. Either we go to The Option Institute, or it's the end of this family." So I said, "Okay." Then I called and made an appointment.

Bryn: It sounds as if things were very difficult for you at that time. When you were finally able to come, did things change?

John: Before we came to the institute, Laura was doing a home program for five hours a day based on the books, including *A Miracle to Believe In*. This went on for almost four months. Julie had started showing good changes. Now she would say a few words, sort of repeat them, not really talking. There was a very small, but substantial change in Julie during those four months that Laura did the program by herself.

Then, when we came to the institute, what really was totally new to us was this concept of a special, amazing room and the idea of using volunteers. At first, that totally floored us.

Bryn: Why?

John: For instance, take this idea that Julie would be in a room all day long. At first we thought "This is not right for her. How is she going to learn anything? How is she going to socialize?"

We would have to go get volunteers to help us. That was really a zinger for us because we were not the type of people to go seeking volunteers. We were very private people. We hesitated to ask anybody for anything. So now to go out and tell people to come in and help us with our autistic daughter seemed impossible to do.

Bryn: What changed for you that enabled you to do it?

John: The whole thing changed. We changed. That was the miracle. We changed in that week. As each day went along, as your father would say, the miracle happened, and inwardly, through what the institute taught, we changed. We changed our beliefs about seeking help, about people helping us, about what this all meant.

Bryn: All in one week! You really embraced what was shared with you. What were some specific things that you changed about yourselves, you, and Laura?

John: Well, I think fundamentally it was the premise about happiness and unhappiness. They are not feelings that happen to you; you create them for yourself, and if you want to be unhappy about something, well, that's the choice you're making. But if you want to be happy, you can be happy. So we basically changed our belief about what Julie's condition meant. Originally, we thought autism was bad, a catastrophe for Julie and our family. Once we changed that belief, we were much more comfortable asking people to help us.

Bryn: So because you no longer saw her autism as terrible, you were able to see everything differently. That's extraordinary. What would you say were the significant ideas and actions that you felt helped turn the tide for Julie?

John: For me—now I'm speaking just for me—the biggest thing was that, before I came to The Option Institute, my feeling was, "Oh, she's an autistic child. She's a special child. She has to be worked with in a very special way that only the experts know. Only these teachers know and special ed personnel know, who have multiple masters degrees and so on and so forth. I'm nobody. I'm just an accountant. I don't know about these things." So I was in a lot of turmoil about even going to the institute. "They'll see I'm a fool; I don't know how to do any of this stuff, and then I'll just make a fool of myself. Even when I go there, I won't learn how to do any of whatever is to be learned because I'm not a special ed person." The most wonderful thing that happened to me when I was there was seeing how easy it was to do what needed to be done for Julie. That was basically quite a departure for me, having been a serious, very methodical, organized, adultish sort of person. From that, changing into being childish, a crazy joker, you know, in order to be with my daughter. When I saw what was needed, I said, "This, I certainly can do."

Bryn: John, you are truly a very special father.

John: I love my daughter very much.

Bryn: That's so obvious in the way that you talk about her. What was it that you learned about working with Julie?

John: Well, I found out that I—and, of course, everybody else—totally had to change my conception of how to work with her and how to be with her, in the sense that she was the teacher now. That was a huge difference. Previously I thought, "I have to teach her." Now I realize I don't have to teach her. All I have to do is motivate her and connect with her. That was my guiding thought throughout the four years we did a Son-Rise Program with her. "I don't have to sit and teach her anything. All I have to do is just encourage her to love me, and she'll want to be with me and, perhaps, learn more. That's all I have to do. If she just loves to be with me, she'll want to do things with me."

Bryn: What a delightful realization for you! Were there also changes between you and Laura?

John: Absolutely. We learned basically how to be more accepting individuals, of ourselves and of each other. And we became more accepting with our other children. What we learned about how to be with Julie has also proved enormously successful not only with our other two children but also with our newest arrival, Patty.

I used to have the situation, before the program, where I'd get up in the morning at six o'clock and be at work at seven o'clock and by nine o'clock have a splitting headache. Now I would get up at six o'clock, work with Julie till ten o'clock, go to work on Cloud Nine, and then smile at all the people who had headaches there. I'd just say, "Hey, I am having a wonderful time!" I just decided that, and it was true.

Bryn: What a transformation! I'd bet everyone always wanted to know your secret. You could have always told them, "I'm lucky; I have an autistic child."

When you finished learning here at the institute, did you put Julie back in the special school or did you do the program full-time?

John: Initially, we took her out of the school just to come to the institute. We didn't tell them our plans. So when we came back the next week, we had to go for some discussions with the staff. The teachers asked, "What did you do last week? Julie seems so happy—so different. What did you do?" Then we told them. Some other teachers said, "Oh, yeah, I've heard about it. I've read *Son-Rise.*"

At that point, we kept her in the special school because we didn't have the program fully set up. She went to school only in the mornings. Every afternoon, Laura would work with her for four hours. On Saturday and Sunday, between us, we would do full days.

In April, about two months after we came back, we had about twenty volunteers, not bad for the Midwest. She was still going to school in the mornings, and the rest of the day, from twelve o'clock on till about six o'clock, she'd have volunteers or Laura and I would work with her. This lasted until June. Then came the second big turning point. Her school finished at the end of June, and the summer session did not start for a week. So we had this one week and now we said, "What are we going to do with her for this one week?" And then I guess I really examined myself and I came to the conclusion, "Well, if there's nobody else to work with her, I'll just have to do it." So I told the people at work that I'd be coming in only from twelve o'clock to four o'clock instead of eight o'clock to four o'clock. So that started the next saga.

We worked with her the first day, then the second. On the third or fourth day, I started seeing really big changes in her, sensed that she seemed happier—relaxed and more connected. I could tell right away. She had much more eye contact, and I could see she was really developing a bond with me, for the first time. I spoke to Laura. And all the volunteers started saying, "She seems so different." It dawned on us that this change happened because we were doing what Bears said was important. "You've got to keep her in a consistent, supportive, nonjudgmental environment. The program won't be effective if she gets conflicting signals," he'd said. And this was the first time we had been able to provide such an environment for her for the full day—every day!

That week was a Godsend. Because if we hadn't seen the full meaning of what you had taught us, really, I think her future would have been very different. I mean, she would have been back in school. Then came the next question, what about the summer? You see, I had been planning to do this just for this one week.

Bryn: So what did you do then?

John: I said, "Really, she is changing. What's going to happen next week when she goes back to school? We finally gave her a consistent environment, the total Son-Rise Program, twelve hours a day, and it's not going to be the same in school." That's when I really examined myself and I came to the next stage of evolution in this process. I said, "I have to change my life. I have to do the whole summer now." I thought, "We'll do the summer, and in September, of course, there is no choice. She's got to go back to school."

I talked to my people at work and took time off. I figured if I worked half days the whole summer, I could still make it. Then we called the school and told them that Julie was not going to come back for the summer session; she would be back in the fall. And in that summer, fantastic things happened.

Bryn: Like what?

John: All her aggressiveness totally stopped. Julie became cooperative, involved, and very interactive. A lot of exciting things happened that summer. She just started progressing. We started teaching her words. Initially, when we started, we'd say, "What's this?" She'd be silent or she'd say, "What's this?" back to us. But Laura made a big breakthrough with her and taught her that when someone says, "What's this?" you are supposed to answer. And that was a phenomenal breakthrough. So she started learning. We'd say, "What's this?" She'd say, "Dog." Julie connected everything more and more.

Also, Laura changed. She seemed so much more solid now, more energetic—and so excited to be working with her daughter. We had hope for the first time. What a difference! And Laura always went the extra mile with Julie, trying to give her extra comfort and love. At night, after the session, she'd lie down in bed with her and sing her a song to help her fall asleep. At first, Julie ignored her and just stared at the ceiling. Laura would hug her and caress her anyway as she sang. After many weeks, Julie started to respond by taking her mom's hand. And then, this one time when Laura rolled over in the bed, Julie, thinking she was leaving, hugged her and clung to her. Laura's eyes filled with tears. Happy tears. Julie showed feelings we thought she would never, ever express.

Bryn: I can imagine that must have been such an exhilarating time, with so many changes. You put your heart and soul into it, and look what you got back! Did you then put Julie back in school and go back to work when September came?

John: Well, I did a lot of soul-searching at the end of August. "Such fantastic progress now; how can she go back to school now?" Then I said, "But this is the end. I won't have a job anymore if I keep this up." But when I asked myself, "What is more important? My job or Julie?" The choice I made was Julie. Julie is more important. I was very nervous because I was thinking, "If I do this, I will have no job." But once I decided, "This is it. I'm going to do this with her," I just became so calm and relaxed. I said, "Well, if this is what I'm supposed to do, this is what I am supposed to do." And with this determination, I went back and talked to my boss. I said, "Look, starting next month, this is going to be my schedule." And he surprised me and said, "Sure, we'll work it out John; you go help your daughter, and we'll work around it."

Bryn: Just imagine! When you totally let go of needing things to happen in a certain way, you get so much more of what you want.

John: Yes. Now, instead of going to work eight o'clock to four o'clock, what I did was go to work with Julie from six to ten and go to my job at ten-thirty. And then I'd work from ten-thirty to six and take just half an hour for lunch. Now, don't forget, I had a second job. I've had a second job all this time in the evening. With three children, it's impossible to make ends meet. Then I spoke to the superintendent at my second job as well. I explained the same thing to him. I told him, "If you want me, I'm going to come from seven to eleven o'clock." And lo and behold, he made sure the building was open for me.

Bryn: So all this time, then, you worked with Julie from six to ten o'clock in the morning, then ten-thirty to six at one job, and then seven till eleven o'clock at night at another?

John: That's right.

Bryn: John, you are extraordinary! So many people would say, "Wow, that's a lot of energy." To what would you attribute your ability to keep that up for so long?

John: I loved working with Julie. Between Laura, the volunteers, and me, we kept up a full-time program for four wonderful years.

Bryn: So you never put Julie back in school, and you did your own home program. How was the experience?

John: We had done the program for a year, and it was going very well and we loved it. Julie was improving beautifully. Then, in the second year, we started to think more and more that we could really improve the program, but we weren't really sure how. We felt we needed more training. We thought we could become even happier and learn to make the program stronger than it was. So that was our motivation, and it brought us back to the institute for a second time.

Bryn: What was the second experience here like?

John: The most crucial thing we learned the second time was that, even though we had done the program beautifully and everybody had done a great job, what we had not done well or fully was to really observe sessions and give ongoing feedback to all the volunteers in the program. During that week, we really learned to trust ourselves and, as a result, be good trainers for everyone else. I always knew Laura was a healthy, strong person with iron determination. And then, when we were in a meeting at the institute and I said, "How are we going to do all this feedback training?" and then very quietly, Laura said, "I'm going to do it." I looked at her and I said, "How are you going to do it?" She said, "I'm going to do it."

When we went back home, we really did it. We trained all the volunteers. We observed every single volunteer working with Julie. We did this consistently for a month or so, and dramatic new things started happening.

Bryn: Like what?

John: Changes in Julie. She was progressing more and more. A few months after that, we had our group meeting with everyone in the program—a dynamic group meeting. From our observations of the volunteers, we had found out exactly what was lacking in the program. The key thing we found was that if Julie was fine and in a good mood, everyone else was, along with her. But once Julie turned off to them and became unresponsive, they really didn't know how to get her back. And that was it. We had identified the problem. Then we videotaped me working with her, just at such a time. We went over the video and showed them over and over again what to do—always to go with her, not to be afraid if she was withdrawn—and then everybody started acting on that. That was in April, and by the following June, she had changed so much. We started thinking, "Hey, maybe she can go to school for a few hours a day; she's talking and interacting easily with everyone."

So the first thing we had to do was again have her physically examined. My friend, the doctor, said, "Bring her down, and let's get this done." Now don't forget, Julie has been working in the room with us this whole time — for years. So we wondered, "Is she really going to cooperate?" And when we were there, we were so shocked. This was the most shocking experience of our lives. Julie went into the office, and she acted almost like a totally normal little girl. We thought we'd have to tell her everything she had to do, and she would probably not do it or refuse to do it. So we went into the examination room, and the doctor, not knowing anything about Julie's background, told her, "Julie, sit down." And Julie sat down. Then, the woman said, "Okay, Julie, now look here," and Julie looked up. And then she said, "I'm going to point here, and you tell me what this is." And she pointed to an apple and Julie said, "Apple." Then, she pointed to a house. Julie said, "House."

Bryn: Was your mouth hanging open?

John: Laura and I were looking at each other; I could feel myself shaking with excitement. I said, "Oh my God, let's not say anything to spoil this." She went through the whole examination beautifully, and then we agreed at that point, "She can do it." So then we put her in school again, part-time. Pre-kindergarten. We wanted to test the waters. So we put her in pre-k two times a week for half a day.

She responded so well that you should see the report card she got at the end of the year! In her second year at the school, the teacher said, "She's an outstanding student — so lovable and so charming and all the kids love her." Julie was talking up a storm — thousands of sentences — and she had no trace of her autism — none at all. They all loved her. She was a very popular kid.

Bryn: It sounds so exciting. Tell me, what are some wonderful times that you have with Julie now that you didn't anticipate you would have?

John: Any time that I come home and see her and she gives me that big smile. She comes over and she hugs me and holds me very tight. I never thought I would see that. She's so lovable. I never thought I would see that. She's more lovable than most other kids.

Bryn: Raun was the same way. John, are there special things that she's said to you, that touched you?

John: Yes. She has a terrific sense of humor. She's so funny. One day she's holding this tooth in her hand and shaking it; she knows about teeth coming out and tooth fairies and all that kind of thing. So, while she's shaking this tooth, I said to her, "Julie, what are you doing?" And she said, "Oh, I'm making the tooth fairy work real hard. This is the third time she's got to come for me."

Bryn: [Laughs.] Oh, what a kid! You know, one of the volunteers in your program who I was giving feedback to—I think it was Charlotte—told me how Julie would come to her house and Charlotte would fast forward through all of the Cinderella videos that they would watch together. She did it to get to what she thought would be the good parts that Julie would like. Then, Julie came over again recently and said she wanted to watch a Cinderella video. This time, she said to Charlotte, "Listen. You don't have to fast forward this time. I'm older now, and I'd like to see the whole thing." I thought that was hysterical.

John: That's how she is, very honest. Another thing I never thought that I would see is her playing with Tommy. The way she and Tommy used to be was frightening. If Tommy would come into her room, she would just go crazy and scream. He's two years younger. So for a long time, years, they were apart from each other. And now, it's so beautiful; they're the best of pals.

Bryn: Really? What do they do together now?

John: Oh, you'd be amazed. I'll come home, or I'll be there, and all of a sudden, I'll hear these two little voices playing and I'll go in and I'll peek, and there they are, the two of them playing make-believe, for about three hours at a stretch. I mean, total interaction, nonstop. "Tommy, now let's do this." "No, Julie, I want to do this." "You did that already. I want to do this." "Okay, I want to play with my men." Tommy loves his men. And Julie says, "No, we played with men already. I want to play with Barbie dolls." Then they'll say, "Okay, let's make a new game: Men and Barbie dolls." That's their favorite game.

  And she's so funny. The things she says. She told me the other day, "When I grow up, I'm definitely getting married." So I said, "Sure. First you're going to do your elementary school; then you're going to do high school; then you're going to do college; then maybe you'll study a little more; and then, after that, you'll go get married." She said, "Oh yeah, but I can't do any of it until I first fall in love." That's Julie, at seven years old. First you have to fall in love.

Bryn: She's so incredibly special. And, you're such a powerful example of what parents can do.

John: Bryn, I believe the single most important factor that contributed to the success of our program was Laura. Without a doubt! You see, even though I worked with Julie those four hours daily, it was nothing compared to what Laura did. Once my shift was over, I left the house and went to work for the next twelve hours. During that time, Laura had to run a very busy household, take care of two other children, manage, observe, and train thirty-five volunteers and then do three- to four-hour sessions with Julie herself. How she managed to do this day after day, in sickness and health, is beyond my comprehension. It was a monumental job, and Laura rose to the occasion and gave it her all. She was the driving force behind the program. The real power.

Bryn: What do you mean by that?

John: She motivated all of us. Cheered us on! She also had this special skill to know what to do next in the program, like when Julie would be ready to learn something new—Laura would seize the opportunity, then teach me and all the volunteers how to do it. The challenge of running a Son-Rise Program had turned Laura into a super organizer. You should have seen her. Julie was in her playroom doing her sessions thirteen hours a day, seven days a week, no matter what. If a volunteer got sick or there was an emergency, Laura would keep the program going. Nothing would stop her. Nothing. For me, Julie's incredible journey will always remain a tribute to Laura's endless and special love.

Bryn: John, you take my breath away. I am so awed with how much you love not only Julie and your other children, but by your deep love and appreciation for Laura.

266

John: What we learned at the institute gave us the attitude, the understanding, the tools, and even the motivation to help Julie. But Laura gave our program its heart! And the volunteers, every one of them, helped make all this possible. They were just regular, normal people offering time, love, and acceptance to our daughter. You cannot imagine how strong the bond became between them and Julie.

Bryn: I hear you. I really hear you. Many parents share with us how their volunteers became a powerful extended family. John, after having put all this energy into your program, how do you feel about having done it?

John: I feel great, because it really changed my life. It changed Laura's life, and all of ours, for the better. And in a way, I really miss it. Like, "Wow, it's over now, that part of our lives." Because I used to love being in the room with Julie. It was a great process of self-discovery for me. Besides finding Julie, I found myself in that room. And that was a real blessing for me. Through this process that you teach, I found that everything I want in life is really within me. All I have to do is seek. I just feel so thankful that this came into our lives: that Julie came into our lives and that The Option Institute came into our lives. We really found ourselves and became happier, better people for it.

*   *   *

The following is a letter written by Julie's mom, Laura, to Samahria on Samahria's fiftieth birthday:

Dearest Samahria,

This month it will be exactly four years since we first spoke to you on the telephone. We were scared and sad, but somehow, your loving and joyful voice convinced us to come to Sheffield to do the Son-Rise Program with our daughter Julie. And since then our lives have changed forever.

We remember when we first met you and you taught us how to work with our Julie. We clung to your every word, and we'll never forget what you told us. You said that you knew that we had what it took to do a great program, and you were positive that our program would be a success. Well, inspired by your confidence and trust in us, we returned home to one great adventure.

The last four years have been the most magical years of our lives. Earlier this year, John was alone in the kitchen one morning making his breakfast. Suddenly he heard footsteps and then a little voice saying, "Daddy! Daddy! I am so excited. Today is the day of my dance recital." He looked up and saw Julie walk into the room with a radiant smile on her face. She looked him straight in the eyes, held his neck, and hugged him tightly.

"Daddy, it's going to be the real thing today," she said. "No rehearsal. I can't wait for my recital! All my friends are going to be there. Are you going to be there with Mommy?" she asked. "Of course, darling," he replied, "I wouldn't miss it for the world." "I am not shy, Daddy, I know all my steps, and I am going to be a good dancer like Mommy and Tina," said Julie.

With that, Julie ran upstairs. John walked down the stairs, turned on the light, and sat down on the chair in Julie's playroom. He was filled with an overwhelming feeling of gratefulness to God. He had blessed us with such a precious and wonderful gift, our Julie. And then, he blessed us further by giving us the means to discover her—you, Samahria; Bears; and your Option Institute. And not only did we discover her, but we also discovered ourselves. And in the process, we achieved great joy, tranquillity, and inner happiness in our lives. What more could we ask for?

John looked around the room. It was some months back that he had stopped doing his morning sessions with Julie, as we started the process of integrating her upstairs with the rest of the family. Before that we had spent about four hours each day with her in this room. For both of us, our time with Julie was an extraordinary process of discovery. While we have now moved to a wonderful and exciting life with Julie upstairs, we do, sometimes, feel nostalgic about our days down in the room with her. We smile when we remember your words, Samahria: "You are not going to be down there forever." It seems strange, but we feel that, in a way, we have not been down there long enough.

Samahria, the love, affection, and gratitude we all feel for you and everyone else at the institute will remain forever in our hearts.

Have a very happy birthday!
Love, Laura, John, Tina, Julie, and Tommy

3

Ruthie—Free at Last!

Carolyn and Her Daughter, Ruthie

Bryn: Before we talk about Ruthie, I want to ask, aren't you involved in teaching special children?

Carolyn: Yes, I'm a special education teacher; I teach preschool to kids with multiple disabilities. One- and two-year-olds.

Bryn: That must be fun. Now, tell me all about Ruthie. First, what was her diagnosis?

Carolyn: The most recent one—before we came to the institute—was schizophrenia. Prior to that, she was diagnosed as having Pervasive Developmental Disorder (PDD) and mental retardation. A diagnosis of autism was considered. But since I adopted Ruth when she was fourteen, we don't have any information about her early years, which is necessary for that diagnosis.

Bryn: Did she live with you before you formally adopted her?

Carolyn: Yes. She was ten when she came to live with me. I actually adopted her over three and a half years later.

Bryn: Tell me, how did Ruthie come into your life?

Carolyn: Well, she was in my class. I taught elementary-age children with multiple disabilities, ages six to fourteen at the time. Ruth never lived with her parents. She has Treacher Collins syndrome. It involves severe facial anomalies. She has downturned eyes, very little cheekbone, no chin, no external ears, no ear canals. She didn't have a cleft palate, but she had a high palate, and was very difficult to feed. Initially, she had to be fed through a stomach tube. Ruth's mother couldn't handle her. So Ruth went from the hospital where she was born to an institution, where she stayed for two years. This child was born without ears, but the people caring for her didn't bother to put hearing aids on her because they didn't really expect her to live.

Bryn: Does she hear now with hearing aids?

Carolyn: She can hear with oscillating hearing aids—bone oscillators.

Bryn: So for all intents and purposes, at that time, she was deaf.

Carolyn: She was deaf for two years. Ruthie also couldn't see. Her eyes are downward slanting from Treacher Collins syndrome. They would look in opposite directions. They did not focus together. Finally, they put a hearing aid on her when she went into foster care at the age of two and got glasses for her when she was three years old.

Most kids with Treacher Collins syndrome have normal intelligence, but some are slightly retarded. Doctors think it's because the skull is sometimes small and the brain doesn't have room to grow. One of the doctors suggested that Ruthie was malnourished as a very young girl and might not have had enough nourishing food for her brain to grow. So it has been suggested that she had normal intelligence and, because of deprivation, was unable to use it.

She was also tube-fed 'til she was three.

Bryn: Because of her mouth?

Carolyn: It was because her doctors did not feel she was getting enough nourishment. Essentially, this kid was sensorially deprived for two to three years—big time. And she was a very strange little girl. Later, when she was older, she was placed in one of my classes because of her "acting out" behavior. Bryn, Ruth acted totally wild. She tantrumed violently. I had heard many Ruthie tales; she threw the teacher's telephone across the room, threw the wastebasket across the room; knocked chairs over. And that's not the half of it! She'd pull curtains off the wall, throw her hearing aid, then her eyeglasses, her shoes—then hit the floor with her body and scream!

She was in the residential unit of the local medical center in the children's psychiatric ward for one semester, and, when she came out, the school system had a hard time finding an appropriate placement for her.

Bryn: She was put in a psych ward? Why?

Carolyn: Well, she went into a multihandicapped class when she was very young. And she did well, but there was a very small pupil-teacher ratio, and she got a lot of attention. They decided that her intelligence was probably higher than that of the other children in that class, so they placed her in a program for children with educable mental handicaps. Unfortunately, she went from a class where she received a lot of individual attention to a class with about ten kids and one teacher, where she was expected to sit down and do seat work. It was too fast a transition for her. She couldn't handle it, and she figured out that if she tantrumed, they would send her home to her foster parents. One time, she had this rip-roaring tantrum. In the middle of the tantrum, she stopped and said, "Well, aren't you going to send me home?" "No," I replied. "Well, that's what they did at my other school. At my other school, when I did this, they sent me home." What she said wasn't this clear; her language wasn't this clear, but I understood. "Well," I said, "that's not what we do here. Here, you stay until the bus comes and you can either have a tantrum or you can work with the other kids." She was so surprised.

Bryn: That was when you first started teaching her?

Carolyn: Yes, that was the first year that I had her in my class. At the end of the year, I asked to adopt her. She had learned that tantruming was a useful way of coping. She did not have good language skills. She wasn't really good at putting into words what she wanted to say and she had difficulty understanding how to ask for things. I remember, the first year we had her, how she used to throw herself on the floor and thrash around when she wanted something at snack time. We tried to teach her how to say, "I want a cookie," instead of tantruming on the floor to indicate she wanted a cookie.

One time, after I had adopted her, we were getting ready to go on a picnic. When I realized the weather could change, I asked her what else she might want to do if we couldn't go to the park; maybe we could discuss alternatives. She shook her head and said, "If what I want doesn't happen, I scream, and then I get it." And she was dead serious. This was her way of coping. It was just incredible.

But, anyway, she came into my class because my team teacher and I had taken a number of children who had problems in other classes; we frankly enjoyed that kind of challenge, which everyone knew, so my supervisor suggested that we put her in our TMH (Trainable Mentally Handicapped) class, which we did.

Bryn: What happened when she came into your class?

Carolyn: Well, we had two classes; in the morning I had the kids with trainable mental handicaps, kids who are supposed to have IQs below fifty, and in the afternoon I worked with kids with multihandicaps. And the poor kid, she was so scared. When Ruthie came, she was supposed to be in the TMH class. And truly, her intelligence level was higher than that, but again, counselors had placed her that way because of her behavior. But she was so scared of these children that walked and talked that she couldn't stay in that class. She would peek around the corner of the door and look at the other children. She just didn't know how to cope with them. She didn't have social skills; she didn't seem to know how to interact with other children or how to get what she wanted. She moved into the other class for the kids with multiple disabilities because they didn't scare her.

At the end of that year, I asked to adopt her.

Bryn: After all that you just told me, I wonder, why did you want to adopt her?

Carolyn: I don't really know. I know that sounds ridiculous.

Bryn: Were you wanting to adopt a child at that point?

Carolyn: Oh, I had thought about it. I'm single. I've never married, and I thought that one day I might want to adopt a child. And I had watched a program called "A Waiting Child" that we have on TV here.

Bryn: I've seen those programs. They present children and try to interest viewers in adopting them.

Carolyn: Uh-hmm. And I had watched that program and thought, "You know, it might be fun to do this some day." But the funny thing is, about a month before I asked to adopt Ruth, I decided I wasn't going to adopt a child after all. I thought, "I'm getting too old."

Bryn: How old were you at the time?

Carolyn: Thirty-three. I thought, "I've thought about getting a kid. I'm probably not going to find one. They're not keen on single parents anyway, so I probably need to get this little fantasy out of my head. And it's probably more work than I really want to go through, anyway, because it would really curtail my freedom." About a month after that, I was talking to Ruthie's foster mother, and she remarked, "Ruth is unadoptable." I asked, "Why is that?" She said, "Well, it's because of her appearance. She's considered unadoptable because people want pretty kids, not children with downturned eyes, a funny mouth, and no chin or ears."

Bryn: Did you agree?

Carolyn: No. In talking to her foster mother, I said I didn't understand why she would be unadoptable because that stuff is such a minor thing; I can understand how her behaviors might make her unadoptable, but not her facial appearance. And she said, "Well, would you adopt her?" I said, "Oh sure," just thinking that this was a hypothetical question. And she said, "No, I'm serious. Would you adopt her?" Then I heard myself say, "Well, yeah, I'd love to adopt her." I actually had thought about it for several months, and I thought, "Here is this available child." There are certain kids who I have worked with that I am very attracted to and really enjoy being with more than others. And she was one of these kids who really turned me on. I wanted more for her. I saw a special soul behind that strange face and those tantrums.

Bryn: What did you see?

Carolyn: I honestly don't know how to explain it to you, Bryn. I truly enjoyed being with her.

Bryn: In what way? Could you give me an example of what you mean?

Carolyn: I remember when we went to the Special Olympics. My team teacher didn't really want to take Ruthie because she always got in a lot of trouble. "Are you sure you want to do this?" she asked. And I said, "Yes." When we first got there, the kids started screaming. It was total chaos. Ruth was scared; she started screaming

273

bloody murder. She was in the stands with my team teacher. So I went over to the stands and pulled her over the stands with me and took her all around the field. Maybe it's because I felt like I was doing something neat for her. I don't know. I just loved her. I thought she was one of the neatest things that had come around in a long time, and I got a kick out of being with her. She was great fun for me. I remember how even before I considered adopting her, I had her over on her birthday just because I wanted to. I thought it would be fun. So, from all those experiences I knew that I was very attracted to her in a way that I'm not attracted to every kid that comes through my class. But exactly what it was—it was love, though I can't tell you what triggered it. It was love.

Bryn: What were the responses of the people in your life when you decided to adopt her?

Carolyn: Beth, my roommate, cried. She is the one who was team-teaching with me. She's a dear friend, and I had known her since we were in college. We were living together at the time.

Bryn: Why did she cry?

Carolyn: She didn't want me to do it. She felt that she did not want to live with Ruth because Ruth was a ton of trouble. And she felt that Ruth would take up a lot of my time and that I would not be able to do the fun things that we usually did together. She just didn't want to deal with everything that Ruth would do at home, in addition to dealing with her at school. But I did. I offered to move out, and she said, "No, if you decided to adopt her, you can still live here, but do be aware that I'm not going to baby-sit." For the first year, she didn't.

My mom was very supportive. She did say, exactly as Beth had said, "Now, don't expect me to baby-sit her; I can't handle this." Most of my friends did not encourage it. My mother was the only one who was really encouraging.

Bryn: I am so impressed with you. Even knowing that you had no support, you still followed through with what you wanted; Ruthie is so lucky to have you.

What was the "prognosis" for Ruth at that point?

Carolyn: Most of the doctors said that she would stay very re-tarded and very dependent.

Bryn: You mean she wouldn't be able to do anything on her own?

Carolyn: Yes. That she would probably be able to develop some self-care skills, but that she would not progress much academically and that she would not be able to do things on her own.

Bryn: What happened next?

Carolyn: She had been in my class a year before I adopted her. The year after I adopted her, she stayed in my class, but she was making progress intellectually and we really didn't feel that a multi-handicapped class served her well. So, since she had hearing problems, we thought about a deaf and hard-of-hearing class. I had noticed in talking to her that she did much better if I signed. She's a very visual person. She would pay more attention to me and her language improved with her signing. So I wanted her in the signing program. She transferred from my class to a deaf and hard-of-hearing class and did fine for the first four years. She still acted weird, though. She still did not know how to interact with people. She didn't know how to make friends. She had some profound social problems.

In tenth grade, the teacher that liked her the best left the school. He had been the department chairman and had run a lot of interference for her. Once he was gone, a major support was gone. People wanted her to be more like all the other kids. And they put a lot of pressure on her and a lot of pressure on me. And I, like a good parent, believed what the professionals told me. In retrospect, I think that's incredible because I have been in special education since 1969. I know that I don't know it all, and so why in the world did I believe that these people did? But I was scared and desperate, and they were saying they couldn't handle her. So, basically, they talked me into taking her to a psychiatrist.

Bryn: Why were you feeling so scared and desperate, Carolyn?

Carolyn: Because they were going to put her out of school. And I didn't know who else would have her. And also I was thinking about the future, thinking, "Dear God, maybe they're right; maybe it is just an impossible situation with all of her problems." I didn't want her mainstreamed, and they convinced me to mainstream her anyway. The reason I didn't want that is that she was still so very scared. I didn't feel that the kids at high school would be the sweetest people in the world to her, especially because of the way she looked. They had her in a regular class for art and gym. They had her in a regular math class for one year, but it didn't work out.

Bryn: What did you do then?

Carolyn: Well, we were going to a psychiatrist.

Bryn: Why were you going to a psychiatrist?

Carolyn: I went to a psychiatrist because the school had had her tested. The psychologist had called me and said, "This child is severely disturbed. We think that she is suicidal. She's been telling us that she wants to commit suicide, and we don't know what to do with her." So basically because I was afraid that they were going to pull her out of school and I had no idea where else she could go and because I thought that they were possibly right and maybe I was perhaps ignoring things that were really seriously wrong with her, I wanted to find out more. So we went to a psychologist who recommended another psychologist and a psychiatrist. They put her on lithium and Melaril.

Bryn: All at the same time?

Carolyn: She was on Melaril and lithium at the same time. She had been on heavy doses of Melaril when she came into my classes at the age of ten. I took her off of it because it was ridiculous. This kid was so zonked she couldn't do anything.

Bryn: What is Melaril?

Carolyn: It's a tranquilizer. She would be coming to life, waking up, and it would be time to give her another Melaril. It was supposed to be used when she was out of control but that was almost all of the time. I couldn't get the doctor to talk to me about it because I was just a foster mom at that point. So I took her off it anyway.

Later, another psychiatrist put her back on Melaril when she was sixteen. It was now used more judiciously and infrequently, still to control some of the wild behavior. The lithium was then used as well because the doctors thought she was schizophrenic and it sometimes helps schizophrenics.

Several things were happening now. For one thing, she was utterly violent. One time, when we were going down the street and I was driving, she tore the rearview mirror off the car and started hitting me with it. She was strong. And her attacks were getting very scary. Also, Ruth fantasized about the Arch of St. Louis; you know, it's a big landmark in that city. Sometimes, she'd wake up in the middle of the night screaming and running up and down the hallway saying that the arch was biting her and she was bleeding green blood. She would get mad and just start beating on me — scratching, biting, hitting.

She was attacking anybody, but particularly me and my roommate, and that was obviously disturbing. Then, on the way to the psychiatrist one day, she said, "You know, I'm only doing this because you want me to." I said, "Huh?" And she said, "I don't really like going to the psychiatrist, and I don't like taking the medicine. I'm doing it because you don't like the way that I am." I thought, "What's wrong with this picture?" I asked her some more about that and she said, "I like the way I am." She was about sixteen then, and I thought, "Wait a minute. What am I doing? Am I doing this for me or for her?" The reason I wanted her to be different was because I wanted her to be happy. It wasn't because I didn't love her the way she was. I was attracted to her, but she was totally crazy. And she wasn't doing anything ordinary. It was just that I thought she would have a better life.

Her violence precipitated my coming to the institute. I came for a three-day weekend.

Bryn: Just by yourself?

Carolyn: With Kay, a friend of mine. It was the craziest thing how we found out about the institute. We had both read *Son-Rise*, seen the movie, and thought it was lovely. Kay was interested in going to a spa and had ordered some material on spas. And The Option Institute was listed in the book on spas. I went to a used-book sale, and I picked up *To Love Is to Be Happy With*, because at that time I was so depressed and so frustrated that I fantasized killing myself and killing Ruth. I don't think I would have done this, you understand, but those were my fantasies. "I'll get a gun and kill both of us, and we'll get out of this." So I was picking up every book at this used bookstore that said "happy" in the title.

277

And I read *To Love Is to Be Happy With* and got so excited about it that I shared it with my friends. About that time, we realized that The Option Institute people were the same people who had written this book. We, immediately, ordered the twelve-tape series — tapes of talks that your father gave. And just on an impulse I said, "I want to go for this weekend. The weekend's fairly cheap. I want to go and see because this might be something that would really do it for me." And Kay said, "Yeah, right, okay." I said, "Would you come with me?" She said, "Well, okay, if you can get in, I'll come." She later said she had thought, "No way, you're not going to get in." There was a cancellation. We both got in. And I knew when I was there that I wanted to bring Ruthie to the institute.

Bryn: Why?

Carolyn: Because my weekend was fantastic. I felt so good at the institute. For one thing, the atmosphere, as I'm sure you're aware, is contagious. It is such a wonderful atmosphere, and it's great to be around so many people who are invested in happiness. And to be in a nonjudgmental atmosphere is just so freeing. It makes you feel like you can do anything. I thought, "I've got to get Ruthie here. We've got to see what would happen." And I did talk to your mom about it a couple of times on the phone. I tried to decide to be okay with me, no matter what happened and to be okay with Ruthie, no matter what happened. And we began to have really wonderful results before I even brought her to the institute.

Bryn: Just from changing yourself?

Carolyn: Yeah, just from realizing that Ruthie was okay. Bryn, I didn't know that before. I thought that there was something wrong with her, and that if I could fix her she would then be okay. The truth was, she was absolutely okay the way she was. I also felt that I had this huge responsibility to make her life okay for her and that, if I couldn't make her life okay, then I was failing her. So I put all this responsibility on me and all this responsibility on her to change. Once I realized that, it took a lot of pressure off me. It took a lot of pressure off her. I got her into a different school where the staff was much more accepting of her as she was. My supervisor helped me locate this class. She had always had a special interest in Ruth and knew that the teachers in this one class were very accepting. In fact, her son was one of the teachers. She was right. They were wonderful!

Anyway, it was at the end of that year that Ruthie and I came up to the institute. I was so scared before I went. I don't know if I would have gone alone. But by now I had so much support. My mother helped me finance the trip. And I was so fortunate to get to bring my very own support group—Beth, my roommate, Kay, the friend who came to the introductory weekend with me, and Joan, who had been doing the institute dialogues with me back home. They all helped me so much—and still do.

Bryn: What happened when you came here?

Carolyn: Oh, my! It was so intense—I think as much as anything else in my life. For one thing, it was so neat to see people enjoy and love my kid. To have somebody else tell me that Ruthie was okay, that she was special, different, and wonderful. And I was beginning to think, "Maybe something wonderful could happen for Ruthie. Maybe it's okay that she's the way she is. Maybe she doesn't have to be like everybody else. Maybe it doesn't matter. But what helped so much at the institute was having a whole week to really just focus on her and ask myself, "What is it that she is wanting? What is it that I am wanting? Why did we think we couldn't have it? Why is it we're not happy?" Because again, I was supremely happy with her when I adopted her. She was an utterly crazy little girl. She was totally obsessed with Raggedy Ann and Andy when I adopted her. The Arch of St. Louis came later. She's always been obsessed with something; that's Ruth. But I was happy with her then.

Bryn: Were you able to be happy with Ruthie again?

Carolyn: Oh, yes. At the institute, I got to know Ruth better. Getting away from the judgmental climate of society, getting away from other people telling me what I ought to be doing with her, I began to look at me and what I wanted to do. Quite frankly, I think I had very good impulses and very good instincts. And when I can stop to really listen to Ruth, really talk to her and find out what she's wanting and access a part of me that relates very well to her, we do get along really beautifully. It's when I begin to get scared and put a judgment on what she is wanting and say, "She shouldn't want that. She shouldn't be doing this. This isn't okay." Or I judge myself and say, "Well, I should be doing this for her, to her, with her." That's when I get myself into trouble. Doing a Family Program at the institute gave me a whole week to have sessions and dialogues — and, thankfully, find answers to my own questions. I didn't have to worry about what anybody else thought. I could just focus on what I was wanting for myself. Why it was that I felt I was failing her. I also realized that I had adopted her to fix her. I really thought that with love and a home and someone that was really caring about her, although she might always be retarded, she would be much more socially adept than she was.

Bryn: Those are some incredible learnings. What other things did you learn that you felt were significant for you?

Carolyn: There are three. I learned, first, that both Ruthie and I are okay exactly as we are; second, that both of us already know what we want and what we need to do; and third, that we are the ones — that we need to look to ourselves instead of to other people for our answers. Every answer I need is inside me. And every answer is there inside Ruthie, too. That's important; Ruth is retarded, but she still has all her answers inside her. That's another thing: She's a much more mature person than I had realized.

Bryn: How did you come to realize that?

Carolyn: It had never occurred to me to ask her. The staff at the institute just asked her what she wanted and what she was doing and why she was doing it. And they also pointed out to her, for example, how her nose ran a lot and how she would not bother to wipe it. And someone at the institute said, "You know, it's okay that mucus is coming out of your nose, but most people won't want to look at it." Just very honestly. Well, I told her to wipe it; it never occurred to me to tell her that I didn't enjoy looking at it. Things like that. It's a different way of speaking — so open, so authentic.

Bryn: You know, my mom told me that you had some amazing conversations with Ruthie during that week here.

Carolyn: I think your mom is absolutely right about the conversations because I learned how to converse with Ruth. In the past,

I had given her a lot of directions, telling her, for instance, what I thought she ought to do, like wiping her nose. I had not thought to explain to her that this was my problem when I saw her with a runny nose. One thing we got into fairly recently. She's really a riot with what she learned at the institute. I had said, "It bugs me; you make me nervous, Ruth, when you do that." And she said, "I can't make you nervous." I said, "Okay, you're right. You can't make me nervous. Let's rephrase that a bit. When you do this, I choose to make myself nervous. I am not comfortable with this." She now reminds me to take ownership of my feelings—reminds me that I choose them. That's great for me.

Bryn: We can all teach each other.

Carolyn: Definitely. I have begun to explain to Ruthie recently, "Okay, you're right. Everyone decides how they want to feel. And you can't make anyone happy; you can't make them unhappy. You can't make someone mad. But sometimes in life, we want someone else to do something and you have to consider their wants if you want to get something back. Basically, if you want somebody to do something nice for you, you've probably got to do something nice for them. Life trades off that way."

Bryn: You can explain to her that you don't have to judge something in order to want something else. Like chocolate and vanilla ice cream. I don't have to hate chocolate to know that I want vanilla. So you can say to Ruthie, for example, "It's not that I hate your runny nose, but I'd just like it if you'd wipe it. Then, maybe I can do something for you that you would like."

Carolyn: That's a very good way to put it. Ruth seems to understand that now. Before, I had viewed her as being too retarded to understand that kind of concept, so I had not tried to explain to her what the institute teaches before I came there. She got it on her own. She really understands quite well now. She keeps it straight, better than I do.

Bryn: What a wonderful teacher she is for you! What do you think was her most significant learning while she was here?

Carolyn: Realizing that she was in control of what she felt. To me, that's the most dramatic thing that you teach—that everything

281

is an option. I picked that up on my weekend here. I didn't always live it, but I picked it up, and that has really been dramatic for her. Now she knows that she has choices. It empowers her. She was a little kid that everyone controlled. And one of the things that she was trying to do with her obsessions was to take control of her own world. Inside her fantasies, she was in charge.

Bryn: Right. Her fantasies did whatever she wanted.

Carolyn: Exactly. And that's when she started to realize that she had some control over herself, her thoughts, and her feelings. At school, the teachers told her what to do. At home, I told her what to do. We even told her whether she was a good or a bad person.

Bryn: We always ask people what they want and how they feel.

Carolyn: Yes. And the staff explained to her that nobody could make her feel anything, no matter what happened in her life. When she would say, "Oh gosh, it's just horrible because of this," one of the mentors would help her understand that, although circumstances might not be what she wanted, she didn't have to feel horrible. She could still choose to feel whatever she wanted to feel about them and decide how she wanted to look at them. She was in charge. And once she understood, something fundamental changed inside her. She made different choices and changed her behavior.

Bryn: Carolyn, you two could inspire the whole world! Wow! Okay, you had said she wasn't really relating to people at home. Was she able to relate to them better here?

Carolyn: Yes, definitely. She related easily and well to the people at The Option Institute.

Bryn: What would you attribute that to?

Carolyn: The staff—everyone accepted her just the way she was. They didn't ask her to change. They might have told her things that she'd perhaps want to consider doing differently (like wiping her nose), but they didn't judge her. And she knew it. Nobody judged her!

Frankly, the world is full of judgments. And I think, for the first time in her life, she felt free. In fact, I knew that she did from the look on her face. I saw a new look on her face—an ease, a softness, smiles. I will send you some pictures I have of her. She doesn't have that worried look anymore. She has a beautiful, free, open expression because she found out what she could be. She's a weird kid, and, Bryn, she knows she's weird. And so what! Everyone at the institute just loved her. By the world's standards, she's a very unusual person. And she's very aware of that. She doesn't want to change. She doesn't want to try to be what other people are. But I think she also very acutely feels that people stare at her appearance and that people judge her quite severely for not looking like other people. And, at the institute, she could be exactly what she was and not have to apologize for it.

Bryn: I have heard so many stories from the staff about Ruthie and how very special she is, how special her time here was for everyone. Since being here, how is she behaving with people?

Carolyn: Oh, she totally spouts what she learned from the institute. People will say, "You're making me mad," and she'll say, "I can't do that. You're making yourself mad." But she did realize also that if she wants other people to accept her, she needs to accept them and become less judgmental. She used to be a very judgmental little character. She's learned so much since then.

Bryn: How did you apply what you learned when you got back home?

Carolyn: Amazing as it is, I brought back a different daughter and a different self! Even more amazing, I found that I was a different mother when I got home! My favorite discovery was that there is nothing to be afraid of—that little bit of understanding has freed me to try things I'd never dreamed I could do. Ruthie continued in school and graduated from high school. I sent the institute pictures of that very, very special day. After the program at the institute, we've tried to find more ways for her to be more independent. I touch base with her regularly about what she's wanting and help her figure out ways to get it. Now that she's out of school, we have tried to find ways for her to get a job. Currently she helps me at school with the other children. She volunteers a couple of days a week in my class and goes to a recreation center for physically limited individuals. She's learned to take the city bus by herself.

Her independence is very important to her. She has begun to understand cause and effect. She now understands, for example, that when the bus comes for her she has to be out at the bus stop. Well, as far as she was concerned before, I was making her be out there. The school bus was making her be out there. That was her concept of time. Now she can see a reason for watching the clock and trying to get to the bus on time. "Oh, there's a reason to get up in the morning. It's not because Mom's going to be mad at me if I don't or because the bus driver is going to yell at me." She's got her own reasons for doing it now. The same thing with planning her day. She has begun to learn to structure her time so that she gets to do things that she wants to do. She loves to go to the library downtown. Oh, and she's learned how to make phone calls to renew her books. She wasn't able to make phone calls before we went.

Most of all, I learned at The Option Institute to let her decide what it is she's wanting to learn. Previously, I didn't. It makes an enormous amount of difference whether *I* decide what it is she needs to learn or *she* decides what it is she wants to learn. She's been interested in learning to cook and much more receptive as a result to learning to read recipes. Once she decides what particular items she wants to buy, she's much more receptive to figuring out how much money it's going to take. And, truly, my big focus now is in helping her realize that she is capable of making such decisions. Before, I did not see her as capable of controlling her own life.

Bryn: What an independent woman she is now!

Carolyn: Just a note. She had one more year of school after we came to the institute. And as I said, she did graduate. Bryn, before I came here, I thought I would have to institutionalize her within a year. She's had only three tantrums since we left the institute over two years ago! This is a miracle in itself. She is becoming a capable, young lady with a sweet disposition. I never would have believed this could have happened. Bryn, I even do dialogues with her and help her sort out what's going on in her life.

Bryn: That is such an incredible transformation. What a difference between now and when you used to tell her that she should be different!

284

Carolyn: It really is.

Bryn: What kinds of experiences do you have with her now? Are you surprised at how different she is!?

Carolyn: Surprised—and grateful. I think several "miraculous" things have occurred. For one thing, I'm able to leave her at home alone and go off, and let her have her independence and me have my independence without having to worry about what she's going to do while I'm gone. She's a responsible, trustworthy person. I can ask her to do something and trust that she's going to be able to carry through with it. I think the most wonderful thing for me is being able to talk to her. Previously, when we would have a regular conversation, if I just said, "How are things going today?" she and I would end up in an all-out fight because Ruthie had a ton of anger toward me and toward everyone else. I would wind up trying to manipulate the conversation so that she would do what I wanted her to do.

Bryn, I think this is the neatest thing—it actually happened a few days ago. I was doing some needlework in the living room, and she just sat down and started talking about life and what she's thinking about and what she's wanting to do with hers. And I thought, "Gosh, I never imagined she would have these thoughts." And I never thought that if she did, she would be able to share them with me. She has such a sweet disposition now. I never thought that I would ever be this comfortable with her. I was scared of her when we came to the institute. Literally scared of her. She was so violent. I would come home scared to death about what she was going to do that night. But not anymore. She's changed so dramatically—so have I.

Bryn: Did Ruthie ever tell you how she felt about the changes you've made since you guys incorporated the attitude you learned?

Carolyn: She told me how much nicer I am since I went. She said, "I'm sure glad we went to the institute so you could straighten out and we could get along better." She's remarked about how much happier we are since we went to the institute. She thinks your work is the best thing that's ever happened and the people at the institute are wonderful. She really thinks that I went to get myself back together, and I guess she's right. Her attitude now is that she was always okay, and it sure is nice that I finally found out.

Bryn: It sounds like both of you are very, very different.

Carolyn: I used to have such a negative self-image. No more! I believe in myself. I'm going to school to work on a doctorate—I plan to go into educational administration. And I used to be an extremely shy person. Totally, totally shy. I could never, ever talk in front of groups. Bryn, now I give workshops on augmentative and alternative communication to professionals and parents working with children unable to speak. Can you believe that?

Tell your parents how very much I love them, what an enormous difference they and the staff have made in my life, in Ruth's life, in our life together. There are so many times—when I am preparing for a talk, when I am preparing for things that I never in my life thought I would ever be able to do—that I realize the major reason is because they touched my life in such a very wonderful way. It's a very special situation here. It's something almost beyond words, truly.

4

Ryan's Ride Into the Sun

Jenny, Randy and Their Son, Ryan

Bryn: Jenny, how would you describe Ryan to someone who doesn't know him and has never seen him?

Jenny: He is honest. He is gentle. He has a very soft, innocent look and a wonderful sense of humor. He just turned thirteen. He must be about five feet, one inch tall, and he is stocky. He wears glasses, and his glasses are kind of thick. He's got big hands, big feet, and he's at that kind of clumsy stage, like a bull in a china shop.

Bryn: How did you first begin to realize that Ryan was different?

Jenny: It started when Ryan was two years old. I took him for a checkup and I felt so lost. I said to the doctor, "Ryan will repeat 'Go bye-bye' all the time. That's all he says. Is this unusual?" "Oh, well, maybe," he replied. I continued, "He doesn't want to ride his little riding toys; he wants to turn them over and spin the wheels. I've had people tell me that this is weird, and I don't know because I've never been a mom before." "Oh, no, you're doing fine. You're a good mother," he told me. Although I hated to say the word, I asked him if he thought Ryan was autistic, because I had heard of autistic children. "No, I don't think so," was all he said.

Bryn: What happened next with Ryan?

Jenny: The doctor said, "If you're concerned about his speech, we will send him to a speech center at the university. They can work with him and have his hearing tested." So we went to the university, and they worked with him a little bit. They said that he was socially immature, that he had no brothers and sisters and needed to go to a day-care center. It seemed strange to me. I mean, I've never had a child before, but I wondered why I had to send him to a day-care center to be socialized.

Bryn: Were there other things about him that you thought were different?

Jenny: Let's see. By this point, I had Lissa, so now I had another child I could compare Ryan to. And, wow, I realized that Ryan didn't hug! There were other things, too. He used to stand in front of automatic doors at the grocery store, get into a very specific and bizarre body pose, put his hands up to the side of his head, and shake them furiously. And he would do that in front of any door, no matter where he was, even in front of the cupboard doors in the kitchen.

Bryn: Did he just look at the doors?

Jenny: At times, he would open doors and shut them. I mean, he would open every single door in the kitchen and then run around and shut them all—over and over and over again. And he had a set of kindergarten blocks. He would build the highest towers, and they wouldn't fall.

Bryn: That is so neat! I've seen so many autistic children do that.

Jenny: Yeah, and he would stand in front of this tower and would move those blocks maybe a quarter of an inch. He knew exactly how to move them—and they never fell. Also, he used to sing. I had a record with twenty-eight nursery rhymes on it, and he would sing them all, word for word, while carrying the tune perfectly. But he wouldn't talk; so, people kept saying, "Have his hearing tested." I'd say, "Come on, people. He can hear. Not only can he hear, he can sing." People were looking at me as if I were crazy. Actually, Bryn, the most disturbing thing that he did was have violent temper tantrums—all the time. He would bang his head on the floor or the wall and then get huge, ugly bruises. That wasn't very easy for us to take.

Bryn: So what did you think?

Jenny: My friends would tell me about some normal kinds of play, like dress up, that they were laughing about their kids doing. And I thought, "Gosh, he's never done that." But it still just didn't hit me that something was terribly wrong.

Bryn: Jenny, how were you feeling at this point?

Jenny: Oh, I kept thinking, "I didn't know being a mother would be this difficult." I would ask advice from friends who were elementary school teachers. Finally, one of them said, "Have you ever had Ryan tested?" I said, "Well, no, not really." And she didn't say anything more. People never said anything directly about Ryan, just little hints, especially at the day-care center where I had him while I was working as a nurse. When Ryan was three, however, an audio specialist came to the day-care center. She screened Ryan's hearing and called me on the phone. "Mrs. Anderson," she said, "We have a problem. We tried to screen your child, but he would not cooperate for the test at all." I apologized. She said, "We're looking at severe emotional and psychological problems. It could be autism, and I have already called a special children's hospital and made an appointment for you and Ryan." And I thought, "Thank you." Because I had been so concerned and finally someone had told me something specific about my son.

Bryn: How was Randy feeling at this point?

Jenny: I think about the same way I was; we were both frustrated. Then, when I told my friends we were taking him to that hospital, one of them, who's in education said, "Well, Jenny, I've been thinking for a long time that maybe you should consider that he might be autistic, but I couldn't say it; I didn't know how to tell you." Then we took Ryan to the hospital, and it was the most horrible experience. I have never taken him back there since.

Bryn: Why? What was horrible about it?

Jenny: Well, one well-known psychologist, who has written a book about autism, examined Ryan. This doctor and her staff were into behavior modification. They tested him, and they tested us.

Bryn: What were they testing *you* for?

Jenny: [Laughter.] I don't know. Maybe they thought we were sociopathic. I wondered, "Are they testing Randy and me to see if we caused this?" We were interviewed for hours, first by a sociologist, then by a psychologist. We were interviewed by others as well, but I don't remember their titles. They all asked us the same questions and told us the same things.

Bryn: Like what?

Jenny: They all looked at me as if I were absolutely crazy when I said that I almost had Ryan potty-trained. He was three and a half years old by then. And they said, "Mrs. Anderson, you'll be lucky if he'll be potty-trained before he's eight. You'll be lucky if he's ever potty-trained." They determined that Ryan had fourteen characteristics of autism. On top of that, I couldn't bear the way they treated him.

Bryn: What did they do?

Jenny: I could have died watching how they handled my son. They held him down; it took four people. Ryan was screaming. No one had ever treated him like that before—and they did it all because they wanted to give him a dental exam as part of a general physical.

Bryn: Why did they have to give him a dental exam?

Jenny: I asked them if it was necessary, and they insisted. They wanted a complete history and physical. And they were so intent on doing what they had to do that they traumatized him. He threw his tantrum (and I could understand why), and they didn't pay any attention to him. After that, finally, he became exhausted and fell asleep.

Bryn: How did you feel during this whole experience?

Jenny: Just awful. I mean, it was the worst day of my life. They sat us down and said, "Mr. and Mrs. Anderson, your child is autistic. He has a moderately severe case, and he will have to go to a special school. He will never go to a normal school. Only three percent of autistic children ever improve, and ninety-seven percent of them get worse, so you're looking at institutionalization by the time he reaches puberty, because a lot of times they become violent." God, Bryn, I'm looking at this little three-year-old, thinking, "I have to put him in a state institution because it's the only place that takes autistic children. And it's the worst place in the world to put a human being." This was in 1982, and I thought, "No, now wait a minute. What can I do right now?" They never told me what I could do right now, though I remember the psychologists saying, "Get a pegboard." Can you believe it? They just told me that my son was headed for an institution and had a ninety-seven percent chance of becoming violent, and the only thing they could suggest was to try to teach him how to put pegs in holes in a pegboard. Good grief!

Bryn: How did you and Randy react to what you were told?

Jenny: We cried a lot. We spent a lot of time feeling lost and sad— crying all the time. The doctor and his staff had given us a list of books to read, but none of them had ever said that they knew about you guys. But later, I found out that all of them did know; they just never put your dad's books on their list. They said, "There are a lot of cures out there; don't believe them. Autism cannot be cured."

The strange thing is the way we did find out about you. I'll backtrack a few years. When Randy and I returned from the Peace Corps, I was pregnant with Ryan. We had spent one year there; I was a nurse. I taught in a nursing school. I taught people with a seventh-grade education how to be nurses. And Randy taught people how to plant crops—cotton and rice and things like that. And he taught some people how to read. When we returned, we didn't know what had been going on here. My dad told us, "Wow! I saw a movie on TV. I can't remember the name of it, but it was about a child with autism and his mother; she worked with him for something like ten thousand hours!" He was telling me about *Son-Rise.*

Bryn: So you heard of it even before Ryan was born.

Jenny: Yes. And, after the diagnosis, I called my dad. I collared him over the phone: "Do you remember when you told me that story about those people who had an autistic child?" "Yeah," he said. "What was the name of it?" I asked. "I don't know," he said. "Do you remember what channel it was on?" I asked. "No," he said. "Just check the major networks." I wondered, "Where do I go to find this information?" I called Channel 12, and nobody knew what I was talking about; I even called New York.

And then my dad was visiting a friend in Indianapolis whose daughter was in special education. And Dad was upset. He said, "I just found out that my grandson is autistic. I don't know much about autism. Can you help me? Can you tell me anything?" His friend said, "You know, I have a book on autism." And she pulled out *A Miracle to Believe In*, and she gave it to him. Can you believe that?

Bryn: And you finally found us!

Jenny: Thank goodness! We gave you a call, and it was five months before we saw you because I was pregnant again. Before we came up, I told one of the original doctors we had seen that I was going to go to The Option Institute, and she said, "Well, that's your decision, but I really wish you wouldn't." I'm so glad I didn't listen to her! I had already stopped going to the seminars given by the National Society for Autistic Children [Autism Society of America] because they were so depressing and awful, and I was really excited to come to the Berkshires.

Bryn: So, when you came to the institute, what would you say were some of the biggest differences you noticed in Ryan during your week here?

Jenny: I'll never forget the biggest difference. Before we came, whenever we wanted a hug from Ryan, we had to approach him very carefully, and he would finally let us hug him, but that was it. After we got home from our week with you guys, my son reached out to me, for the very first time, and initiated a hug. I'll never forget the way I felt having his little arms around me.

The second difference I noticed was that he never again engaged in head banging. Not even when he was angry. He used to bang his head every single time he was irritated or agitated. After our week here, he just didn't do it anymore. These two things were the first dramatic changes that we saw. But the biggest thing that changed was me. I mean, my attitude. I didn't use to think of him as this child that belonged to me. As a result of all the input we received from the doctors and hospitals, I saw him as a clinical entity: He was autistic. With all the diagnosis and foreboding predictions, I couldn't see that this was my son. It was like I had a certain number of years to deal with his autism, and then he was going to be taken away to live in some institution. And I never stopped to sit down and say, "I don't care what you are; you're just so cute. I love you so much. Even in your autism, I love you so much." I never thought of him as cute because everybody said his autism was so awful and everything I read was so depressing. And I never stopped to say, "It doesn't matter. You are beautiful just the way you are right now." And since I left The Option Institute, I can't stop telling him how beautiful and cute he is. And that is the one thing that I think changed the whole course of our lives and our son's life.

Bryn: What you are sharing is really the heart and soul of what we want for these children and their families.

Jenny: Samahria and all the staff worked with him in the gentlest and most respectful way. I watched him respond in ways that I never thought he could. I remember saying, "Wow! We're getting smiles! He doesn't look like a robot!" He always used to remind me of a little robot before, but then, right before my eyes, my child blossomed.

Bryn: That must have been so special for you.

Jenny: Oh, it was. We couldn't wait to do our program ourselves.

Bryn: How long did you do your program for Ryan?

Jenny: We did it for two years, and we used college students. We have a small university nearby, and these kids were great. They were so enthusiastic.

Bryn: How many hours did you spend working with Ryan each week during the two years that you ran the program?

Jenny: At first, we did eight to twelve hours a day. We would go from eight in the morning to eight in the evening. From the time Ryan woke up till the time he went to bed. We went over to a town that's about twenty or thirty miles from here; their university has a very large education department. At first, I wasn't sure I wanted to go there, because they used behavior modification, but then I thought perhaps there would be some students there that would want to try doing something different. And the students there were wonderful. They gave us a copy of the movie *Son-Rise*, because they used it in their special education classes. Most of them had read the book *Son-Rise* because the professor made it assigned reading in her class. So we found a lot of excitement among her students. "Oh, my gosh, there is somebody actually doing this near our town!" they said. We always had a good response. That was my biggest job, recruiting volunteers. And I learned so much from doing it. And as the program went on, we decided to go back to the institute again. "Why not learn even more?" we said.

Bryn: How many times have you been here?

Jenny: We came on three different occasions, for a week each time.

Bryn: Couldn't stay away, huh? [Laughs.]

Jenny: Actually, besides coming with Ryan, Randy and I came ourselves to some of the group programs offered at the institute. Those programs were sensational, and the more we got our heads together just as people, the better we were with Ryan. Hey, the better we were with everything in our lives! After the first year, we began to cut back the time we spent working with Ryan, and I did a lot of the work. At that time, I was working only two evenings a week. The biggest thing that the program taught Ryan was how to love people. He was just beaming. All these people were coming to the house to see him; we all made a lot of friends. To this day, two of our best friends are people who came to help us with Ryan's program. One volunteer switched her major from business to special education. Another switched from math to elementary education for the learning disabled. We met some really neat people.

Bryn: So did we. We still have dear friends from Raun's program. Were there changes you and Randy noticed in yourselves after you completed the Son-Rise Program here at the institute?

Jenny: Absolutely. The sadness disappeared. It was as if a black cloud had lifted and we could see the sun again.

Bryn: What do you think would be the most significant thing that you and Randy learned from doing the program?

Jenny: I think the biggest change came in me. I think we gave Ryan enough help so that he could grow and change. I don't think that would have happened if I hadn't changed and if Randy hadn't changed. We would have never been able to help Ryan. And who knows, then, what would have happened to him?

I was very critical of myself, of the kind of mother I was, to the point that I wasn't aware that I was blocking out love I could have given Ryan. The single most important thing I learned was to love and accept him right now where he was—not for what he could be or what he was going to be tomorrow, but for who he was today. Whatever he was doing, I learned to love him right now. That's powerful; it really is. That realization not only changed the way we related to Ryan, but the way Randy and I related to each other. What a treasure!

Bryn: What were you like before you realized that? What were you like afterward?

Jenny: Before, I used to get frustrated any time Ryan exhibited autistic behavior. I would either physically or verbally try to stop his behavior. You know I believed that if I could stop it, it wasn't there. I can see how he would think we weren't accepting him. After coming to the institute, we imitated him. We were cheerleaders. It was just so different. He would stare at us as if he were thinking, "What has happened?" It was as if he had turned on a light bulb; his face just became animated when we started doing that, and it's never stopped being that way. School psychologists have said to me, after seeing his changes, that they have never seen an autistic child change like him—never. They always ask, "What did you do? What did you do differently?" I have heard that more than once. It is amazing. And I think that is the single most important thing: accepting him, going with him. You know, we always had the love, but we just didn't know what to do with it—or how to express it. The Son-Rise Program taught us how.

Bryn: It sounds as if you have really taken what you learned and made it your own. You had said before that you tried to physically stop his autistic behaviors and that didn't work. You tried the pegboard and that didn't work. Were there other things besides accepting him—mirroring him—you learned that you felt did work?

Jenny: Eye contact. I think that made a super difference. You guys taught me to do anything to get his eye contact; crawl around on the floor with him, bark like a dog, dress up like a clown, whatever it took. Once I got eye contact from him, things started to move. And imitating him was so powerful. I remember how one volunteer in her first session with Ryan got eye contact, and then Ryan started his stick-banging ritual. Ryan started pounding the table, and she mirrored his action. Then, wow, he suddenly stopped to see if she was following. So she stopped, just like he'd done, and looked back at him. Then he gave her the biggest grin. They stared at each other and not at the toys for what seemed to be five minutes. She was amazing. It was just the most incredible scene to watch.

Bryn: It sounds beautiful. When I'm with children at the institute, imitating them and loving them is truly a precious experience for me.

Jenny: For me, too. The volunteers that not only took on the attitude of accepting Ryan, but also really went with him into this world—without a doubt, they got the most from him.

Bryn: Were there other things he seemed to respond to?

Jenny: Something really funny, Bryn. He wanted to go out and play in the rain one day. The workroom had a bathroom connected to it, and I remember that one of the volunteers said, "Oh, you want rain! We'll make rain." She gave him what he wanted, but inside the room. That was their big thing. They made rain in the bathroom. A lot of rain. They ruined the bathroom. We were going to redo that room anyway. [Laughs.] We loved our house, but we loved our son more.

Bryn: Wow! It sounds like you had some very creative volunteers.

Jenny: Oh, we did! They were wonderful. Our volunteers helped create magic in our home. Ryan has made amazing progress, and it is documented by school psychologists who said that it wasn't necessary that we take him back to the special children's hospital because he was doing so well. He skipped kindergarten and went on. He's a little learning delayed, but he does phonics beautifully. He reads. He is doing so well. He's got the best teacher-pleasing behaviors in the world He's never had a teacher who didn't love him. And, Bryn, remember they told me that he would never be potty trained, and that he would be in an institution by now? You guys helped me give Ryan back his life.

Bryn: Jenny, tell me a story about one of the wonderful times you've had recently with him—one you never anticipated you would ever have.

Jenny: Okay. He and I ride bikes. All my kids can ride, but Ryan could ride forever. He can ride probably twenty miles at a time. My other kids ride ten to fifteen miles, maybe, and they're complaining. But he and I can get on our bikes and ride like the wind. One time this summer, we did this while I was home and Dad was at work. Well, his dad was so excited when he heard the news that he got on his bike the next weekend and rode with us. But he stopped every five minutes; he kept finding a reason to stop and rest. Being a loan officer, he's used to sitting on his butt. Finally, Ryan turned around and said, "You know, Dad, riding with you is like riding behind a school bus; you have to stop every five minutes." And Randy just laughed and laughed, and I thought, "What a sweet way of saying, 'Get with the program, Dad.'" And he does that; he will tell people what the problem is, but he says it in such a way that they are not offended. You know? I was ready to say, "Look, Randy, you can't do this. Just give it up and go home. We're riding here. We're not stopping; we're riding." But my son showed me a different way to see this situation—and a much, much sweeter way to handle it.

Bryn: He sounds like an excellent "people person." What are some of his other interests?

Jenny: He loves cars, trucks, and baseball cards. He plays baseball and soccer and enjoys swimming. Also, he still has the funniest sense of humor. He has a lot of friends, and they all come from the fifth grade. He should be in the sixth grade, but right now he's doing fifth-grade work, and I am the proudest mom ever!

Bryn: What does he like to do with his buddies?

Jenny: He has them come and sleep over—oh, and they called 911 in the middle of the night and the police came out. They did that one night because they thought they heard a burglar in the house. We have a large house, and they know that when you hear noises you're supposed to call 911. So, at three o'clock in the morning, the police came and searched the yard, the house, the basement; finally, they asked the boys where their parents were. We were upstairs sleeping; we were zonked. We hadn't heard anything. So, there we were—the policemen with their flashlights in our bedroom.

Bryn: [Laughs.] Hey, look at how conscientious he is! He takes good care of you.

Jenny: Very much so. And he is very responsible. He just started mowing the yard this year, and he looks at the grass on a daily basis. He even measures it. He's a little compulsive, but it's cute. We can give him responsibility, and he can handle it. He is doing so well!

Bryn: Jen, do you ever have experiences with Ryan where you are just so moved by what he does? I know that Raun recently came home on a university holiday, and he was talking to me about who I should vote for in the upcoming election. I had that feeling where it seems that time stops, and I was humbled by the wonder of him and the seemingly "ordinary" things that he does. Does that ever happen to you?

Jenny: Oh, absolutely! I know what you mean. I see all the amazing changes in Ryan. We were somewhere, and I reached over to give him a hug and a kiss and he pulled away from me. His friends were around. He later said, "Mom, would you please not hug me around my friends anymore?" And I said, "Oh, but Ryan, I can't help it; you're just so wonderful!" And he said, "Mom, a hug and a kiss at night before I go to bed is fine. I love you, Mom." That's something that happened recently. And it was just such a normal reaction for a teenager.

Bryn: So how do you feel now after having done this program?

Jenny: I wish we could have done it longer because it was such a great time in our lives. I never regret a minute.

Bryn: At this point, what would you want to say to other parents who have special children?

Jenny: I would say, "Do it!" I would say to any parent with a special child, "If you're feeling frustrated, if you're feeling any kind of sadness or anything, just give The Option Institute a weekend; then give them a week." I'd say, "You can do anything you want with what you learn because it's your choice, but I guarantee that you will feel so much better about yourself and about your child."

Bryn: Jenny, I have to tell you: You have created something so amazing.

Jenny: It is amazing. Even after all these years, it never leaves— the miracle never leaves.

5

Danny and the Bathtub
to Heaven

Marie, Robert, and Their Son, Danny

Marie: My son Danny is small, small boned. He's got kind of almond-shaped eyes and a beautiful face. He's got this china-doll complexion. His hair, when he was born, almost stood straight up. It's calmed down quite a bit, but he was always really electric looking.

Bryn: Would you tell me some experience that you had before you came to the institute, for instance when you were going to have him diagnosed by the doctors or the schools?

Marie: We knew something was not quite right; he wasn't putting words together in sentences, and he would often not respond to our requests. I had him in a play school setting, and he was sort of lying around a lot. He would alternate between being extremely high-strung and hyper or being very sluggish. Finally, his teacher said, "You know, he almost never answers me when I ask him a question. I think you should get his hearing tested." I made an appointment immediately. Tests proved his hearing was fine, but the hearing and speech specialist sensed other problems and recommended that he see a psychiatrist for further evaluation. The first time I heard the word *autism* was when our pediatrician was looking for a code to precertify the evaluation with our insurance.

Bryn: How old was he at this point?

Marie: By the time we got him to the psychiatrist, he was three. I don't think the psychiatrist had ever given a diagnosis of autism. In other words, the doctor literally read the symptoms of autism off a list and said, "Well, Danny shows these characteristics, but

300

he doesn't show this one." It was as if he were saying, "So, maybe he's not autistic." But he never really gave us a clear diagnosis. We were left with nothing definite and that was very, very difficult for us. I was really frustrated because something was wrong with my child. I wasn't able to connect with him, and he was having a lot of problems.

Bryn: Like what else?

Marie: Like having screaming fits sometimes for hours. Intense screaming fits. And I couldn't comfort him, no matter what I did. He had minimal eye contact; he was very echolalic. He would answer almost every question by screaming "No!" He would have a tantrum at the drop of a hat, sometimes scratching and biting me. I was petrified to take him anywhere alone because his moods were so unpredictable.

He didn't do the classic sit and rock ritual, but he lined things up. It was hilarious, but also a pain! For instance, I would take him to play groups and he would get all the cars and line them up and not want anybody to touch them. We spent a very frustrating first few years as a family.

Bryn: At this point, then, you didn't consider him autistic?

Marie: I really thought that his symptoms matched those of autism. But I was so distraught. I thought maybe I was the problem. Everyone said, "You are a new mom; you've got to learn to relax." So I went to a family therapist, and she asked me to describe Danny. At one point, she looked up and she said, "Does he spin plates?" I said, "No, he doesn't." And she went on to another subject. It was as if she thought, "Maybe he's autistic, but, since he doesn't spin plates, I guess he's not." Now I look back on that and I think, "Oh, we could have known that much earlier." But it shows me how many professionals really don't understand autism and developmental problems.

Bryn: Did he continue to go to the play groups?

Marie: We continued to try to have him in limited day care. He was really miserable. Often, he screamed all the way to school. He hated school, and I know now that it was total sensory overload for him. At one particular school we tried, I would leave him crying under the assumption that after I left he would calm down. That wasn't what happened. It wasn't until three months later that the teacher finally said, "You know, he never has made any friends, and it took him forever to just quit sobbing in the corner for an hour after you left him." And I'm thinking, "Why the hell didn't you tell me sooner?" For three months, they didn't tell me.

Bryn: That's really surprising. How were you handling the scream-ing fits at home?

Marie: It was horrible. That was the worst time of my life. I would get really scared that I was going to hurt him. I mean, I had a new-born baby, and Danny was out of control. So I would end up put-ting him in his room, tying the door closed with rope, and sitting in front of the door—just begging him to calm down. I wouldn't leave him, but I was so frightened. I couldn't cope.

I'll speak for mothers. This is a very broad generalization, but I do believe that one of a woman's biggest fears is not being a "good mother." And when that seems to be happening in your life and you're trying your hardest, it shakes your foundation. I was mortified.

Bryn: Many parents have shared that with me. They get scared when all the general information they've been given about parent-ing doesn't work. I can understand why that would be difficult for parents.

Marie: I also heard, "It's just the terrible two's" from doctors and people who didn't witness Danny's uncontrollable behaviors. I lived in fear of my younger son, Sam, turning two because I thought I was going to have to live through it all over again. It had been a living hell when Danny was around two.

Bryn: What happened then?

Marie: Well, the ice broke when we got a second diagnosis from the Child Development Center at the university here. There was a team of specialists: two pediatric psychologists, a speech/language pathologist, an occupational therapist, a pediatrician, and a social worker. They see kids from all over the state. There was quite a waiting list to get him in there and when he did, he had just turned four. They unanimously assessed Danny as having autism. That was very validating in a way; it was our suspicion all along. I remember the psychologist commenting that we were taking this news really well compared to other parents who are usually quite shocked. We said, "We've traveled a long road to get this diagnosis."

It was after this that I started looking in earnest for your mom and dad. I had read all their books by then and knew that I wanted to work with Danny the way they had worked with Raun. But I felt I needed a solid diagnosis first.

Bryn: What did the team tell you about autism when they gave you the diagnosis?

Marie: That it was a communication disorder, an organic brain dysfunction of some kind. They were quick to point out that nobody really knows for sure what brings it on. And also, that it is considered incurable. In my naïveté I thought, "Oh, you get this diagnosis; then they're going to give you all this information, all these references, all these places to go." But that wasn't the case. It's like you get the diagnosis and then you're on your own.

Bryn: Did they have anything to offer you?

Marie: Well, they referred us to the regional autism specialist and advised us to continue his speech therapy, and they also gave us the pamphlet the Autism Society of America puts out. The first thing I read in that pamphlet was that autism is a lifelong disability. That is a grim prognosis that doesn't leave open many avenues for hope, and I *wanted* hope.

Bryn: What was it like for you when you came here? What did you notice? I worked with you and Danny, but I want to hear it from you.

Marie: Before we got to the institute, we actually started using what I had read in the books as a model because we had to wait six months for an opening before we could come. I took Danny out of school, kept him at home, and did a program as best I could.

Bryn: How had he been doing in school at that time?

Marie: It was overwhelming for him. It was a Montessori setting, which was actually a very calm, structured environment. He couldn't bond with the kids, and he would often scream about going. He would wander out of class—twice he was found in the parking lot.

When I came to the institute, I learned how not to react to Danny's anger. He had this great wellspring of anger. When he would scream, I would jump so high in response. I had no idea that I was doing that. Mainly, I wanted to avoid any sort of confrontation with him. At that point, I was afraid of him. And at the institute, I learned that it was okay to tell him what I wanted. I learned that I could handle whatever reaction he decided to give me. What a thing to learn! And what a loving way to be.

Bryn: Sensational! Would you say that was one of the most significant learnings for you?

Marie: Absolutely!

Bryn: Do you know what was the most meaningful thing for Robert at that time?

Marie: He opened up and shared his feelings in a way that he never had before. He felt so safe at the institute, and he was really able to express himself. Plus, I think he really learned how to play with Danny in a whole new way. Robert and I had made a point to both attend the introductory weekend offered by The Option Institute before our family week. So we were already familiar with the dialogue process and the attitude of happiness as a priority. As a result, our family week was fast paced, allowing us to cover a lot of issues, work through a lot of doubts.

Bryn: Were there changes that you noticed in Danny during that week and after?

Marie: Yes! For the first time, he said, "I love you, Mom." Not a repeat, like echoing me. He just told me on his own. I just about died and went to heaven. And he has just been saying it ever since. Danny also began to make more eye contact. Not incredible amounts of eye contact, but much more than before.

Bryn: What about the screaming and crying? Did that change?

Marie: Yes, because of the work we did with him in our program the following year, his fits have diminished greatly. They are practically nonexistent now. I mean maybe one every six months or so, and they usually can be linked to other stresses such as illness. What's so different now is we as parents are confident in our ability to deal with them. We don't judge them as "bad" anymore.

Bryn: How do you deal with them on the rare occasions that he has one?

Marie: If he is having a major fit—screaming, getting really aggressive—I will pick him up and take him to his room. I'll sit in his room with him and say, "Just go for it, Danny." And I'll scream with him wholeheartedly. Then, I'll talk to him calmly about how he is feeling. I'll do deep breathing with him. He'll just let it all go. And he remembers that he can control his anger. I know the main thing is having learned not to judge his anger, but to accept it.

Bryn: That is such a huge difference—not to judge the anger, not to judge him.

Marie: I used to judge everything. I still find myself judging sometimes, but now I see it isn't really necessary. Bryn, I'm a different person. I have to say that I've embraced what I learned from our work with Danny as a life-style. I love it, and it has changed my life.

Bryn: In what ways?

Marie: It's been very life affirming to know that I can be faced with a situation like this and still be happy, that I can come to un derstand myself as I deal with difficulties, that I can use them to grow and keep growing. I know that there's plenty more growth ahead for me, and I'm excited about it, too. I love what I learned in Sheffield, Massachusetts!

Bryn: As much as we love teaching it! How long have you been doing the program?

Marie: One full year since we learned the Son-Rise Program.

Bryn: As you look back now on your program, do you remember any specific challenges?

Marie: Sure. Developing the confidence to do a program, and saying, "Yes, this is what I want to do," was a challenge. When I dealt with some of the professionals—autism consultants, etcetera—I would say, "I'm going to do this home program with my child." The support was not overwhelming, to say the least. The widely held belief is that children with autism need early intervention and that means classroom intervention. The focus is on training them to function in a classroom setting as soon as possible so they will get used to structure, to the school system's expectations. I really had to ask myself, "Well, what do I want for him?" And I thought, "I want this kid to be able to make eye contact. I want this kid to be able to say what he is feeling. I want this kid to love the world, not be scared of it." He simply wasn't ready to socialize and be in school. So the challenge was to go ahead and do what I believed in. Also, training and working with the volunteers was an incredible challenge, all the time.

Bryn: How many volunteers did you usually have?

Marie: We had a total of sixteen volunteers over the year. Mostly, they would work two-hour shifts. Usually, I had five to seven at a time.

Bryn: How many hours a week were you running the program?

Marie: Danny was in the room between four and five hours a day. Sometimes longer.

Bryn: And how many hours did you and Robert do?

Marie: Robert did about five hours on the weekends and worked some evenings. When Robert and Sam got home, we would have dinner and then Robert would do a lot of playing with them together. Sam was a great helper. He is one of the most enthusiastic kids I've ever known, and he helped Danny just by his manner of approaching life full force.

And for a long time, it was challenging for me to say, "I'm not Samahria Kaufman; I'm doing *my* version of the Son-Rise Program. I do want to be in there three hours a day. I want my volunteers in there for two or three hours a day. I want Danny in the room four or five hours a day. And that's okay."

Bryn: So were you pressuring yourself?

Marie: Yeah. But, when I let go of that, things really started to happen for me.

Bryn: Marie, what would you say were the most significant things you learned that made the difference in your work with Danny?

Marie: I remember several key turning points. One was understanding how excited I could get doing the same thing over and over, and actually thinking, "I really want to build this ship for the twelve hundredth time." To me, that was fantastic and Danny sensed it. I mean, one day I turned a corner and thought, "I'm not getting into this, and I really want to be into it. I want to be excited about it." And then it was instantaneous; when I really participated with genuine enthusiasm, I saw Danny's contact and communication increase dramatically. When I observed volunteers, it was always obvious when they were into it with their whole hearts—Danny's response level would reflect it.

Bryn: Tell me the bathtub story again. I love that story.

Marie: Oh, yes. Thank you for remembering. There have been so many stories. This was hilarious. We had a session. It had just ended and Danny wanted to take a bath. I said, "fine," but I realized that I didn't want to stop working with him. So I went into the bathroom and sat with him while he was in the tub. I sat on the floor and talked to him. He kept looking away, not answering me. I got up, feeling frustrated. I remember thinking, "Doggone it, I've lost him, and he's in the bathtub." I walked out, feeling defeated. And then I thought, "I don't want to feel this way." So I turned around and jumped into the bathtub with all my clothes on. I sat down and said, "Now, will you play with me? Now will you look at me?" And I was soaking wet; my clothes were wet. I had my shoes on. And he just started to laugh so hard. He cracked up. He looked at me and wouldn't stop looking at me. We ended up having the session of our lives in the bathtub—together, in the bathtub.

Bryn: I always say to parents, "When you feel like you've given one hundred percent, then give two hundred!"

Marie: That was very much on my mind when I jumped into the tub. I call it the two hundred percent solution. I learned that in the Advanced Family Training Program at the institute.

Bryn: You and Danny in the bathtub—it's such a great story; that's why I've always remembered it. Marie, was that event pivotal in helping you be there in a better way for Danny?

Marie: Definitely. Also, I will say again that learning not to judge people and their reactions made a huge difference for me. Even their anger! It's so easy to judge anger because we're all hung up about it. First of all, I learned not to judge it myself. And then I was able to help the volunteers see that Danny's anger was just an emotion that they didn't have to see as bad, and they didn't have to be frightened of. When they could let go of that, they were so much freer—more able to really be there for him. That was a very important lesson for Danny, learning that anger wasn't going to get him what he wanted anymore.

Bryn: Were there changes in your relationship with Robert and Sam as well?

Marie: Yes. Robert and I are continually trying to enhance our relationship. There were times when our marriage felt kind of rocky. Sometimes he wasn't as involved in the program as I wanted him to be and so there was real friction there. Working through that has been great. I think we feel as if we have created and we can always keep creating what we want in our marriage and in our lives. If something's not quite going the way we want it in our relationship, we can look at it and say, "Well, what do we want? Can we create what we want and work through this?" And deep down, we always have this core feeling, "Yes, we can."

Also, we trust each other inordinately, more than your typical couple will trust each other. The whole dialogue process we learned at the institute has given us a means to work out our confusions. Our copies of *To Love Is to Be Happy With* and *Happiness Is a Choice* are dog-eared!!

As for Sam, I have to say that his presence in our lives has been as big a blessing as Danny's. He has been a real grounding force for us. Our work with Danny has helped us to be better parents in general. We can use the same attitudes with Sam that we use with Danny. When we share that happiness quotient, it just builds on itself.

Bryn: Marie, now that you're approaching your life so differently, what are some situations or interactions that maybe you never anticipated you'd have with Danny?

Marie: Just recently we went to a street fair where there were a lot of people and clowns and activity. Even to this day, we're sort of tentative about putting him in such busy places, bombarded by frantic stimulus. But there he was and he did everything the other kids were doing. Everyone wanted to play putt-putt golf. There were tons and tons of kids in line, waiting. Having to be patient. Having to understand about taking turns. We thought, "Oh, Danny's not ready." But then he said, real excited, "I want to play putt-putt. I'm going to stand here in line and wait."

Bryn: Really?

Marie: And he did. And he waited there patiently. And he played putt-putt. He had a blast, and we were having a blast right along with him. We were in awe, watching our son play. What an appreciation we've developed for the little things in life.

Here's another story that's been heart stopping for us. I know for most parents this might be a nonevent. For us, it was a bit of heaven. One day, we were going to a play group for both Danny and Sam at their friend Angela's house. In the car Sam said, "Angela doesn't really like Danny." And I asked, "Why do you say that?" Sam answered, "Last time we were there, she chased him all around the house with a rubber Halloween ax." "Oh," I laughed, "you know that Danny loves to play chase games. I bet they were having fun." Danny just sat in the backseat and listened to us. He didn't say a word. Well, after being at the play group for over an hour, Danny went up to Angela and said, "Angela, do you like me?" Her answer: "Yes, Danny, I like you a lot." Later that night, when Robert came home, he asked the boys what they had done that day. Sam said, "We went over to Angela's." And Robert asked, "Oh, who is Angela?" Then Danny, who had been in another room, obviously listening to our conversation, chimed in and said, "She's my friend!" All those connections. He made them easily and communicated so clearly with us. Heaven, Bryn, that's heaven.

Bryn: It's a heaven that you and Robert created. What other things does he like to talk about?

Marie: He comes up with some very interesting analogies. He is very visual. For instance, he stacked up a few double-A batteries the other day and said, "Look, Mom, they look like the log pile at the mill." He has started to ask "Why?" questions. For instance, "Why are trees bigger than us?" That one stumped me!! It is wonderful to see him expanding into these more complex ways of thinking. Using language fluidly is still a challenge Danny faces, but his skills just keep improving.

On many occasions I've said, "I cannot believe I'm getting to do this with him." For instance, going on long strenuous hikes, or going to a birthday party and seeing him participate. Having him want to be in school. That was real hard—deciding to put him back in school. We didn't know how he would respond, but we felt that he was ready to socialize and he could now express himself verbally, if he felt uncomfortable. We held him back a grade so that he could catch up. Our one-year home program paid off. Instead of hampering his ability to socialize, we feel he learned how to socialize in the playroom. Now he loves to go to school! It's a real miracle. Also, he has learned how to ask for what he wants and how to accept the fact that he won't always get what he wants and that is okay. So, Bryn, he's now in a regular kindergarten class.

Bryn: A regular kindergarten! What do his teachers say about him?

Marie: They love him! They comment on how polite he is, and I know that is a direct result of us reminding him over and over that he can ask for things in a nice way. We have continued to be very involved even within the school setting. Robert is a parent volunteer one day every other week. When we first enrolled Danny in school, I was holding my breath, knowing how much it used to overwhelm him. But I have to say that I was floating on a cloud the other day as I observed him participate in phys-ed class; he was so involved, so happy! We made sure that he had the support services we thought necessary to make the transition a smooth one. There is an instructional aide available to help him when he doesn't understand a particular direction or needs assistance with transitions. At this time, the school team has recommended Danny be placed in a regular first-grade class next year. At our last team meeting, his teacher expressed that Danny's skills are equal to, and in some areas, above the other students'. The whole team feels confident that with the right support services Danny will continue to shine in the school environment. It's wonderful to see him respond and want to connect with the other children. He's reaching out and making friends.

Bryn: Really? Marie, that's remarkable!

Marie: He's a very bright child. We were actually able to verify that because now he will cooperate with testing. Although he still has a way to go with complex speech interactions, he is able to communicate what he wants, what he knows, and how he feels. He has come amazingly far! And he is the greatest teacher any of us could ever have had. What he has brought to other people is astounding. All the volunteers have learned so much from him—because of him.

Bryn: Special children have always been my most powerful teachers. That's why I have always surrounded myself with them. People have always said I was the teacher—but, really, they teach me!
   Tell me, what kind of time and energy went into doing your program?

Marie: Most of my time and energy has been devoted to helping Danny find a way out of the confines of autism. We have tried to help him by researching the literature on autism and making selective treatment choices. We incorporated other treatments in our program, including diet modifications and nutritional supplements, and auditory training. To varying degrees, I think they all contributed to his improvement. But I will say, without a doubt, that our home program made the pivotal difference in that it gave him a nurturing and exciting environment where he could be himself and be accepted. I believe that is why he is as comfortable and interactive with the world as he is today. I would choose to do the Son-Rise Program again in a heartbeat. Because I've changed so much! Bryn, I used to have the most negative attitude of anybody I've ever known in my life!

Bryn: Listening to you speak now, it's hard to imagine that you were ever that way.

Marie: I mean, I was pessimistic, cynical, very judgmental. My family has seen me drop all that. And they think, "There's hope for the world. If she can drop that, then maybe we can." I just approach life so differently now. I really do. I try not to judge others. It just opens up so much space, so many possibilities. Also, Bryn, learning how to know what I want and to go ahead and go for it just fills me with energy and hope. Me, the former pessimist—I've become an optimist!

Bryn: Isn't life much more fun that way?

Marie: Absolutely!

Bryn: Let me ask you one last question. After doing this program, what statement would you want to make to other parents who have special children?

Marie: I would love for them to believe that the possibilities are absolutely endless—that they can say, "I can do something." I want every parent to know that they absolutely have everything they need inside them to make a difference for their son or daughter. And that their special child, I really feel, will be their greatest teacher. Or could be. If their child has autism or has any other serious problem and they're thinking about doing this kind of home program, it's well worth it. It's the most powerful thing that's ever happened to me in my whole life. That's what I would say. And it's touched my whole family—my mom, my dad, even my grandfather—everybody.

One more thing, Bryn. With all my heart, I want to thank all the volunteers. They came to help us; they were open to learn and change themselves—all to help Danny. Their love and energy helped him to become who he is today. But I'm not only thanking my volunteers, but all the volunteers in every Son-Rise Program everywhere—they proved to me how much love there is in the world.

6

Justin—The Opportunity of a Lifetime

Janine, Scott, and Their Son, Justin

Bryn: Can you give me a thumbnail sketch of your life right now?

Janine: Currently, I'm directing the program for Justin, but before that, I worked in accounting and worked on building my own freelance photography business. Scott is and has been working in the auto business. He's the general manager of a new-car dealership. And, Bryn, we live in a very rural area, smack-dab in the middle of a cornfield.

Bryn: Janine, could you paint a picture of Justin? Also, how old is he now?

Janine: He's five and a half and a strikingly beautiful child. He has absolutely gorgeous, haunting eyes. Hazel. He is somewhat large for his age. He gives the impression of being someone who's enchanted. He just glows.

Bryn: What about his dimples?

Janine: Oh, how could I forget his dimples? Yes, he has big, big dimples and a real round, adorable, lovable, pinchable type face. Don't I sound just like a mother?

Bryn: You're allowed. You sound like you appreciate and delight in your son. That's a model for any parent. Tell me more about Justin.

Janine: Where do you want me to start? In particular, it used to be virtually impossible for Justin to relate to us. He preferred to do everything alone. If Scott or I tried to read a book to him, for example, he would hit us, act out, and tantrum. That was not all the time, but a large percentage of the time. Putting him with other people was absolutely impossible. When we took him to our relatives, the kid would cry from the minute we got there until the minute we left. Just having a simple family meal at his grandmother's house was utterly impossible. Taking him anywhere was a gamble. There was no way of knowing whether he was going to completely lose it; most of the time he did.

Bryn: What do you mean: "completely lose it"?

Janine: He would be so overstimulated and so frightened and so unable to process all the stimuli around him that he would just shut down—either by withdrawing totally, or more likely, by completely falling apart. Becoming inconsolable and crying to the point where we thought he was going to have seizures. As a matter of fact, we later had him screened for epilepsy because of these crying episodes; he would literally jerk and twitch and lose control of his body.

Bryn: How old was he at this point?

Janine: This happened from the time he was two until the time he was three.

Bryn: Was this when you started seeing doctors?

Janine: We started seeing doctors when he was around two and a half.

Bryn: For what reason?

Janine: Because of these unusual behaviors and especially because he wasn't talking. At that time, we said, "Oh, he's such a self-amused child." Looking back now, we can say, "Yeah, he was autistic." He wasn't interested in other people. He wasn't playing with other kids. Everybody kept saying, "Don't worry. Next summer, he'll be out there with all the other kids." It just never happened. But, primarily because he wasn't talking, we were concerned that he might not hear. He often didn't seem to hear us. So, we had him undergo hearing tests and speech evaluations. The people testing him said, "There's no biological reason why he can't talk. We see autistic behavior." So we began speech therapy and also we went and had a complete global development evaluation. He was diagnosed: Pervasive Development Disorder/Autistic.

Bryn: What did the people evaluating him say that meant?

Janine: The gist of what they said was: "Well, yeah, he has autism, but it could be worse. It could be a classic case. Instead, he seems to be one of the more highly functioning children." Because, at this point, by the time we had him diagnosed, he had started to say some words. But it wasn't communication! He didn't develop meaningful communication until we came up to The Option Institute. So his first speech, for example, he memorized from a storybook tape he had listened to. His first words were: "Don't Cry, Big Bird. Story by Sarah Roberts. Pictures by Tom Lee." While they diagnosed him, he sat there in the examination room saying, "Thirty, twenty-nine, twenty-eight, twenty-seven, twenty-six," and so on. He never said, "Mommy" or "cookie" or "juice" or "I love you."

Bryn: How did you and Scott feel about the diagnosis?

Janine: Like we had run into a brick wall. Only we were very lucky because, in addition to the diagnosis, we got a recommendation to read *Son-Rise*. From a division of Children's Hospital, believe it or not. Now, I will tell you that they prefaced their recommendation by saying they didn't believe in a cure. They thought *Son-Rise* was a really great story and the people in it seemed to have had more success than anybody else with this kind of child — so check it out. The next day, I was at the library checking out *Son-Rise* and *A Miracle to Believe In*. We were devastated, but I feel that we got past that a lot quicker than most people because of those books.

Bryn: When you say that you were devastated, what did you think his diagnosis meant? What did you think would happen to Justin?

Janine: We were told, "There's no way of knowing if he'll ever communicate meaningfully. There's no way of knowing whether he'll ever be able to progress beyond rudimentary special education. He may need it for life." And we felt like every dream that we'd ever had for our child had just been pulled right out from under our feet. And we weren't offered any kind of hope whatsoever.

So we freaked out. But, as I said, that didn't last too long be-

315

cause I started reading *Son-Rise,* which I actually had read before when I was in high school. It didn't take me long to get to a point in the book where I started to believe that we, at least, had the right to hope. We were even more hopeful when we learned of The Option Institute's programs and we started planning for a trip there. But there was still a lot of pain and a lot of concern: "God, will he ever be like other kids?" And it was really hard when I would see kids who were around his age, and the contrast would be so stark, and I would find that painful. Scott didn't experience that to the same degree that I did. I think Scott lived more of an Option Institute's attitude right from the start. My whole family was convinced that he was in complete denial because he never cried when we got the diagnosis. He said he just didn't believe he had to be unhappy to show he cared. He also didn't make assumptions about what the diagnosis meant about Justin's abilities. We were at a wedding once and saw a little boy Justin's age. I just fell apart. I mean, I had to leave, and I said, "It is just so painful when I see other kids his age and have to acknowledge how different he is." And Scott said, "You know, I don't feel that way because I would never prefer that this other little boy was my child—not only because I love Justin so much, but because ultimately Justin will be capable of achieving more." I said, "Well, gee, I hope you're right." But really I was thinking, "Yeah, right pal."

Bryn: So what changed things for you?

Janine: Coming to The Option Institute. The first thing that happened when we came to you was that we were in complete shock. Matt greeted us in the parking lot and he was so loud, so boisterous, so dynamic, and so enthusiastic—and we were thinking, "Oh my God, he's going to scare Justin to death." And that was the first time it occurred to us that we had been walking on eggshells around our son. And what we saw happen was the complete opposite of what we could ever have expected. For the first time in Justin's life, he checked to make sure that Matt, another human being, was watching. He would reposition himself to get Matt's glance before he would do something. So we saw it click in his mind: For the first time ever, we saw him make the connection that people were worth it—and all that happened in the parking lot of the institute!

316

Then, on the second day we were there, we had a major toilet-training success. For the first time in his life, Justin became willing to have a bowel movement in the toilet. He was so comfortable there, he got over his fear of the toilet and graduated from the "kiddie potty." He didn't even have any accidents while we were there!

Bryn: That's wonderful. I know what a difference it makes to parents when their children are potty-trained. How old was he at that point?

Janine: At that point, he was three and a half. Also, another major event took place while we were there. For the first time, he understood that, when someone asks you a question, an answer is the desired response. Before, if people asked him a question, he would either completely ignore them or he would just echo back to them what they had said. Someone would ask, "You want juice?" And he would just repeat, "You want juice?" At the institute, he started answering questions with "Yes" and "No." I remember how on Wednesday night, when we were preparing our notes for the Thursday group meeting with the staff, it hit me like a ton of bricks; "This kid is answering questions!" He finally got it, this interpersonal communication thing. He understood: You say something to people in order to achieve something and they say something back to you. He became conversational! You have to understand, up to that point, what speech he had was strictly echolalic. At some point, he was doing some one-word naming. For example, if he wanted Snoopy, he'd say, "Snoopy." But he wouldn't direct his words at us or say, "You get Snoopy." It seemed never to have occurred to him that people were useful, that he could get something from us. So that was a biggie. It was like the whole world cracked open and he figured out: "Wow, people are worth the effort! They're not the enemy, and when I say something, stuff happens."

Bryn: Janine, that's incredible!

Janine: I know, and that was just within the first three days at the institute.

Bryn: Were there any specific challenges that you came up against when you returned home and started doing your own program?

317

Janine: Well, one of the challenges was being able to come back home and sustain the momentum. Also, figuring out how to deal with the fact that, at that point, we had only two volunteers. Also, we really couldn't afford to build a playroom. Justin and I built the playroom together. He sat there with his little Fisher-Price tools, and I sat there with the real tools. As far as the interpersonal dynamics of running the program, we learned a lot about how to trust ourselves and how to train volunteers.

Justin was the antithesis of what we would have expected— we never had any trouble getting him to go into the playroom. He lived to go in that room. He would come wake us up and say, "Time to do a session!" My God, in one short week, you guys had him conversational and loving the room. Well, we had so many fears about working with him all day in one room and they completely vanished. That was something that really gave us confidence that we were doing the right thing. This kid wanted to be in there!

He went through all kinds of different stages in the program. For six months straight, all he wanted to do was eat toys. So we sat and chewed them with him. Boy, did we chew up a lot of little toy people. But it was amazing because that was the only thing that would stop that behavior. If we asked him to stop chewing, or if we took his toys away, he would just chew more. And when we would imitate him, he would laugh at us and tell us that we were being silly, and he would stop.

Often, if he felt that he was not in control, he would hit himself in the mouth. Not hard—I wouldn't call his behavior self-injurious—more like self-stimulatory. Imitation was the only thing that ever succeeded in stopping that, too. Another challenge was Justin's unusually hypersensitive hearing. With tons of love and acceptance, we dialogued with him to prepare him for a treatment that normalized his hearing. Acceptance and imitation were especially important afterward, as he used his old rituals to adapt to his new hearing. In general, in regard to every difficult behavior that we encountered, the whole Son-Rise Method of feeling accepting of his behavior and joining him got us through it. Being with him in this way and showing our volunteers how to be with him in this way, we found it never took him more than a couple of weeks with each person to get to the point where he was genuinely interacting with them.

318

Bryn: You and Scott must have been very inspiring teachers, show-ing your volunteers how to be truly accepting of Justin's rituals. How were the two of you, you and Scott, doing with each other.

Janine: We were okay, but we wanted more; so we attended The Happiness Option Weekend Introductory Program. The different issues that Scott and I had all came down to one great big kernel. We really got it during that visit to The Option Institute: that all the things that we'd used in our lives, such as unhappiness, frus-tration, judgments, either to motivate ourselves or to motivate other people, like each other or our families, all the things that we've tried in order to make people be what we wanted, or to change ourselves, actually moved us further from what we wanted. We really finally got it! And the books helped us so much as well—especially *Happiness Is a Choice* and *To Love Is to Be Happy With.* We didn't have to be unhappy in order to motivate ourselves to go for more. We didn't have to be afraid of illness in order to strive for health. We didn't have to be terrified of death in order to love living. That really clicked for us. We realized that in going for anything that we want in our life, we're going to be ultimately more effective and happier if we can do it from a positive stance. And more so with Justin than in any other arena in our lives. But we definitely ap-plied it to everything in our life. Scott, for example, has had excit-ing major changes in his career as a result of learning that, and I experienced positive changes in my friendships and other rela-tionships. So, what we learned really has spilled over into every aspect of our lives.

Bryn: Janine, after having made all these changes, did you han-dle the situations in your life differently?

Janine: Absolutely! I'll give you a very specific example. Before I came to the institute, I thought I had to see myself as a bad per-son for any mistakes that I might have made either before Justin was born, during my pregnancy, or after he was born. I felt I was a horrible person for everything I had done in my entire life that could be in any way construed as being related to his disability, and I believed I had to remember that so that I wouldn't do any-thing "wrong" again. And I finally realized during the institute's Advanced Family Week in February—I worked on this during a dialogue with Annie—that I could just forgive myself for things that I had done in the past, that I didn't have to hate myself in order to decide that I didn't want to do certain things again. I don't have to think that I am a horrid mother for yelling at Justin in order to motivate myself not to yell at him anymore.

Bryn: Janine, you are a dynamo.

Janine: I have really changed. So can I say I'll never cry again? I don't know. But when I do, I'll really revel in it and enjoy it. [Laughs.] Samahria said something very meaningful to me that first time we were there, when I was feeling guilty for crying. She said, "God, if you're going to cry, you might as well wallow in it and enjoy it." I laughed. I couldn't believe she'd said that. But it made so much sense.

Bryn: I know that was really significant for you. Did you learn other perspectives that also impacted on Justin?

Janine: During our time there, we learned that we'd be far more effective in getting whatever we wanted from him or for him if we went at it from a very accepting, loving, and positive stance. Let's take a real simple example: In the past, if I wanted him to clean up his toys, and if he didn't do it, I had to show him how angry and unhappy I was that he wasn't doing it. And, ultimately, that approach was just disastrous. He'd be writhing on the floor, near a seizure. I mean, he'd throw a tantrum. I would think he was making a personal statement about me, and I'd throw a tantrum back. We'd end up at opposite corners of the house, literally steaming. And ultimately neither of us got what we wanted.

Bryn: How was it different after you returned home?

Janine: What I did after leaving the institute is to realize that I can really, really, really want something and be completely accepting if I don't get it. And truly, I became genuine in that. I mean, I didn't have it mastered right from the start, but it wasn't very long before I could sincerely say, "It's perfectly all right with me if he cries forever. If he cries forever, so be it. He's doing the best he can. I don't want him to cry, and from the most loving place on God's earth, I'm going to try to show him that he doesn't have to. But if he does, so be it. God love him, that's okay."

Take the toy story for example. I could show him in the most positive, energetic, and exciting way how fun it would be for him to clean up his toys and also how much I would love it, and I could show him that I would love him and be completely happy if he didn't. Once the pressure was taken off—it's amazing—this kid was jumping through hoops to pick up his toys! Scott and I finally understood that we were definitely going to be far more effective at motivating him from a happy and accepting place.

And we also really did get to the place—and this I think is probably at the core of it all—where we could say—and I really swear to God that this is true—Justin having autism is the best thing that's ever happened in our lives. Even if he had never gotten any better than he was at the start, I still wouldn't trade him for anything on earth. We gained a true appreciation of Justin and life in general because of what you people taught us. We gained several insights from imitating him and joining him in all his activities. We really came to understand that (a) he's doing the best that he can; (b) this kid is instinctively treating his own disorder; and (c) he's really lovable. He's funny. He's amazing! Okay, so most people don't line their toys up at a forty-five degree angle in all the doorways, but, lo and behold, in his mind, he may have been building bridges. So we were able to really appreciate him exactly as he was, and that's been the key to everything.

People still can't believe me when I say, "I swear to God, Justin's autism is the best thing that ever could have happened. Both for him and for us." Certainly for me personally. Before I had Justin and before he was diagnosed with autism, I didn't have a clue what I wanted. I was a business administration major who, throughout my entire four years of college, thought that I was in the wrong major and should be changing to something more artistic and creative and never had the confidence in myself to change direction. I didn't have any idea whether I'd ever be able to go after my dream of becoming a photographer. I had no clue what I wanted to do next. I had no idea whether I'd be a good parent or not. I had no idea what I wanted out of my marriage, didn't know whether it would ever survive. And then, boom! We have an autistic child. Now, for most people, that would be the end. For us, it was the beginning. I finally got it together. I've never before been more clear or had more purpose in my life.

Bryn: You really used your circumstances as an opportunity to grow. My parents always thought that Raun's autism was the best thing that ever happened to them, too. What do you think it was that helped you to see it that way?

Janine: I guess because for the first time in my life I felt motivated to do something. And, because I was so motivated, my purpose was clear. "Whatever else happens, I want to do the best I can to help my child." Although I wanted him to be cured, I didn't keep thinking, "I want him to be cured." I kept thinking, "Whatever else, I want to do the best I can to help him, and if nothing else, I want him to live his life being completely loved and accepted." I never before experienced such an intense love as the love I now have for my child.

Bryn: You must have had so many precious experiences with him. Tell me about one of them.

Janine: This will be the perfect example: When I first had Justin, one of the things that was difficult for me was not knowing whether I would be able to pursue my photography career, especially when we found out he had special needs. And now Justin has his own camera, and he and I go on photo outings, and he takes pictures, and I take pictures, and we take pictures of each other. And he loves to go to the photo store. Actually he wants to be allowed to do darkroom work, but I'm concerned because he's chemically sensitive. Still, this kid is actually enjoying and joining me in one of the greatest loves in my life—which is photography. Not only that, he is loving it himself and is totally involved and connected. I mean, he knows what an enlarger is! I never in a million years would have believed that this could ever happen. I hoped for it, and I thought, "Maybe," but if anyone would have ever told me that in such a short time he'd be joining me in one of my biggest interests in life—I never would have believed it.

Bryn: Maybe that's just a cosmic gift, given to you for all the times that you loved his interests and joined him in his world. Janine, what is he like now?

Janine: Now Justin is a very special, very extroverted, very happy little boy. He has a real zest for life. He loves people. He is wasting no time making up for lost time, that's for sure. He now loves being around people, both individually and in groups. He is extremely bright. In many areas, he is very advanced for his age. By five and a half, he read somewhere up to a fourth- or fifth-grade level, was totally computer literate, and seemed mathematically inclined. His vocabulary and expressive skills were tested this past fall, and his scores ranged from a six- to ten-year level.

Bryn: Well, he is certainly not the child he once was. Is he going to school?

Janine: Yes, at age five and a half he began going to school part-time in a regular preschool program — not a handicapped class! To prepare for this, we did a video feedback and telephone conversation with the institute that really helped. We also trained a very loving one-to-one aide who was there for support in his preschool class. Our hope was that the preschool would act as a bridge from the home program to kindergarten. Our dream came true — Justin grew so much in the first half of this year in preschool, just after his sixth birthday we made a gradual transition to kindergarten. This went so great — he doesn't even have a one-to-one aide anymore. He really is fitting in! Now the school believes he'll be ready for the first grade next fall. So do we!

Through all of this, we've continued our program part-time. Justin comes home from school wanting the input to continue. Also, it's funny, at first glance, most people don't know there's anything different about him. If they spend some time with him, they might start seeing that he's somewhat different from other children, even though for the most part, he appears to be a really exceptional little kid. I mean, academics are easy for him — more so than for most kids. But he still has to work extra hard at the social stuff that most people take for granted. He's really such an incredible little kid who's just not going to let anything stop him now. Since he'll still be only six and a half, he'll be at grade level! My God! After only two and a half years of working with him, look what's happened!

Bryn: Isn't it incredible? All of us here at the institute are so excited for you, Scott, and Justin. You have really taken the ball and run with it. What kinds of things do you talk to this little guy about?

Janine: Well, he's got the whole concept of asking questions now, so we spend a lot of time with him answering his questions. Like, "How can fish breathe under water?" He has a clear understanding of past, present, and future, so he may talk to us about something special that we did before or something special that he wants to do. He conveys his experiences to us, like what he did at school, or he comes home and tells me what he did with his dad, and he shares with us on just about every level.

Bryn: How is he with physical expressiveness?

Janine: Oh, he's very, very physically affectionate now. He loves hugs and kisses. He comes and spontaneously says, "I want to give you a hug," and tells us spontaneously, "I love you." He writes us love letters. Simple stuff like, "Mom, I really love you. Love, Justin." He only just became able to write last spring. So he's not writing a whole bunch. He's a lot better at verbally expressing himself than he is in writing, but God, he's only six years old. What's really funny is that on the reading, we figured out he also reads cursive, not just printing. And a lot of people say, "That's not reading with comprehension. He's just hyperlexic. He doesn't really know what he's reading." Absolutely not true. His comprehension has been tested and, furthermore, when this kid sees a word he doesn't know, he asks the meaning; you explain it to him, he's got it forever. I mean, I would say his vocabulary exceeds that of many adults. It's actually limitless the kind of stuff that we talk about with him because he's interested in everything.

Still, many of his interests are similar to those of other kids his age; for instance, he wants to play baseball. He just went to his first baseball game with his dad. Actually, he recently hit his first baseball. Believe me, that was a significant event. Scott was going to call every relative on earth. I was thrilled, too, but you know how a dad is about his son hitting his first baseball. Now Justin is starting to be interested in sports, and he rides bikes and he gardens with me. He's really into the garden. So we talk about rosy fat magenta radishes. He pretty much shares in all our interests. He likes to cook. He loves music. So he's totally into sharing with us just about anything we want to do with him.

Bryn: What does he especially like to do?

Janine: Justin really loves to play games of any kind! Board games, travel games, cards, you name it. He even invents his own games. Most importantly, he wants to play them with people. He even takes horseback riding lessons singing "Home on the Range" the whole time. He also really loves reading. And in particular, reading to us, if we'll read with him. He loves reading on his own, but, mostly, he loves reading together. This is the same little kid who used to beat me up when I tried to read to him—I mean, hurt me, bruise me. Now, he loves to go to the library and look up books in the catalog and pick them out. And they use a computerized catalog system at our library, so it's no small affair. He's got it down to a science, boy. And he likes to read books that parallel something we're doing, like, for example, books about gardening. So, like when I spoke of "rosy fat magenta radishes," we went to the library; we checked out a book about a girl who grew a rosy fat magenta radish. He would go outside every day and read the story to the radishes and every day measure how tall they got. And then, after his radishes grew, he painted a picture of them in one of our sessions together. So he's bringing all the areas of his life together. He can really generalize from one experience to another.

Bryn: He sounds like such a multifaceted young child.

Janine: I think he lives an extremely full life for a child his age. From the five to six year olds I've known, and from what I remember of my life at around that age, I think that most children his age are interested in one or two things—he wants everything.

Bryn: It seems like so much changed for you in relation to Justin. Were there also changes that you noticed between you and Scott?

Janine: Oh, gosh, yes. In particular, we dealt with Scott and I each using unhappiness to try to motivate each other. For example, if I wasn't being loving enough to Scott and he felt that I was wrapped up too much either in Justin's program or my photography or whatever, sometimes he thought the best way to get through to me, to let me know that he wanted more of my attention, was to give me the silent treatment or to mope around. Just like me, at times he used unhappiness to send me a clue that he was not getting what he wanted. And ultimately, I would become frustrated, reactive, and even more distant from him. We'd create a stalemate with each other.

What we came to later was that he could sit down and say to me, "I really want to be closer to you. I want more time for us together." Or whatever. And when he'd approach me like that, I'd instantly feel so much closer to him. He was amazing! Instead of defeating himself as before, he moved toward what he wanted by taking a positive approach. I learned a lot for myself from that. We developed a much clearer, more open line of communication. And we also became profoundly respectful of each other's relationship with Justin in very much the same way. If there was something that I wanted Scott to be doing with Justin, I didn't any longer feel a need to use anger or unhappiness to motivate him, and vice versa.

And that's not all. When Scott and I spent that week at the institute, he worked with the staff doing dialogues exploring his concerns about his asthmatic condition. He visualized the source of the problem coming from within him and realized his breathing felt so restricted because of his beliefs that the doctors must be right about his need for medication. He really worked at that one. He changed his attitude and some core beliefs. Do you know that since we came home, he stopped using the medicine and the asthma is no longer a problem?

Bryn: It really sounds like you've both done a lot of changing, even in your ways of being with each other.

Janine: Oh, heavens, we've changed tremendously. Especially since going back to the institute and taking the weekend program together.

Bryn: With so much going on in your family, what kind of energy would you say went into doing the program?

Janine: Tremendous, tremendous amounts of energy. Timewise, it varied. For the most part, we and our staff spent between six and eight hours a day working with Justin—I did some of the sessions and the volunteers and other staff did the rest. We convinced both our school district and a Respite Care Program for the Disabled that the Son-Rise Method was the only available treatment program for Justin. They supported our home program by sending personnel to help that I then trained myself.

Bryn: What did you tell the school that convinced them that this was the only treatment for Justin?

Janine: Well, we hit them with a fifteen-page proposal that completely ripped apart much of what anybody had ever thought about autism. We explained why the physical environment of other programs was inappropriate, why the teaching methods were inappropriate, why the discipline methods were totally inappropriate, why emotionally they would be harmful for him. We mentioned specific characteristics of his that would have made it impossible for him to learn in a judgmental environment. And then we also documented professional recommendations regarding The Option Institute's work and methods.

We also backed up everything we said in the proposal with references to the law. For example, in the State Code it says you cannot discipline a child for a behavior that is a characteristic of that child's disability. But, in our schools, teachers do that all the time. When kids flap their hands, they yell at them and tell them to stop; they even hold them down. So we quoted the code right up front to show that the law was on our side. As a result, the school district didn't even bat an eyelash or take us to mediation. Instead, both the school and the respite program gave us really positive support, help, and input all along.

Bryn: Have you told them about any of the changes that you've seen in Justin since you started doing your Son-Rise Program?

Janine: Yes. Both in writing and in person. Only one section of the proposal discussed harmful things that we felt had come out of his being in school. The other section detailed positive things that we'd seen since he was in our home-based program. What we did next was to have them come over to observe our work because we felt that seeing firsthand was going to be more convincing to them than anything that they could see written down. And, indeed, it took only two home visits and they were convinced. They even said they wished I could be a teacher in their district.

Bryn: Wow! How do you feel at this point about having done the program?

Janine: Oh, God, fabulous. Not just for Justin and not just for us, but for other people too. Because of our program, we are one of the first families in our state to get support of the kind we got from the school system. I mean, for goodness sake, the school district even paid for Justin to go to a private preschool. They allowed him to continue there during the gradual transition to kindergarten. Even now, we still have one school staff member in the home program! Have you ever heard of such a thing? It's laid down a precedent for other people that says, "There isn't just one right way, and if there is one right way, it certainly isn't what they used to think it was." It has laid the groundwork for other people, who now have such a program as an option for their child.

Bryn: You have really paved the way for other families to receive more support from their school systems. Is there anything that you would want to say to parents who have special children?

Janine: If there's any one thing on earth that you can do to help your child, this would be the most impactful and effective thing. And it will be worth any amount of time, money, effort, and whatever else that has to be put into it; it will come back to you tenfold, even if your child never overcomes autism or any other serious developmental difficulty. Personally, there was nothing that I wanted more for my child than for him to be in a program where he was not going to get the message that there was something wrong with him. I wanted him in a program that did not begin like all the others. The programs I'd seen all seemed to begin from the premise: There's nothing you can do; so the best you can do is teach your child some minimal, rudimentary skill. I wanted a program that started from a premise of hope—that anything is possible. Granted, we can't know what is possible, but, at the very least, we can try and go for what we want. All the other programs start from the premise: There are limits to what's possible; your child won't get over this problem. Even to be able to teach them minimal skills, they must first learn to stop acting autistic, be quiet, sit still, and stand in line. And they were wrong—dead wrong!

We wanted Justin in a program that started from the premise: Let's see what we can go for. We don't know what he's capable of; so let's go for it all and give it everything we've got.

In our proposal to the school, we said that no one ever suggested that if a child has leukemia their parents might as well not bother to try and find a cure for leukemia, but just teach that child to be quiet and stand in line, in spite of their disease. No one would ever say that. But when it comes to autism, or other serious learning disorders, people say, "Oh, we know it can't be cured, so you might as well just teach him to behave, since you can't cure the disability." And we just thought that was ludicrous. I mean, we haven't given up trying to find a cure for cancer. And that was how we felt. We just wanted Justin to be in a program that told him, not that there was something wrong with him, but rather that we loved him for who he was, that maybe he could get better, and that, hey, we don't know, but let's try. And that is the kind of program we were offered by your parents and The Option Institute.

Bryn: And that is the kind of program you continued to do with him.

Janine: Absolutely. Actually, I knew I wanted that before I went to the institute, but it was confirmed when we were there. To this day, and I'm familiar with just about every approach to autism that's out there, I feel there isn't anything else that even comes close. I'm a member of the Autism Society of America and other groups about autism and developmental disabilities, and I've learned a lot from these groups. But what they couldn't give me is the kind of individualized program with the positive approach Justin needed. People say things to me like, "Oh, I'd never be able to do a program full-time." Well, I completely advocate doing the program full-time. But, at the same time, I think that two hours a day of the Son-Rise Method beats a full day of any other program there is. That's how much I believe in it. And my son is living proof of its power.

  Any amount of time that you could do this program would benefit your child more than putting them in some catchall handicapped class where teachers start from the premise that your child cannot improve.

Bryn: You are so passionate about what you're saying! Is there anything else that you'd like to share?

Janine: Oh, gosh, we just love you guys so much. Being involved with The Option Institute has really opened up our world. We're just so much happier than we used to be. Now we want to pass the torch to all the other families who call us. We'll be involved with the institute for the rest of our lives, I'm sure. It showed us that Justin is the best thing that has ever happened in our lives.

Being with him in this way has benefited him tremendously and benefited us tremendously. The happiness we feel has affected him enormously and spilled over into the lives of all the people around us. At this point, I really just want to pass it on. Because it's the best thing that ever happened to us and for our son.

*　　*　　*

Two weeks ago, a mom and dad came with their special son to observe Justin's program. When Justin saw Joey, he asked, "Is Joey autistic?"

"Yes he is," Janine answered.

Justin replied, "We should tell them that he can get better like me."

Epilogue

Several months ago, I taught a workshop on personal empowerment to a large group of participants, including people from the helping professions, educators, businesspeople, lawyers, physicians, homemakers, artists, factory workers, and college students. An awesome, diverse group of individuals, we explored together the collective perspectives we all might share regarding beliefs that empower us and beliefs that inhibit us from going for and getting what we want.

We isolated three commonplace core beliefs that undercut our passion and optimism as we pursue our dreams. First, most group members believed they couldn't get what they really want—even before they tried. Second, many envisioned a universe of limited possibilities. And third, they concluded the universe was unfriendly, even hostile, and would not readily support them. As a result, they believed they would have to produce almost superhuman thrusts to make real and lasting changes in their lives.

We adopt the beliefs we have for the best of reasons: to take care of ourselves and those we love. However, if the visions we hold do not serve us, we could consider changing them and reeducating ourselves in order to take another position—create another perspective. One member of the group cautioned fellow participants to keep the framework of our exploration realistic—don't start to believe you can live after hearing from doctors that your illness is terminal; don't think you can facilitate peace among people who make war with one another; don't think you can reach children, help, and even possibly heal them after experts have deemed their condition irreversible. The message has been given loud and clear to all of us: Be realistic! However, the "realism" most of us have learned leaves us without hope or the impetus to reach out passionately and try for more. We turn away, paralyzed by our own pessimism and distracted by the discomforts and distress that accompany our viewing ourselves as powerless and the world around us as unresponsive and unsupportive.

After facilitating the discussion for several minutes, I made

331

a simple suggestion: Perhaps, in this moment of time, we could consider the possibility of living our lives unrealistically. Oftentimes, we use conventional realism and skepticism to limit our thinking and creativity. I reminded the group that most of the progress in the world comes from unrealistic people who dare to do what others have not done before: Galileo with his telescope, Pasteur with his test tubes, Robert Frost with his pen and pad, Frank Lloyd Wright with his architectural designs.

Most of us, in our efforts to do the very best for ourselves, have used the beliefs we have been taught to limit our dreams rather than bring them to fruition. What would happen if we decided (made a conscious choice) to hold only those beliefs that would serve to empower and inspire us?

To that end, I whimsically suggested alternative beliefs with which to replace the three disempowering ones the group had discussed. My suggestions: First, we can get what we want or at least have the joy of trying for it; second, we live in a universe of limitless possibilities; and, third, the universe can be truly supportive, even user-friendly. Some people laughed sweetly as if to express kindly their skepticism in the face of my fanciful meanderings and hypothesized worldview. However, everyone did agree that for those holding such a perspective, wonder and optimism would abound. Would that determine success? Not absolutely! But some group members insisted that folks with that viewpoint probably wouldn't place their emphasis on "success"—but on the act of doing; they'd be counted among the happy few—enjoying a state of mind that might, in fact, energize them to try again and again or pursue another dream undaunted.

Our beliefs not only create our worldview and attitude, but shape the way we feel about ourselves, others, and the events of our lives. Given that most of us have learned a vision for our lives that inhibits us and creates discomfort, we can still unlearn it— choose again and blaze a new trail. In effect, that is exactly what the families portrayed in this book did for themselves and their children.

Some of us see walls and only walls; others see not only the walls, but the windows!

*　　*　　*

At the conclusion of the keynote address I gave to three thousand guidance counselors and school psychologists, I had the opportunity to share personally with hundreds from the audience. One woman gave me a big smile and hug. She said, "You really believe so much is possible, don't you? So I started to think," she continued, "'Yes, I can do. Or at least I can try.'"

"How did you feel thinking that?" I asked.

"Great!" Then her expression darkened. "But, you know, people will tell me I've got to keep my feet on the ground." She paused, then laughed again—a big belly laugh. "I guess what they really mean is for me to keep my feet in the mud."

* * *

A woman came to our teaching center to do a series of private dialogue sessions with me and some of our staff. She had previously attended several workshops at The Option Institute and knew us and our work. Donna had been diagnosed recently as having an advanced case of lymphoma. The cancer cells had spread to other parts of her body. Doctors gave her a grim prognosis. Upon hearing the news, her family and friends rushed to express their sorrow. She stopped taking their phone calls. Instead, she listened to the messages they left on her answering machine—messages meant to comfort her—and found herself getting even more frightened.

I encountered her in the dining hall immediately after her arrival. Walking to greet her, I smiled. As we opened arms to hug each other, I said, "Congratulations! I hear you've begun an amazing adventure!"

Donna stopped short and started to laugh. "Only in this place would someone give me such a positive and hopeful greeting!" She thanked me repeatedly for my welcome, calling it a needed relief from everyone else's pessimism and depressed commentaries.

Over the next four days, Donna cried, laughed, shouted her protest to God, and questioned deeply so many of the fundamental principles that had guided her life. In the end, she transformed what she had initially viewed as a curse into an opportunity—casting aside her victim mentality, finding her own power, guiding her healing process, and using each unfolding moment to prioritize happiness and love with herself, her husband, and her children. The disease did not go away in those four days. What changed was Donna's vision—her beliefs and perspectives of her changing life experience. Just by changing her attitude, her "new eyes" enhanced profoundly the quality of her life. Additionally, I am sure her improved sense of well-being, inner conviction, and optimism will serve her well as she faces challenges that lie ahead.

∗   ∗   ∗

We can make an endless list of specific difficulties that many of us would want to avoid but that most of us, nevertheless, will encounter in some way. The death of a parent. The loss of a job. An investment gone sour. Divorce. Disease. Or—having a child with apparent, even severe, difficulties.

Some people will buckle under the stress and experience their life situation as overwhelming ("Bad things happen to me"; "I am unlucky"). Others will survive and attempt to cope ("Life is a series of ups and downs"; "You have to take the bad with the good"). A rare few will have learned to take their apparent difficulties and transform them into inspiring growth experiences ("I always do the best I can"; "Let me find the unseen possibilities").

To break the mold that might keep us in a defensive position and to begin approaching the events of our lives with new openness (that is, welcoming our experiences instead of fighting them), we would first have to adopt a new vision—a new principle. What about the one I suggested earlier in this book? *Good fortune is an attitude, not an event*; therefore, every problem can become an "opportunity" by virtue of our embracing it as one.

Such is our vision of every adult and child we try to help—especially the special child. Every person is individual, precious, and wondrous to behold. Often, when we hear words like autistic, brain impaired, pervasive developmentally delayed, schizophrenic, cerebral palsied, mentally retarded, epileptic, and the like, we recoil fearfully, overwhelmed by our different child and the possible difficulties we face. The belief: Something "bad" has happened to our child and to us. In the end, we lose touch with our appreciation and delight in the presence of the youngster in our midst.

A special child is a gift that challenges us to respond with enormous energy and dedication. Finding a way to help that child, to be there in the most loving, supportive, and facilitating way possible is, in effect, learning to express the most powerful and humane part of ourselves. Such a process is a daily, moment-to-moment treasure for all of us teaching and using the Son-Rise Program — for the Family Program staff at The Option Institute, for the volunteers who give so much, and for the families and professionals who cross our threshold.

*   *   *

I don't remember asking God and the universe for a profoundly neurologically disabled child. Sure, both Samahria and I wanted the best for ourselves and our family. What we didn't know in the first moments of realizing that our son was different is that God and the universe had given us the best—we had only to discover it. And the discovery was not so much a revelation as a creation. We had to teach ourselves how to see differently and be far more open and loving than ever before. I used to think we were so alone—our family and our son. I used to think no one really cared or wanted to understand. Perhaps, for a time, that might have been true. But now, as I watch the courage and magnificence of other parents using an attitude of love and acceptance to help their children, I am profoundly moved. Their commitment to change themselves for the love of a child speaks to a deep place inside. No one can ever guarantee whether someone you love will change or be healed, but embracing that person with respect and happiness can only be a gift—a gift for the giver and a gift for the receiver.

I don't know what's around the corner. I don't know what unanticipated challenges tomorrow will bring. But I do feel blessed to realize that I can continue to teach myself to be openhearted and to search for the lesson of love in every moment.

For information regarding workshops, seminars, and motivational talks by Barry Neil Kaufman, Samahria Lyte Kaufman, and The Option Institute, as well as for information about their services helping individuals, families, and groups, please write or call for free literature:

> The Option Institute
> P.O. Box 1180-SR
> 2080 South Undermountain Road
> Sheffield, MA 01257
> Phone: (413) 229-2100
> Fax: (413) 229-8931

Please Help Us Reclaim Children's Lives
Your tax-deductible contributions to The Option Institute can assist us to serve even more special children and their families. We require funds to expand facilities for families, to create scholarships for families unable to meet the program fees, to fund ongoing support services for families now using the Son-Rise Program℠ at home, and to train more Son-Rise Program teachers. The Option Institute is a nonprofit charitable organization.

For a free catalogue of Barry Neil Kaufman's audio and video tapes and other books, write:

> Option Indigo Press
> P.O. Box 1180-SR
> Sheffield, MA 01257

Or for your ordering convenience with MC or Visa, call 1 (800) 562-7171 Mon.–Fri. 9:00–5:00 EST.

Suggested Reading

During our travels throughout the world, people ask us continually for support materials regarding our work with families with special-needs children. Our answer is similar to those families and individuals that attend any programs at our learning center, The Option Institute. The core of what we teach is attitude—making happiness and love tangible and useful—to help a special child, to deal successfully with an illness, a relationship, or a career challenge, or to simply put new vigor into our everyday lives. Unhappiness is not inevitable. We have been systematically taught to use discomfort and distress as a strategy to take care of ourselves. We can unteach ourselves—and begin again. But first, we have a choice to make—to become students of what we want and make such personal change a priority in our lives.

The path is neither long, difficult, nor painful. Although we, ourselves, are still very much students of what we teach, there are now written materials as well as audio tapes to help people on this journey:

Happiness Is a Choice: Presents a simple blueprint not only to empower the decision to be happy (create inner ease, comfort, and peace of mind inside) but also shares six shortcuts to happiness, each of which opens a doorway into an openhearted state of mind. This book contains the best of twenty years experience working with tens of thousands of people—synthesized into an easily digestible, step-by-step journey to self-acceptance and empowerment. Note: This book and the other books listed were written by Barry Neil Kaufman. There is another book with the same title, unrelated to Barry Neil Kaufman's work. Mr. Kaufman's book is published by Fawcett Columbine (Ballantine Books/Random House).

To Love Is to Be Happy With: Details the dialogue process and how to change beliefs that inhibit us to beliefs that liberate us to be happy, loving, and empowered. This has become the cornerstone book and manual in helping people redesign their attitude and their lives. Additionally, families, professionals, and volunteers use it to train themselves in adopting an open and embracing attitude as a foundation for helping their special children. Published by Fawcett Crest (Ballantine Books/Random House).

Giant Steps: Illustrates ten intimate and uplifting portraits of the dialogue process in action. In this book, the reader comes along for special journeys with young people who learn to break through their pain and triumph even in the face of extreme crisis. Published by Fawcett Crest (Ballantine Books/Random House).

A Miracle to Believe In: Shares a most revealing portrait of Barry and Samahria Kaufman's working life-style as well as an in-depth study of their family and the group of volunteers who came together to love a special child back to life. This book also provides a format for work with children, adolescents, or adults with special problems. Published by Fawcett Crest (Ballantine Books/Random House).

These books are available at local bookstores, libraries or can be ordered by mail through Option Indigo Press, P.O. Box 1180-SR, 2080 South Undermountain Road, Sheffield, MA 01257. Phone: 1 (800) 562-7171.

Audio tapes, including *Special Children/Special Solutions* by Samahria Lyte Kaufman, *No Fault/No Risk Parenting* by Barry Neil Kaufman, *The Twelve Tape Option Process Series, The Keys to Option Mentoring* (the Dialogue Process), *Body Vital/Stress Free Living, The Empowered Leader,* and many others are also available by mail order from Option Indigo Press.

Index

About the Author

Barry Neil Kaufman teaches a uniquely self-accepting and empowering process (The Option Process®) that also has educational and therapeutic applications. He and his wife, Samahria, are cofounders and codirectors of The Option Institute and Fellowship (P.O. Box 1180-SR, 2080 South Undermountain Rd., Sheffield, MA 01257, (413) 229-2100), which offers programs for people either challenged by adversity or trying to improve the quality of their lives. The Kaufmans, with their staff, also counsel individuals, couples, and families. Additionally, Mr. Kaufman and his wife lecture at universities, presents motivational talks at conferences, guides workshops and seminars, and has appeared in mass media throughout the country.

Their teaching modality has been adopted by teachers, therapists, businesspeople, families, and individuals worldwide. Their books have been translated into fourteen languages. As a result of their innovative and successful program, The Son-Rise Program℠, which they developed for their once-autistic child, the Kaufmans also counsel and instruct families wanting to create home-based teaching programs for their own special children. They teach professionals in this area as well.

Barry Neil Kaufman has written nine books, coauthored two screenplays with his wife (winning the coveted Christopher Award twice and also the Humanitas Prize), and has had articles featured in major publications. His eighth book, *Happiness Is a Choice,* is one of the most inspiring and hopeful statements of his work to date, a blueprint of simple concrete methods to empower the decision to be happy. In *Happiness Is a Choice,* he pulls together the best of his twenty years experience helping tens of thousands of people to achieve happiness.

His first book, *Son-Rise,* which details his family's inspiring journey with their once-autistic child, was dramatized as an NBC-TV network movie presentation and has been seen by three hundred million people throughout the world. His subsequent books include *Giant Steps,* which documents intimate and uplifting portraits of young people he has worked with and touched during times of

346

extreme crisis, and *To Love Is to Be Happy With,* which shares the specific applications of the attitude and the dialogue process of self-exploration he, his wife, and staff teach.

A Miracle to Believe In recounts the emotional and oftentimes miraculous story of the journey to love a little Mexican boy back to life. *The Book of Wows and Ughs* is a playful collection of sayings and insights. *A Land Beyond Tears,* coauthored with his wife, Samahria (formerly Suzi), presents a liberating approach to death and dying, and *A Sense of Warning* details the Kaufmans' life-changing psychic experiences.

His most recent book, *Son-Rise: The Miracle Continues,* presents an expanded, updated version of the original *Son-Rise* story with additions that include his son's blossoming into manhood and heartwarming stories of other families who have reached their once "unreachable" children with the Kaufmans' guidance.

ALSO FROM H J KRAMER

FULL ESTEEM AHEAD
100 Ways to Build Self-Esteem in Children and Adults
by Diane Loomans with Julia Loomans
"*Full Esteem Ahead* is the best book on parenting and self-esteem that I know."—Jack Canfield, author of *Chicken Soup for the Soul.*

HEALING YOURSELF WITH LIGHT
How to Connect With the Angelic Healers
by LaUna Huffines
The complete guide to the healing power of light for physical, mental, and emotional health.

THE LIFE YOU WERE BORN TO LIVE
A Guide to Finding Your Life Purpose
by Dan Millman
Dan Millman's popular Life-Purpose System features key spiritual laws to help understand your past, clarify your present, and change your future.

UNDERSTAND YOUR DREAMS
1500 Dream Images and How to Interpret Them
by Alice Anne Parker
The essential guide to becoming your own dream expert—makes dreaming a pleasure and waking an adventure.

THE ALCHEMY OF PRAYER
Rekindling Our Inner Life
by Terry Lynn Taylor
The Alchemy of Prayer is an original, inspiring, empowering, and loving look at a timeless subject by best-selling angel expert Terry Lynn Taylor.

If you are unable to find these books in your favorite bookstore, please call 800-833-9327.

ALSO FROM H J KRAMER

RECLAIMING OUR HEALTH
Exploding the Medical Myth and
Embracing the Source of True Healing
by John Robbins
In his rousing and inspiring style, John Robbins, author of *Diet for a New America*, turns his attention to the national debate on health care.

THE AWAKENED HEART
Meditations on Finding Harmony in a Changing World
by John Robbins and Anne Mortifee
An inquiry into the issues and concerns of the heart.

TARA'S ANGELS
One Family's Extraordinary Journey of Courage and Healing
by Kirk Moore
The singular account of a father's journey through grief and the awakening of the soul of a family to profound love and spiritual purpose.

WAY OF THE PEACEFUL WARRIOR
A Book That Changes Lives
by Dan Millman
A spiritual classic! The international best-seller that speaks directly to the universal quest for happiness.

CREATING MIRACLES
Understanding the Experience of Divine Intervention
by Carolyn Miller, Ph.D.
Discover the book where science and miracles meet. The first scientific look at creating miracles in your life, these simple practices and true stories offer new wisdom for accessing the miraculous in daily life.

If you are unable to find these books in your favorite bookstore, please call 800-833-9327.